BRITANNICA
BRAINBUSTERS

Challenging Puzzles
for the Curious-Minded

Theodore Pappas and Jeff Knurek

TRIUMPH
BOOKS

ENCYCLOPÆDIA
Britannica

This book is available in quantity at special discounts for your group or organization. For further information, contact:

Triumph Books LLC
814 North Franklin Street
Chicago, Illinois 60610
(312) 337-0747
www.triumphbooks.com

Printed in U.S.A.
ISBN: 978-1-62937-095-8
Design by Preston Pisellini

CONTENTS

INTRODUCTION

Welcome to *Britannica Brainbusters*!

The riddles and puzzles that follow are designed to be challenging, informative, and—most importantly—fun. But first a few words about the layout of the book.

The riddles are grouped into seven categories—Famous & Infamous; Pop Culture & Entertainment; Food & Drink; the Sporting Life; U.S. Presidency & First Ladies; Science, Space & Technology; and Literature & the Arts—and the category is given for each riddle, thereby serving as a clue to the answer.

There are also five puzzle types. Four kinds (Alphabet Soup, Criss Cross, Fill in the Blanks, and Word Search) are presented in four separate chapters. A letter box is provided for the first three puzzle types (for all but Word Searches), and if letters used in an answer are crossed off in the letter box, the remaining letters will serve as additional clues for completing the other puzzles on the page. At the end of each chapter is an extended answer key, with each riddle explained in detail.

The fifth type of puzzle (Mind Lines) is interspersed throughout the four chapters. This game can be played individually or by teams, and it can even be played simultaneously with the other puzzles. Using the riddles and answers found throughout the book, the Mind Lines challenge is to see how efficiently a player or a player's team can move from the top line of subject categories to the bottom line. Each correct answer to a riddle is one "move" on the Mind Lines board.

The Word Searches, too, can be played different ways. If stumped by a riddle in a Word Search, players may look at the end of the chapter and learn the answer to the riddle without also immediately learning the *location* of the answer within the puzzle—the two types of information are intentionally kept separate. This way, even after learning the answer to a riddle, a player can still enjoy the challenge of *finding* the answer within the Word Search.

Additionally, in order to enjoy these rhyming riddles to their fullest, they should be read aloud. For rhythm and rhyme have a special effect on us, and whatever our age and however we encounter them—whether in the verse of Dr. Seuss, the sonnets of Shakespeare, or the rapped lyrics of popular music—the effect of their twin presence remains: we listen more attentively and our brain engages more acutely, enhancing (for most of us) the experience at hand.

Finally, I would like to thank several people for making this book possible, including Jorge Cauz, president of Encyclopædia Britannica, and Dale Hoiberg, former editor in chief of Britannica, for allowing me to pursue this project; my Britannica colleagues Robert Lewis and Thad King, for thoroughly checking my work and for their kind suggestions along the way; Jeff Knurek, for his great puzzle designs; the folks at Triumph Books, for their partnership in this venture; and, most of all, my children—Oliver, Cecilia Jean, and Demetrius. It was for my children, in fact, that I began writing these couplets in the first place—to pique their interest in learning, to test what they had learned, and to show them that education can occasionally be fun.

Enjoy!

—Theodore Pappas
Chicago, Illinois

BRITANNICA
BRAINBUSTERS

Alphabet Soup

Fill in the blanks with letters from the letter box below. All letters will be used only once in answering the riddles.

FAMOUS & INFAMOUS

1 According to some, I'm a polygon of doom,
A place where great mayhem and much mystery loom.

_ _ R _ _ _ _ _   _ R _ _ _ _ _ _

2 I was the largest ever built, I was all the rage,
Till I burst into flames and brought an end to this age.

_ _ N _ _ _ U _ _

POP CULTURE & ENTERTAINMENT

3 I tried to kill myself one cinematic Christmas Eve,
But then an angel showed me the wonderful life I'd leave.

_ _ M _ _   _ _ E _ _ _ _

4 My cool and sexy songs have won me quite a bit of fame,
I also caused that wardrobe mishap at the football game.

_ _ _ _ _ I _ _   _ _ _ _ _ _ L _ _

B I W H M M I D A Y E N N T T I R
N S U J E N M T R I K L E U A G D
R E G R B L R J E A T I S U T A B M E

Alphabet Soup

Fill in the blanks with letters from the letter box below. All letters will be used only once in answering the riddles.

FAMOUS & INFAMOUS

1 Of U.S. disasters I was one of the worst,
Barriers all along the Gulf Coast did I burst.

_ U _ _ _ _ _ _ _   _ _ _ _ I _ _

2 I was a humble beekeeper, I really was quite meek,
But fame came fast and furiously when I reached the peak.

_ _ _ _ _ D   H _ _ _ _ _ _

THE SPORTING LIFE

3 I was named after a famous white abolitionist,
But changed it as a famous black leader and pugilist.

_ _ _ S _ _ _   C _ _ _

4 I'm one of the four Majors, associated with green,
And "Amen" is uttered at 11, 12, and 13.

_ _ S _ _ _ _   _ O _ _ _ _ _ _

U T N I T C R S M S A A R R C L C K
Y A E I H A O L R M Y T E N A A A L M N U
E D I U S N I U R H R N E S D T S A

Alphabet Soup

Fill in the blanks with letters from the letter box below. All letters will be used only once in answering the riddles.

FAMOUS & INFAMOUS

1 Have we a republic or a monarchy, the lady asked in anticipation, "A republic, if you can keep it," I replied with trepidation.

_ _ _ J _ _ _ _   _ _ _ _ K _ _ _

2 To Mother I gave 40, and seeing what I'd done, Folks say I turned to Father and gave him 41.

_ _ Z _ _ _ _   _ _ _ _ _ E _

LITERATURE & THE ARTS

3 Although I failed to be mayor, I knew the naked and the dead, And I even managed to stab twice one of the six wives I wed.

_ O _ _ _ _   M _ _ _ _ _ _

4 "So you're the little woman," Abe said to me, Whose book caused our national catastrophe.

_ _ R _ _ _ _   _ _ _ _ _ H _ _   _ _ _ W _

N A B B E N M M R D B R I E O E E F
H I R L I O E Z I K N R T C E Z N L A R
N O T H I R M A A R A S N N L W I J E E E

Alphabet Soup

Fill in the blanks with letters from the letter box below. All letters will be used only once in answering the riddles.

FAMOUS & INFAMOUS

1 To products I widely sold my name, a novel move with flair,
And I shocked the highfalutin with lines of ready-to-wear.

_ _ _ _ R _ _   _ A _ _ _ _

2 I sold out 12 for 30 instead,
I then wrapped a noose around my head.

_ _ D _ _   I _ _ _ _ _ _ _

POP CULTURE & ENTERTAINMENT

3 With rope, locks, and boxes, and even strong chain,
They'd try to contain me but always in vain.

_ _ R _ _   _ O _ _ _ _ _

4 I received millions in pay for a mere ten-minute part,
Because my name was "super" in the cinematic art.

_ _ R _ _ _   _ _ _ _ D _

P I R S H L N I R U R R Y I A A D
M D N E E H O A I S J O C O R A C
R T I A R U D N D R A B N I O

12

Alphabet Soup

Fill in the blanks with letters from the letter box below. All letters will be used only once in answering the riddles.

FAMOUS & INFAMOUS

1 My Union prisoners were kept in a horrible state,
And many thousands of them died at a staggering rate.

_ _ _ _ _ _ _ N V _ _ _ _

2 My location, for years, I would closely conceal,
Until sinking at sea at the hands of a SEAL.

_ _ A _ _   _ _ I _   L _ _ _ _ _

SCIENCE, SPACE & TECHNOLOGY

3 My oath is tied to graduation day,
But am I still relevant or passé?

_ _ _ P _ _ _ R _ _ _ _

4 Some called my work science, others called it pornography,
I did "for sex what Columbus did for geography."

_ _ _ F _ _ _   _ _ _ _ _ Y

N	S	O	P	A	N	P	D	A	R	N	C	R	A	D	N
A	V	E	I	F	O	E	S	K	L	A	L	M	E	L	R
I	H	E	L	S	D	T	I	A	E	I	O	B	S	N	E	Y

13

Alphabet Soup

Fill in the blanks with letters from the letter box below. All letters will be used only once in answering the riddles.

THE SPORTING LIFE

1 Individuals compete in me but as part of a team,
I'm my sport's top event, with a strong yellow theme.

_ _ _ _ R _ _ _ _ _ _ _ _ C _

2 Nearly no one has been better at the sport that I do,
Though hubris cost me millions and the life I was used to.

_ _ G _ _ _ _ _ _ _ S

FOOD & DRINK

3 We're tiny, tart, and juicy, with shiny bright red skins,
We're common on the pancakes of Scandinavians.

L _ _ _ _ _ _ B _ _ _ _ _ _

4 In the wake of a divorce and in need of recovery,
Three things were pursued on this trek of discovery.

_ _ T _ _ _ _ _ _ _ _ V _

T R O N L E E A S F O O E G G
O R O I L E E T V A R W B D D R
I U E E S Y P I A T N R N R C

14

BRITANNICA
BRANINBUSTERS

Mind Lines

Try to get from the top line of categories to the bottom in the fewest moves. Check off each box (or mark initials in the box if playing opponents) after each correct answer to a riddle. Once a player "owns" a box, an opponent must find another path.

Fam - FAMOUS & INFAMOUS
Sci - SCIENCE, SPACE & TECHNOLOGY
Lit - LITERATURE & THE ARTS
Pres - U.S. PRESIDENCY & FIRST LADIES
Pop - POP CULTURE & ENTERTAINMENT
Sprt - THE SPORTING LIFE
F&D - FOOD & DRINK

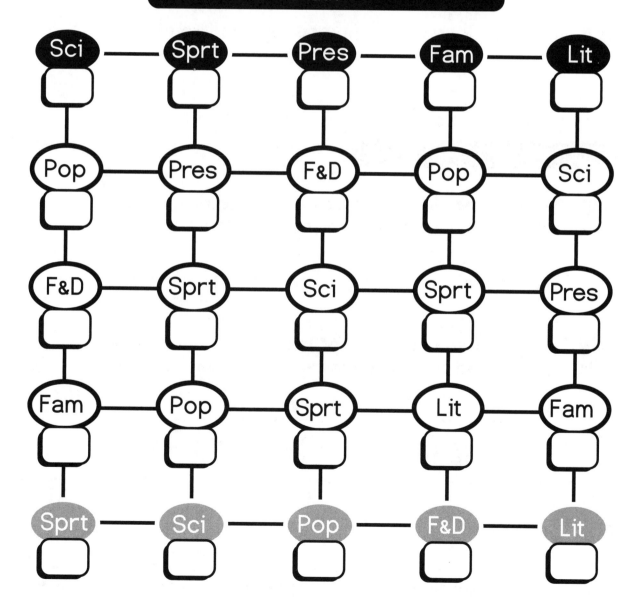

Alphabet Soup

Fill in the blanks with letters from the letter box below. All letters will be used only once in answering the riddles.

THE SPORTING LIFE

1 I am famous in my sport but seldom do I win,
Few male fans seem to care, though, as long as I show skin.

_ _ _ _ C _   _ _ _ _ _ _ C _

2 I'm a good-looking star, no one bends it like me,
Just don't mess with my clothing—I have OCD!

_ _ _ _ I _   _ _ _ _ _ H _ _

LITERATURE & THE ARTS

3 My characters waited for someone who didn't show,
Just another part of mankind's existential woe.

S _ _ _ _ _   _ _ _ _ _ _ T _

4 I chummed around with "Hef" and his cuddly friends,
I understood trees and where the sidewalk ends.

_ _ _ L _   _ _ _ _ V _ _ _ _ _

H	H	T	T	E	I	B	I	S	C	V	I	I	K	N	L	I	U	C
E	T	E	A	L	K	A	V	S	A	E	E	C	M	P	A	M	B	
R	A	D	A	S	D	K	E	C	N	R	T	D	S	L	E			

Alphabet Soup

Fill in the blanks with letters from the letter box below. All letters will be used only once in answering the riddles.

THE SPORTING LIFE

1 I refused to retreat as I was told,
"Manassa Mauler" was how I was sold.

_ _ C _ _ _ _ _ P _ _ _

2 Of brawn and brain I am a novel, weird mix,
Based on cerebral and violent conflicts.

_ H _ _ _ _ _ X _ _ _

FAMOUS & INFAMOUS

3 My crush on an actress and sick fascination,
Is what led me to try an assassination.

J _ _ _ _ _ _ _ _ _ _ _ _ Y _ _ _

4 I felt like the protagonist in *The Catcher in the Rye*,
And put a bullet through the maker of Lucy in the sky.

_ _ R _ _ _ _ _ V _ _ H _ _ _ _ _

C V J O M C H A A N C S B H E
D A R P N S N E P K J Y D I R M S I X Y
H L C G M N E K K H D A O A E I J

Alphabet Soup

Fill in the blanks with letters from the letter box below. All letters will be used only once in answering the riddles.

THE SPORTING LIFE

1 The Olympics cut me as a competitive event,
But in gym class I remain a most popular ascent.

_ _ P _   _ _ _ _ M _ _ _ _

2 I'm a famed event where mushers can mush,
I wind through the paths of the old gold rush.

_ D _ _ _ _ _ D

SCIENCE, SPACE & TECHNOLOGY

3 I'm a famous table, without legs but weights,
And plenty of numbers and nuclear states.

_ _ _ _ _ _ _ _ C _   _ _ _ L _

4 Though I won a Nobel, and protested Soviet rule,
I staked my claim to lasting fame by making canines drool.

_ V _ _   _ _ V _ _ _

O	O	R	M	G	I	L	L	L	E	N	I	I	D	I	A
T	T	R	V	B	C	V	R	A	B	P	A	C	V		
I	D	A	P	O	P	O	E	I	L	E	I	D	N		

18

BRITANNICA
BRAINBUSTERS

Alphabet Soup

Fill in the blanks with letters from the letter box below. All letters will be used only once in answering the riddles.

SCIENCE, SPACE & TECHNOLOGY

1 A newborn is a rated by this test, providing information,
On appearance, pulse, grimace, activity, and respiration.

_ P _ _ _   _ C _ _ _

2 I saved several industries—beer, wine, as well as silk,
But most famous were my vaccines and un-soured milk.

_ _ _ _ _ S _ P _ _ _ _ _ _

U.S. PRESIDENCY & FIRST LADIES

3 I brought comfort to the country with my fireside talk,
And seldom did the public ever see me try to walk.

_ _ _ _ _ _ _ _ N _ _ L _ _ _
_ _ O _ _ _ _ _ _

4 Upon age 40, I did something extreme,
I gave up all drinking of beer and Jim Beam.

_ E _ _ _ _ _   _ _ _ S _

O O K U A G E L A E P E U N L S E G
F T O L R G B O H R S R P A N I R I C
E U S R R V S N E E S T W O D O A A L

19

Alphabet Soup

Fill in the blanks with letters from the letter box below. All letters will be used only once in answering the riddles.

SCIENCE, SPACE & TECHNOLOGY

1 A great tragedy I suffered, school teaching was my life,
I was a devoted mother, space pioneer, and wife.

_ H _ _ _ _ _   _ _ A _ _ _ _ _

2 The father and sons were surgical masters on their own,
But their surname and their center are more famously known.

_ _ Y _   _ L _ _ _ _ _

FOOD & DRINK

3 I was easy to make but hard to eat,
The worms inside me were considered meat.

_ _ R _ _ _ K

4 I'm creamy and I'm sweet with a crispy top shell,
But ramekins you'll need and a blowtorch as well.

_ _ E _ _   _ _ _ _ _ E

H I R I E C T A A A L F C O S Y
I U C B E H I A T M C E C E
A D K M C F U R L E R R N M L

BRITANNICA
BRAINBUSTERS

Mind Lines

Try to get from the top line of categories to the bottom in the fewest moves. Check off each box (or mark initials in the box if playing opponents) after each correct answer to a riddle. Once a player "owns" a box, an opponent must find another path.

> Fam - FAMOUS & INFAMOUS
> Sci - SCIENCE, SPACE & TECHNOLOGY
> Lit - LITERATURE & THE ARTS
> Pres - U.S. PRESIDENCY & FIRST LADIES
> Pop - POP CULTURE & ENTERTAINMENT
> Sprt - THE SPORTING LIFE
> F&D - FOOD & DRINK

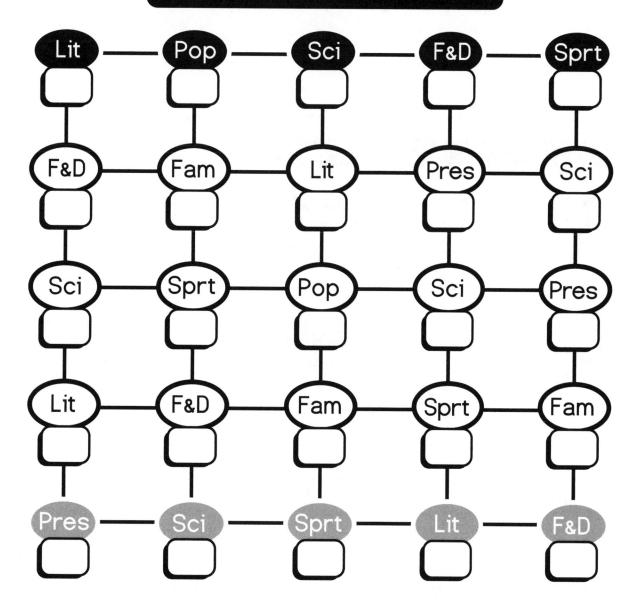

Alphabet Soup

Fill in the blanks with letters from the letter box below. All letters will be used only once in answering the riddles.

SCIENCE, SPACE & TECHNOLOGY

1 My view is very special and unique in history,
Launched in 1990 by the shuttle *Discovery*.

_ _ B _ _ _   _ _ A _ _

_ _ _ _ _ _ _ _ P _

2 I was the top Greek inventor of my day,
And my screw-shaped device is still used today.

_ _ C _ _ _ E _ _ _

POP CULTURE & ENTERTAINMENT

3 A film icon was I, an idol in capris,
And my breakfast I adored at famed Tiffany's.

_ _ D _ _ _   _ _ _ _ _ R _

4 Hunk, Hickory, and Zeke would all join Ms. Gale,
In this classic film journey and famous tale.

_ _ Z _ _   _ O _   _ _

I C E Z F O I E R E S A W M O E U R
B H S A E E U A L D O H D C D P
E E R L U A B N T H P P Z Y E B S C R

Alphabet Soup

Fill in the blanks with letters from the letter box below. All letters will be used only once in answering the riddles.

SCIENCE, SPACE & TECHNOLOGY

1 I'm a biologist not seeking absolution,
For my books with such titles as *The God Delusion*.

_ _ _ _ _ _ _ D _   _ _ W _ _ _ _

2 I witnessed warfare in my lab at the microscopic scale,
And the mold that I discovered is a legendary tale.

_ _ E _ _ _ _ _ _   _ _ _ _ M _ _ _

LITERATURE & THE ARTS

3 Women bathers and girls of ballet I painted,
With the Impressionists was I well acquainted.

_ D _ _ _   _ _ G _ _ _

4 Lilly pads, haystacks, and cathedrals, oh my!
No impression escaped my painterly eye.

_ _ _ _ _ D _   _ _ N _ _ _

I A M R D D U A G D R I D N L E R N
M L A F S A N O G E N E R D W T X
K A E L C C S H I E D G A A E E

Alphabet Soup

Fill in the blanks with letters from the letter box below. All letters will be used only once in answering the riddles.

LITERATURE & THE ARTS

1 The statue comes to life and demands that I repent,
And once I fail to do so, I start my dark descent.

D _ _   _ _ _ _ _ _ N _

2 I have long lived inside a circle and a square,
And Leo's drawing of me is without compare.

_ _ _ _ _ _ V _ _ _   M _ _

FOOD & DRINK

3 I was loved by the Spanish who pushed the Aztecs to the brink,
And some 50 cups of me would Montezuma daily drink.

_ H _ _ _ _ _ T _

4 I'm a choice cut, so scrumptious and tender,
For which you will pay more to the vendor.

_ _ _ _ T   _ _ N _ _

G	I	E	N	N	A	T	N	N	O	O	R	N	V	O	D
L	N	A	I	L	V	E	A	I	U	M	N	F
A	V	I	M	T	C	O	T	I	G	C	I	H	O

Alphabet Soup

Fill in the blanks with letters from the letter box below. All letters will be used only once in answering the riddles.

LITERATURE & THE ARTS

1 After fighting Vincent, which left the man unglued,
I left for Polynesia, bold hues I pursued.

_ _ U _   _ _ _ G _ _ _

2 The movable type that made me also brought me fame,
How we learn and spread ideas would never be the same.

_ _ _ _ _ B _ _ _   B _ _ _ _

U.S. PRESIDENCY & FIRST LADIES

3 My children's cocker spaniel, a coat worn by my wife,
On matters such as these hung my political life.

_ _ _ H _ _ _   _ _ _ O _

4 I was the last major presidential candidate to sport facial hair,
And to the *Chicago Tribune*, I was last president to so dare.

_ _ _ _ _ A _   _ _ W _ _

A E A N O R O B I X L D G Y R N U
I U L U H B G S W I T T A E G C
G N H B R E D N M U P I A E E

25

Alphabet Soup

Fill in the blanks with letters from the letter box below. All letters will be used only once in answering the riddles.

LITERATURE & THE ARTS

1 My shows set records, they're enormous hits,
My productions are famous for their glitz.

_ _ _ _ E _ _ L _ _ _ _ _ _ B _ _

2 My paintings are endearing but hardly sublime,
Projecting an innocence of a simpler time.

_ _ _ _ M _ _ _ _ _ _ _ _ _ L

THE SPORTING LIFE

3 "Say it ain't so, Joe," was the boy's plaintive plea,
About the scandal tainting baseball and me.

_ H _ _ _ _ _ _ _ O _ _ _ C _ _ _ _

4 The stade was the very first Olympic race,
Inspiring the term for a sporting place.

_ _ A D _ _ _

D O O C S E A T N A R S E N O R S O
L S R L K A O M W E W O L R K L N E J
H E E B D I W J C D E U M Y B S N L A

BRITANNICA BRAINBUSTERS

Mind Lines

Try to get from the top line of categories to the bottom in the fewest moves. Check off each box (or mark initials in the box if playing opponents) after each correct answer to a riddle. Once a player "owns" a box, an opponent must find another path.

Fam - FAMOUS & INFAMOUS
Sci - SCIENCE, SPACE & TECHNOLOGY
Lit   - LITERATURE & THE ARTS
Pres - U.S. PRESIDENCY & FIRST LADIES
Pop - POP CULTURE & ENTERTAINMENT
Sprt - THE SPORTING LIFE
F&D - FOOD & DRINK

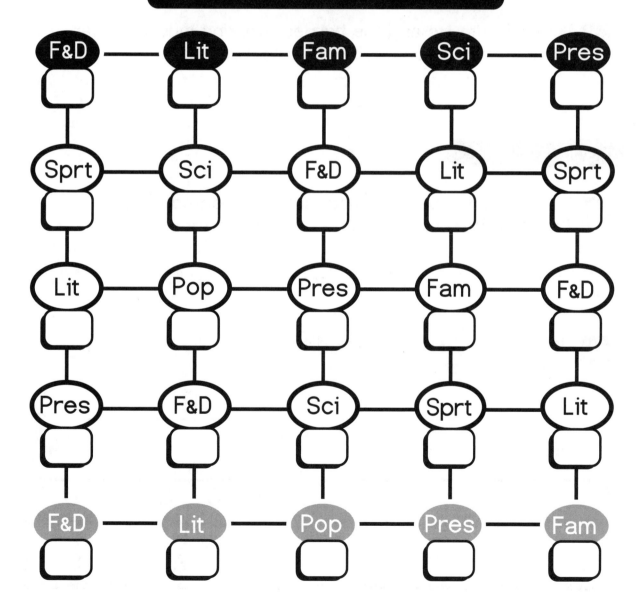

Alphabet Soup

Fill in the blanks with letters from the letter box below. All letters will be used only once in answering the riddles.

SCIENCE, SPACE & TECHNOLOGY

1 I'm the largest human muscle, I can look great in jeans,
And without me you would lose important balancing means.

_ _ _ _ T _ _ _   _ _ X _ _ _ _

2 I'm critical to life and the hardest working muscle by far,
Moving 2,500 gallons daily, I'm a workout star.

_ E _ _ _

FOOD & DRINK

3 I came from Japan, I'm made from fermented rice,
I'm most often served warm but can also top ice.

_ A _ _

4 Sauerkraut's German name disgraced it,
This "new" wartime dish then replaced it.

L _ _ _ _ _ _ _   _ _ _ B _ _ _

G	Y	L	B	M	B	S	E	C	G	X	U	T
I	E	K	R	H	B	A	T	U	A	T	S	
A	R	E	M	L	A	E	I	A	U	S	E	

BRITANNICA
BRAINBUSTERS

Alphabet Soup

Fill in the blanks with letters from the letter box below. All letters will be used only once in answering the riddles.

FOOD & DRINK

1 I'm the most famous white wine grape around,
To drinkers and growers am I renowned.

__ __ A __ __ __ __ __ N __ __

2 How do you rule a country, this leader would tease,
That has 246 kinds of cheese!

__ __ __ R __ __ __ __ __ E __ __ __ __ L __ __

FAMOUS & INFAMOUS

3 From Paris to Constantinople did I run,
My plush accommodations would not be outdone.

__ __ I __ __ __ E __ __ __ __ __ __

4 I'm notorious for the murderous knife I'd wield,
My identity may finally have been revealed.

__ A __ __ __ __ __ __ __ P __ __ __ __

C A O P O E J S N A X R E D G E C A
Y R L L E U P K E H P I C A H T
R E E A R N T E S R I N D R H L S

29

Alphabet Soup

Fill in the blanks with letters from the letter box below. All letters will be used only once in answering the riddles.

FOOD & DRINK

1 I'm famously served at the Kentucky Derby each year,
With green herbs mixed with bourbon, I'm more powerful than beer.

_ I _ _   _ _ _ _ _ P

2 My dinners for four, said my doctor, had to cease,
Unless there were three others allowed to the feasts.

_ R _ _ _   _ E _ _ _ _ _

POP CULTURE & ENTERTAINMENT

3 No waitress was cuter than I at the Perk,
My "do" was a critical part of my work.

_ _ _ _ _ _ _ F _ _   _ N _ _ _ _ _

4 I was the most famous festival of the Sixties,
Three days of peace and music, and plenty of hippies.

_ O _ _ _ _ _ O _ _

I	L	D	T	E	F	W	L	E	P	S	N	T	N	I	R	E
N	R	O	K	E	N	N	J	I	S	C	M	O	E
O	A	S	N	L	O	W	S	T	O	U	J	O

Alphabet Soup

Fill in the blanks with letters from the letter box below. All letters will be used only once in answering the riddles.

FOOD & DRINK

1 I'm a meatless dish with a meat-based name,
A grilled cheese sandwich comes close to the same.

W _ _ _ _   _ _ _ _ I _

2 I'm a traditional dish in the Middle East,
And now the world over I'm a common street feast.

_ A _ _ F _ _

U.S. PRESIDENCY & FIRST LADIES

3 My presidency began with an awkward start,
When the chief justice and I flubbed the swearing-in part.

_ _ _ _ _ K   _ _ _ M _

4 Young John-John enjoyed crawling through my spaces,
Spaces once covered for FDR's braces.

_ E _ _ _ _ _ _   _ _ _ K

L B O F R C K B E K B A E
I E M R A S H A L R B E A
T W E A F A L S A L T O U D S

Alphabet Soup

Fill in the blanks with letters from the letter box below. All letters will be used only once in answering the riddles.

FOOD & DRINK

1 I'm a common British dish, far humbler than steak,
Partially named for the exploding sound I make.

_ _ _ G _ _ _   _ _ _   _ _ _ H

2 I'm boneless meat rolled tight so my butter won't drain,
I'm a classic dish named for the capital of Ukraine.

_ _ _ _ K _ _   K _ _ _

SCIENCE, SPACE & TECHNOLOGY

3 I'm seen atop church spires and ship masts, too,
I'm sparky and typically violet or blue.

S _ _ _ _   _ _ M ' _   _ _ R _

4 I'm the largest in the world, I'm a U.S. national monument,
But around my severe environs no vacationer ever went.

_ _ _ _ _ _ N _   _ _ _ _ _ C _

A V A N H R D A I A H E O N I C S
E S N R R T S G H K L B F I E A E
N R C E E M T S M N A K M A I N C I

BRITANNICA
BRAINBUSTERS

Mind Lines

Try to get from the top line of categories to the bottom in the fewest moves. Check off each box (or mark initials in the box if playing opponents) after each correct answer to a riddle. Once a player "owns" a box, an opponent must find another path.

Fam - FAMOUS & INFAMOUS
Sci - SCIENCE, SPACE & TECHNOLOGY
Lit - LITERATURE & THE ARTS
Pres - U.S. PRESIDENCY & FIRST LADIES
Pop - POP CULTURE & ENTERTAINMENT
Sprt - THE SPORTING LIFE
F&D - FOOD & DRINK

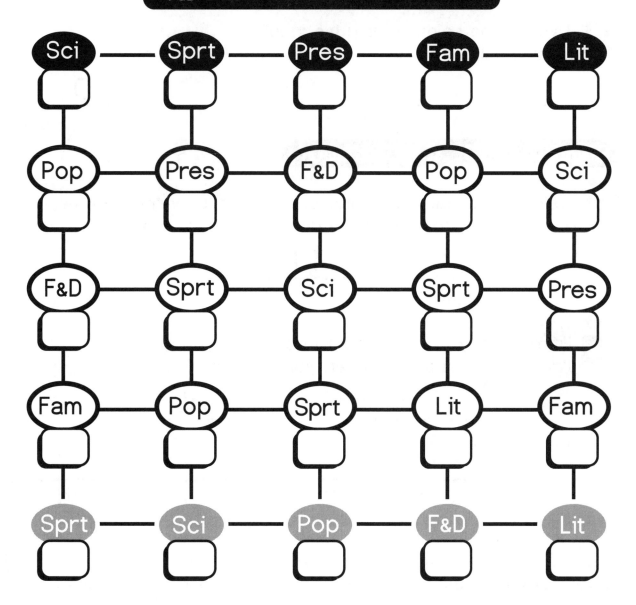

Alphabet Soup

Fill in the blanks with letters from the letter box below. All letters will be used only once in answering the riddles.

POP CULTURE & ENTERTAINMENT

1 Sexy con men and doomed lovers are roles I take,
My movies are famous like my famous namesake.

_ _ _ N _ _ _ _ _   _ _ _ _ _ P _ _ _

2 Twenty-one soloists sang me in 1985,
Raising millions to help feed and keep Africans alive.

_ _ _ R _ _ _ _ _ _ _ _ _ _ D

SCIENCE, SPACE & TECHNOLOGY

3 We're communal furry critters, in the North we're found worldwide,
And contrary to legend, we don't commit mass suicide.

_ _ _ M I _ _ _ _

4 I'm not funny or a bone but I can make you groan,
I'm what you really hit when you hit your "funny bone."

_ _ _ N _ _   _ _ _ V _

E	L	G	I	U	O	O	W	R	L	E	A	W	E	N	R
C	D	A	A	D	S	O	R	V	T	L	M	D	R	I	N
R	E	A	R	M	N	E	P	L	I	N	E	O	H	E	

34

Alphabet Soup

Fill in the blanks with letters from the letter box below. All letters will be used only once in answering the riddles.

POP CULTURE & ENTERTAINMENT

1 I worked on the waterfront, made many women swoon,
And mumbled to an Oscar as a mobster-tycoon.

_ _ _ _ O _   _ _ _ _ _ D _

2 Law and order were lost on that infamous day,
We left a man dead at the Altamont Speedway.

_ _ L _' _   _ _ G _ _ _ _

U.S. PRESIDENCY & FIRST LADIES

3 Lincoln said he owed his presidency to me,
My photo of him helped his popularity.

M_ _ _ _ _ _   _ _ _ D _

4 My good-looks wooed the ladies, I thrilled men on stage,
But Lincoln hardly welcomed my last role and rage.

_ _ _ N   _ _ L _ _ _   _ _ _ T _

```
A R W E O S Y N L S D R H N O M
A L O T O W A S E O L B J B H I N
E G A K R D E N A L M H B H L T
```

35

Alphabet Soup

Fill in the blanks with letters from the letter box below. All letters will be used only once in answering the riddles.

POP CULTURE & ENTERTAINMENT

1 Of SNL's many hosts, I was the first,
My "seven dirty words" got me praised and cursed.

_ _ _ _ G _ _   _ _ _ L _ _

2 From the Europe of Hitler did we all flee,
The sound of music filled our group with glee.

_ _ _   _ _ _ P _   _ _ _ _ _ _ Y

THE SPORTING LIFE

3 "Baseball is 90% mental," I once proclaimed,
"The other half is physical," I quickly exclaimed.

_ _ _ _ I   _ _ _ R _

4 I never had sails, despite my name,
I scored the blonde with the worldwide fame.

_ O _   _ _ _ _ _ A _ _ _

E	I	C	P	O	I	Y	I	P	G	O	B	G	D	A
G	Y	G	M	R	O	E	I	R	N	A	T	I	L	A	O
R	E	J	G	E	L	N	M	A	A	R	V	F	R	O

36

Alphabet Soup

Fill in the blanks with letters from the letter box below. All letters will be used only once in answering the riddles.

POP CULTURE & ENTERTAINMENT

1 I'm rank propaganda battling drugs and related crime,
A cult classic I became, as the worst film of all time.

_ _ _ _ _ E _   _ _ _ _ N _ _ _

2 From war hero to gun-runner to singer in beret,
Atop the music charts my stunning ballad would long stay.

_ _ _ _ _ Y S _ _ _ _ _ _

FOOD & DRINK

3 I started civilization, writing, as well as wine,
And my name is the location where two rivers entwine.

_ _ _ _ _ P _ _ _ _ _ I _

4 I caused his death after he drank me,
I killed the towering Socrates.

_ E _ _ _ C _

E	I	S	M	T	S	R	R	A	E	C	R	S	M	E
H	E	M	A	A	B	A	O	L	D	P	O	S
F	L	M	Y	O	A	E	D	R	E	E	R	N	K

Alphabet Soup

Fill in the blanks with letters from the letter box below. All letters will be used only once in answering the riddles.

U.S. PRESIDENCY & FIRST LADIES

1 My séances at the White House sought the spirit world,
Around my lavish spending much controversy swirled.

_ _ _ _ Y   _ _ _ _   _ _ _ C _ _

2 From legumes and the Navy I came to D.C.,
A coup and malaise ended my presidency.

_ _ M _ _   _ A _ _ _ _

THE SPORTING LIFE

3 When this place held the Games, 60 nations wouldn't go,
The boycott set the stage for a bad Olympic show.

_ _ _ _ _ O _

4 The stars were football players, each one a Chicago Bear,
In this classic drama about the friendship they would share.

_ R _ _ _ '   _ _ N _

A	I	S	T	N	O	M	A	W	O	T	L	R	Y	O
S	N	G	I	I	S	M	C	N	D	C	R	B
Y	M	O	A	R	O	R	L	M	E	D	J	C	N

Alphabet Soup

Fill in the blanks with letters from the letter box below. All letters will be used only once in answering the riddles.

U.S. PRESIDENCY & FIRST LADIES

1 I was the fattest president, heavy on the scale,
And the tub at the White House once snared me like a whale.

_ _ _ _ _ _ _ M _ W _ _ _   _ _ _ _

2 Ending Reconstruction was my dubious fame,
For it re-enchained blacks by a new, novel name.

_ _ _ _ _ _ _ R _ _ _ _   _   _ _ Y _ _

FAMOUS & INFAMOUS

3 My brand smacks of money, style, and class,
And on the back of a pony would an empire I amass.

_ _ _ P _ _ _ _ _ R _ _

4 Legend says I was sold out by the "lady in red,"
Although she really wore orange, I still ended up dead.

_ _ _ N _ _ _ _ _ _ _ _ R

E B A R L A G L H O J R W W L A F R
U R S I R N I H T A E I D A P T D H T H
E L O N F Y D R M L I L H R O N A U E

Alphabet Soup

Fill in the blanks with letters from the letter box below. All letters will be used only once in answering the riddles.

U.S. PRESIDENCY & FIRST LADIES

1 The women who followed me followed my lead,
And I saved U.S. treasures from British greed.

_ O _ _ _ _   _ _ D _ _ _ _

2 I had Midwestern roots, and my speeches seldom bored,
I helped bring down a curtain and stem a chilly war.

_ _ _ _ _ _ D   _ _ _ _ G _ _

FOOD & DRINK

3 I'm tiny but strong and widely consumed,
And I joined King Tut when he was entombed.

_ U _ _ _ _ _

4 When France denounced the Iraq War in 2003,
This U.S. food then became a hit, temporarily.

_ _ _ _ _ _ D _ _   F _ _ _ _

O	U	R	D	N	E	E	L	R	G	O	M	F	F	A
L	S	D	R	O	E	R	N	N	I	S	M	E	A	
A	E	M	D	A	O	D	D	R	S	L	I	T	Y	A

Alphabet Soup

Fill in the blanks with letters from the letter box below. All letters will be used only once in answering the riddles.

U.S. PRESIDENCY & FIRST LADIES

1 For just 200 days the country I led,
"I am a Stalwart," my killer calmly said.

__ __ M __ __   __ __ __ __ F __ __ __ __

2 Several amendments were passed during my eight years,
Allowing women to vote and prohibiting beers.

__ __ O __ __ __ __   __ __ __ __ __ N

SCIENCE, SPACE & TECHNOLOGY

3 "ROY G BIV" reflects the seven layers of me,
Which in a rain or in a mist you might just see.

__ __ __ __ B __ __

4 Mark Twain nearly predicted exactly when he'd die,
Tying his prediction to when next I would fly by.

H __ __ __ __ __ __ ' __   __ __ M __ __

A N E I S O O O A O Y N A D J A R
W I E G O S O O W C M W I
L S F H L D R B T M L E R W L E

Alphabet Soup

Fill in the blanks with letters from the letter box below. All letters will be used only once in answering the riddles.

THE SPORTING LIFE

1 I stressed the forward pass when I did coach,
And to football I brought a new approach.

_ _ U _ _   _ _ _ K _ _

2 I always host, on the weekend of a holiday,
The best-attended sports event on a single day.

_ _ _ _ _ N _ _ _ _ _ I _

POP CULTURE & ENTERTAINMENT

3 I wrote a hit song, creating game shows was my passion,
I also claimed to serve as a CIA assassin.

_ _ _ C _   B _ _ _ _ _

4 My influence was mighty, and all because,
"And that's the way it is" was the way it was.

_ _ _ T _ _   _ _ _ _ K _ _

N B I C O L O I T C R R P O I N I
U R E K E T A S N H C N W U C
K T E N A K K R S L A D A R I E

Alphabet Soup

Fill in the blanks with letters from the letter box below. All letters will be used only once in answering the riddles.

FAMOUS & INFAMOUS

1 I was the real Dracula behind the lore,
Who impaled his victims and relished in gore.

_ _ _ D _   _ _ _   I _ _ _ _ _ _ _

2 I was weak until donning my famed leopard trunks,
I turned skinny weak punks into muscular hunks.

_ H _ _ _ _ _   _ _ L _ _

LITERATURE & THE ARTS

3 A classier trio of singers could not be found,
Our concerts in two decades were globally renowned.

_ _ _   T _ _ _ _   _ N _ _ _

4 I created my own steps, with Shirley did I tap,
No one ever better put my art form on the map.

_ _ _ L   _ _ _ _ _ S _ _

L D B H L T T B A R H S N E O C I O
H M R R A R V T A E T E E A I E
R N L S E N L P E S L A S T I H L O

43

Alphabet Soup

Fill in the blanks with letters from the letter box below. All letters will be used only once in answering the riddles.

FOOD & DRINK

1 Korean tacos as well as Tex-Mex,
Both are samples of this movement's effects.

_ _ S _ _ _   C _ _ _ _ _ _

2 I'm a Japanese delicacy, I'm a poisonous fish,
And thin slices of me make up a very expensive dish.

_ U _ _

U.S. PRESIDENCY & FIRST LADIES

3 My meal of milk and cherries on a hot summer day,
Is what clearly caused my death five days later, some say.

_ _ C _ _ _ _   _ _ _ Y _ _ _

4 I took the oath and then talked for two hours,
I died after only four weeks in power.

_ _ _ L _ _ _ _   _ _ _ R _

_ _ _ _ _ S _ _

U O R L A H R C I Y T L Y N E W A I
Y R R I N O G U I A Z L S O I M
R F C F U H N A I H S N U S E A

Alphabet Soup

Fill in the blanks with letters from the letter box below. All letters will be used only once in answering the riddles.

FAMOUS & INFAMOUS

1 Tales of my deformity and depravity abound,
And my 500-year-old bones were just recently found.

_ _ C _ _ _ _   _ _ I

2 To the powerful I famously offer seats,
Amid circles and squares and letter-named streets.

_ A _ _ _ _ _ T _ _   _ _

FOOD & DRINK

3 Post-meal coffee and ice cream usually served separately,
Are combined into one in this dessert in Italy.

A _ _ G _ _ _

4 To deal with hunger in Ireland there was this deal,
A tongue-in-cheek one to serve these darlings as a meal.

_ H _ _ _ _ _ _

F	H	I	N	N	A	A	H	W	N	I	O	G	I
C	C	F	O	H	C	L	E	I	G	R	R		
A	R	D	T	T	S	A	I	D	D	O	I		

ALPHABET SOUP
Answer Key

Page 9

1. Reports of unexplained occurrences in the region known as the **Bermuda Triangle**—an area roughly bounded by Miami, Bermuda, and Puerto Rico—have been common since the mid-19th century. Scores of planes and ships have seemingly disappeared without a trace, leaving some observers to turn to the supernatural for explanations.

2. The *Hindenburg*, the German dirigible that was the largest rigid airship (zeppelin) ever created, dramatically caught fire and exploded while landing at Lakehurst, New Jersey, on May 6, 1937, killing 36. The tragedy was captured on film and brought an end to the era of using dirigibles for commercial air transportation.

3. **Jimmy Stewart** was already one of Hollywood's major stars when he joined the armed forces in 1941, eventually rising to the rank of colonel and logging more than 1,800 hours in bombing missions. His role in the Christmas classic *It's a Wonderful Life* (1946)—in which his character decides to commit suicide on Christmas Eve— was his first film upon returning to Hollywood.

4. **Justin Timberlake** achieved fame as a member of the hit "boy band" *NSYNC and as a solo performer, but he made headlines worldwide at the 2004 Super Bowl when he pulled off part of costar Janet Jackson's top in what was famously termed a "wardrobe malfunction."

Page 10

1. The costliest natural disaster in U.S. history, **Hurricane Katrina** struck the southeastern United States in late August 2005 with winds in excess of 175 mph, claiming more than 1,800 lives. New Orleans' levee system failed, flooding 80 percent of the city. When aid was slow in coming, crime and looting became rampant, only compounding problems.

2. On May 29, 1953, New Zealand beekeeper **Edmund Hillary** and Tibetan mountaineer Tenzing Norgay became the first climbers to reach the summit of Mount Everest, the highest point on Earth. Hillary left behind a crucifix, and Tenzing, a Buddhist, made a food offering.

3. Boxing champion Muhammad Ali, born in Louisville, Kentucky, in 1942, was originally named **Cassius Clay**, Jr. He and his father (Cassius Clay, Sr.) were both named after the Kentucky-born abolitionist who bravely led the antislavery movement in the South and who became one of the founders of the Republican Party in 1854.

4. The **Masters Tournament**, one of the four "Majors" of golf, is held annually each April at the Augusta National Golf Club in Augusta, Georgia. It is noted for the impeccable condition of the course, the green sport coat afforded the winner, and for the 11th, 12th, and 13th holes, known collectively as Amen Corner and the site of many momentous shots in the tournament's history.

Page 11

1. At the end of the Constitutional Convention in Philadelphia in 1787, as **Benjamin Franklin** exited Independence Hall, a lady asked him, "Well, Doctor, what have we got—a republic or a monarchy?" "A republic," he said, "if you can keep it."

2. According to the famed ditty, "**Lizzie Borden** took an axe / And gave her mother forty whacks; / And when she saw what she had done / She gave her father forty-one." Borden was acquitted of murder charges in 1893, and in point of fact, her mother and father had been hacked 19 and 11 times, respectively.

3. **Norman Mailer** was famous for his writings, such as the World War II classic *The Naked and the Dead* (1948) and his Pulitzer Prize-winning *The Executioner's Song* (1979), as well as for his tumultuous non-literary life, which included a failed run for mayor of New York City and a double stabbing of the second of his six wives.

4. According to legend, when Abraham Lincoln met **Harriet Beecher Stowe** in 1862, he said, "So you're the little woman who wrote the book that started this great war." Her anti-slavery novel, *Uncle Tom's Cabin* (1851-2), was an international sensation and made Stowe a celebrity.

Page 12

1. In 1959, trailblazing fashion designer **Pierre Cardin** was expelled from the Chambre Syndicale (the Parisian association of haute couture designers) for releasing a ready-to-wear line. He then shocked the establishment again when he began widely licensing his name to non-clothing products, from eyewear and watches to pens and even automobile interiors.

2. **Judas Iscariot** was one of the Twelve Apostles of Jesus Christ. For 30 silver coins, he betrayed Jesus to the chief priests and elders, an act leading to the Passion of Christ (his arrest, trial, suffering, and crucifixion). Filled with remorse, Judas returned the "blood money" and hanged himself. His name subsequently became synonymous with treachery.

3. **Harry Houdini** was the greatest illusionist of his day and perhaps the greatest escape artist ever. In a typical act he was shackled with chains and placed in a box that was locked, roped, weighted, and then submerged under water.

4. **Marlon Brando** received a record salary of $3.7 million for his ten-minute part as Superman's father in *Superman* (1978). Some reports say his ultimate salary for the meager part reached some $14 million, due to a negotiation for a percentage of the box-office take. Memorization of lines was not even necessary: his lines were written on props.

Page 13

1. **Andersonville**, in southwest-central Georgia, was the site of the Confederacy's largest prison for captured Union soldiers during the Civil War. It was notorious for its unhealthy conditions and high death rate. Between February 1864 and May 1865, nearly 13,000 Union prisoners died at Andersonville from disease, malnutrition, and other causes.

2. **Osama bin Laden** was the founder of al-Qaeda and the mastermind of the Sept. 11, 2001, attacks on the World Trade Center in New York City and the Pentagon near Washington, D.C. On May 2,

2011, a small force of U.S. Navy SEALS, transported by helicopters, raided bin Laden's compound in Pakistan, shot and killed him, and then carried his body to sea for burial.

3. Reciting the Hippocratic Oath, the renowned ethical code of conduct associated with **Hippocrates**, the ancient Greek "Father of Medicine," remains a ritual of medical school graduation ceremonies. But conservative critics have wondered whether an oath predicated on the principle of first doing no harm can be relevant in an age of legalized abortion and physician-assisted suicide.

4. **Alfred Kinsey** became president of Indiana University's Institute of Sex Research in 1942 and published the groundbreaking Kinsey reports (on males in 1948, on females in 1953). Irregularities in his sampling methods, as well as his own open marriage and bisexuality, only added to the controversy that shadowed him. *Time* magazine compared his impact to that of Christopher Columbus.

Page 14

1. The **Tour de France** is the world's most prestigious bicycle race. Begun in 1903, it was established by cyclist and journalist Henri Desgrange, whose publication was printed on yellow paper. Yellow thus became the color of the jersey worn by the cyclist with the lowest cumulative time each day during the three-week race.

2. Few athletes have dominated their sport as thoroughly as golfer **Tiger Woods** did from the 1990s until 2009, when news of his multiple infidelities broke, costing him his marriage and causing a disruption of his career from which he struggled to recover.

3. **Lingonberries** come from a small creeping plant, related to the blueberry and cranberry, whose fruit is popularly used in jelly, jam, and juice by northern Europeans and Scandinavians. Lingonberry jam, for example, is a common topping on Swedish pancakes.

4. Elizabeth Gilbert's best-selling memoir, **Eat, Pray, Love**: *One Woman's Search for Everything Across Italy, India, and Indonesia* (2006), chronicles the author's travels across Europe (especially Italy, where she delights in Italian cuisine) and Asia in the wake of a painful marriage and divorce. The film version (2010) stars Julia Roberts.

Page 16

1. American race car driver **Danica Patrick** was the first woman to win, in 2008, an IndyCar championship event. Her win quieted some critics who, in light of her sexy modeling and lucrative endorsement deals, wondered whether she was merely a marketing phenom.

2. English football (soccer) star **David Beckham** is famous for his ability to "bend" the ball. He is just as famous for his good looks and highly publicized personal life, which includes his marriage to pop singer Victoria Adams ("Posh" of the Spice Girls) and his struggle with OCD (obsessive-compulsive disorder).

3. **Samuel Beckett**, recipient of the Nobel Prize in Literature in 1969, is perhaps best known for his play *Waiting for Godot* (1952), in which two men wait hope-filled but in vain for the mysterious Godot. The play spurred the so-called Theater of the Absurd, whose works reflected an existential view of the absurdity of life.

4. Writer and cartoonist **Shel Silverstein** drew for the military newspaper *Stars and Stripes* while serving in Japan and Korea, contributed to Hugh Hefner's *Playboy*, and gained a wide audience with his classic children's books such as *The Giving Tree* (1964) and *Where the Sidewalk Ends* (1974).

Page 17

1. On Sept. 22, 1927, former heavyweight boxing champion **Jack Dempsey** of Manassa, Colorado, met champion Gene Tunney in the famous "Battle of the Long Count." After Dempsey knocked Tunney down, he failed to go to a neutral corner. By the time the referee escorted Dempsey to the corner, Tunney had received extra seconds to recover, and he eventually won the match.

2. The hybrid sport of **chess boxing**, invented in 2003, is now played worldwide and managed by professional organizations. A match consists of two competitors and 11 rounds—six rounds of chess and five rounds of boxing. Victory is gained by knockout, checkmate, referee's decision, or an opponent exceeding the time allotted for the chess portion of a match.

3. On March 30, 1981, **John Hinckley, Jr.**, fired six shots as Ronald Reagan exited a hotel in Washington, D.C. One bullet entered Reagan's lung, and he nearly died. Hinckley had become obsessed with Jodie Foster, a teenage actress in *Taxi Driver*, a film about a loner who plans to kill a presidential candidate. By killing the president, Hinckley thought he could win Foster's affection.

4. On Dec. 8, 1980, **Mark David Chapman** shot and killed ex-Beatle and pop icon John Lennon, famous for such songs as "Imagine" and "Lucy in the Sky with Diamonds." Chapman had become obsessed with the confused and disillusioned protagonist of J.D. Salinger's *Catcher in the Rye* and angry over Lennon's statement that he and the Beatles were "more popular than Jesus."

Page 18

1. **Rope climbing** was part of the gymnastics competition in nearly every Olympics between 1896 and 1932. The goal was to climb a vertical rope using only one's hands, beginning from a seated position; the rope was a daunting 45 feet long (reduced to some 25 feet later). Considering the strength the event required, it was a natural complement to the gymnastics competitions.

2. The annual **Iditarod** is Alaska's famed sled dog race. Covering approximately 1,100 miles, it partially follows the old Iditarod Trail sled dog mail route blazed from the southeastern coastal towns of Seward and Knik to the goldfields and mining camps of northwest Alaska in the early 1900s. Sled teams delivered mail and supplies to such towns as Nome and Iditarod and carried out gold.

3. Russian chemist Dimitry Mendeleyev (1834-1907) invented one of the foundations of chemistry, the **periodic table** of elements, the basic building blocks of matter. He discovered that, when chemical elements were arranged in order of increasing atomic number—i.e., the total number of protons in the atomic nucleus—the resulting table revealed a pattern called the "periodic law."

4. Russian physiologist **Ivan Pavlov**, who won the 1904 Nobel Prize for Physiology or Medicine, developed the concept of the conditioned reflex from his famous experiment with a dog trained to salivate at the sound of a bell. An anticommunist who was not allowed to transfer his lab abroad, Pavlov bravely remained in Russia in the 1920s and 1930s while boldly denouncing Soviet rule.

Page 19

1. The **Apgar Score,** named after Dr. Virginia Apgar who invented it in 1952, is a medical rating procedure used to assess a newborn's health immediately after birth. A score of 0, 1, or 2 is assigned to each of five conditions, whose first letters spell out Apgar's name: **A**ppearance, **P**ulse, **G**rimace, **A**ctivity, and **R**espiration.

2. Chemist and microbiologist **Louis Pasteur** (1822-1895) had an extraordinary influence on the development of science, technology, and medicine. He discovered that microorganisms cause fermentation and disease, developed vaccines against anthrax and rabies, and created the heat-treatment process called pasteurization that kills microorganisms in food and beverages.

3. **Franklin Delano Roosevelt**'s radio broadcasts (called "Fireside Chats" for their informal nature) did much to restore public confidence during the Great Depression and World War II. Roosevelt also did not want his physical limitations due to polio to hinder the public's faith in his abilities, so he requested that the press not photograph him in his wheelchair or while attempting to walk.

4. **George W. Bush**, who had been arrested for drunk driving in 1976, decided to change his ways after a drunken weekend celebrating his 40th birthday. Said his wife Laura, "George just woke up and he knew he wanted to quit. . . . He just stopped cold turkey."

Page 20

1. American high school social science teacher **Christa McAuliffe** was chosen out of some 10,000 applicants to be the first private citizen and nonscientist to travel to space. She was among the seven-member crew that died when the space shuttle *Challenger* exploded 73 seconds after launch on Jan. 28, 1986.

2. Three generations of the Mayo family established at Rochester, Minnesota, the world-renowned nonprofit **Mayo Clinic** and the Mayo Foundation for Medical Education and Research. Charles Horace Mayo (1865-1939), the youngest son of his father William who established the family practice, was called a "surgical wonder," pioneering numerous surgical techniques.

3. Some form of **hardtack**—the bland cracker or biscuit made from flour, water, and salt and hardened by baking—was a staple of soldiers and sailors for centuries. If kept dry, hardtack was nearly imperishable, but when not stored properly it could easily become infested with worms, as happened frequently during the U.S. Civil War.

4. **Crème brûlée**, French for "burnt cream," is a popular dessert of rich custard with a crispy, caramelized top, the stark contrast giving the sweet treat its appeal. It is usually served in small ceramic dishes called ramekins, and a small blowtorch is used to caramelize the top into a crispy shell.

Page 22

1. The **Hubble Space Telescope**, the most sophisticated optical observatory ever placed into orbit around Earth, was named after famed American astronomer Edwin Hubble and launched by the crew of the orbiter *Discovery* on April 25, 1990.

2. **Archimedes** (*c.* 290-211 BC) was the most famous mathematician and inventor of ancient Greece. He formulated the law of buoyancy, known as the Archimedes' principle, and invented the famed "Archimedes screw," a machine used for raising water from the hold of a ship and still employed today in sewage treatment systems.

3. **Audrey Hepburn**, the slender, stylish, Belgian-born film actress, was famous for her radiant beauty, her charming mix of sophistication and innocence, and her tireless efforts to aid needy children as a special U.N. ambassador. Her hit films included *Roman Holiday* (1953), *Sabrina* (1954, in which she sported her famed capri pants), and *Breakfast at Tiffany's* (1961).

4. Farm hands Hunk, Hickory, and Zeke became the Scarecrow, Tin Man, and Cowardly Lion, respectively, who joined Dorothy Gale on her dream journey in *The **Wizard of Oz***. The movie (1939) made a star out of Judy Garland, who sang the film classic "Over the Rainbow."

Page 23

1. British evolutionary biologist and popular writer **Richard Dawkins** has outraged many with his energetic defense of atheism. He also famously introduced, in a 1976 book, the idea of "memes," the cultural equivalent of genes through which ideas, symbols, and practices migrate and mutate from person to person in writings, speech, gestures, and rituals.

2. On Sept. 3, 1928, Scottish bacteriologist **Alexander Fleming** noticed that mold accidentally growing on a dish of bacteria was inhibiting the growth of the bacteria. This chance discovery of one of the most widely used antibiotic agents (called penicillin after the name of the mold) earned him a share of the Nobel Prize for Physiology or Medicine in 1945.

3. A prominent figure in the Impressionist movement, **Edgar Degas** (1834-1917) often chose for his subjects the laundresses, cabaret singers, milliners, and prostitutes of Paris in the late 19th century. He is particularly well known for his depictions of ballet dancers and of women bathing.

4. **Claude Monet** (1840-1926) is synonymous with the Impressionist movement in painting. His repeated studies of the same scene but in different light—as seen in such series as *Haystacks, Rouen Cathedral,* and *Water Lilies*—rank among the most famous and popular works in Western art.

Page 24

1. Although not fully appreciated in its day (it premiered in 1787), Mozart's ***Don Giovanni*** was soon recognized as one of the greatest of all operas. The music by which the vengeful ghost (a stone statue that comes to life) appears at the end is some of the most formidable Mozart ever wrote. The music foreshadows and accompanies Giovanni's descent into Hell.

2. Created in about 1490 to illustrate the theory of symmetry as propounded by Roman architect Vitruvius, ***Vitruvian Man*** is Leonardo da Vinci's most famous illustration. Leonardo drew a perfectly proportioned human figure whose outstretched arms and legs fit perfectly within both a circle and a square.

3. The cacao plant, from which chocolate is produced, thrived in Mesoamerican civilizations. **Chocolate** was venerated as "food of the gods," and the pods were used in religious rituals, traded as currency, and even decorated and used as vessels from which the chocolate would be drunk. Aztec Emperor Montezuma II reportedly drank 50 cups of chocolate each day.

4. **Filet mignon** is widely considered the king of steaks. An expensive cut, it is taken from the back rib cage of the animal, a non-weight-bearing area that remains tender and not toughened by exertion.

Page 25

1. **Paul Gauguin** was one of the most influential of the Post-Impressionist painters. After his argument with Vincent van Gogh on Christmas Eve, 1888, van Gogh cut off part of his own ear. However, some recent scholars have suggested that it was not Vincent, but Gauguin, who actually severed the ear. Gauguin later resided in Tahiti, the setting for many of his most famous works.

2. Completed in 1454-5, the **Gutenberg Bible** was the first major book (and is the oldest extant book) printed in Europe with movable type.

Johannes Gutenberg's mechanical press was the first instrument of mass production in Europe. His invention revolutionized the spread of knowledge throughout the world.

3. After **Richard Nixon** was accused of using campaign funds for personal use while running as Dwight Eisenhower's vice presidential candidate in 1952, he saved his political life with a televised talk later called the "Checkers Speech" in which he described his moderate means, his wife's simple cloth coat, and his children's dog Checkers—a gift from a supporter he said he'd never give back.

4. Clean-shaven looks have been the norm among the major presidential contenders since the moustached **Thomas Dewey** ran against Harry Truman in 1948. That election set the stage for arguably the most embarrassing newspaper mistake in history, when the *Chicago Tribune,* trusting polls, released its early Nov. 3, 1948, edition with the headline, "Dewey Defeats Truman."

Page 26

1. **Andrew Lloyd Webber** is the most famous living composer in musical theater. His productions—including *Jesus Christ Superstar* (1971), *Evita* (1978), *Cats* (1981), and *Phantom of the Opera* (1986)—rank among the most successful and longest-running musical productions in history. He was knighted in 1992 and made a life peer (Baron Lloyd-Webber) in 1997.

2. Painter and illustrator **Norman Rockwell** (1894-1978) is best known for his widely reproduced magazine covers (322 in all) for *The Saturday Evening Post.* His works typically depicted small-town life and traditional American customs. They were, and remain, widely popular with the public.

3. The Black Sox Scandal involved eight players from the Chicago White Sox who were accused of accepting bribes to lose the 1919 World Series. All were banned from baseball. "**Shoeless Joe**" **Jackson**, the biggest star among the disgraced players, was supposedly confronted by a young boy with the famous line, "Say it ain't so, Joe."

4. There was apparently only one event at the first Olympics in Greece in 776 BC: a footrace, known as the *stade,* that covered one length of the track at Olympia. The word stade also came to refer to the track itself where the race was held; it is the origin of the modern English word *stadium.*

Page 28

1. The **gluteus maximus** is the largest of the three gluteal muscles of the human buttocks. It is used in standing up, balancing, and climbing.

2. The **heart** pumps some 2,500 gallons of blood every day, making it the hardest-working muscle in the body. The heart is estimated to beat more than three billion times in an average human's lifespan.

3. **Sake**, a Japanese alcoholic beverage made from fermented rice, is served with a special ceremony. It is typically first warmed in a small earthenware or porcelain bottle and then sipped from a small porcelain cup. Premium sake is served cold or on ice.

4. During World War I, Americans anathematized anything German or related to German culture, including food. Amid the war fervor, "sauerkraut," a staple of German cuisine, was renamed "**liberty cabbage,**" especially by manufacturers who feared a patriotic public would stop buying their product otherwise. "Kraut" remains a derogatory term for a German.

Page 29

1. **Chardonnay** is the most famous white wine grape and is grown in nearly every wine-producing area of the world. Used most famously for producing dry white wines, the grape can also be used for sparkling as well as sweet ice wines.

2. **Charles de Gaulle** (1890-1970)—French soldier, writer, statesman, and architect of France's Fifth Republic—once humorously asked about his native country, "How can you govern a country that has 246 varieties of cheese?"

3. The famed **Orient Express** ran between Paris and Constantinople (Istanbul) from 1883-1977. With its Oriental rugs, velvet draperies, mahogany paneling, deep leather armchairs, and fine cuisine, the train was unmatched in luxury accommodations. It was called "The King of Trains and the Train of Kings."

4. "**Jack the Ripper**" is perhaps the best-known serial killer in history. He killed at least five women, all prostitutes, in London between August-November 1888. In 2014, a researcher, using DNA analysis of a bloody scarf recovered from one of the crime scenes, concluded that long-time suspect Aaron Kosminski was the Ripper. Not everyone has accepted his conclusion.

Page 30

1. The Kentucky Derby, one of the races that comprise the Triple Crown of American horseracing, is noted for the blanket of roses that adorn the winning horse, giving the race its nickname, "The Run for the Roses"; for the extravagant spring hats worn by the women spectators; and for its signature drink, the **mint julep**, made with Kentucky bourbon.

2. Few figures in Hollywood history were more influential than **Orson Welles**. His *Citizen Kane* (1941), which he produced, directed, co-wrote, and even starred in, is considered by some to be the greatest movie ever produced. He grew quite fat later in life, reportedly topping some 350 pounds.

3. **Jennifer Aniston** will forever be known for her role as Rachel on the popular TV sitcom *Friends* (1994–2004), which also launched a successful film career for her. An important part of her popularity was her bouncy, face-wrapping hairstyle dubbed "The Rachel," which became one of the biggest style trends of the '90s.

4. **Woodstock**—billed as "Three Days of Peace and Music" and held from Aug. 15-18, 1969—was the most famous rock festival of the 1960s. The city of Woodstock, New York, actually refused to host it—it was held in Bethel instead—but the name was retained because of the cachet of hipness associated with the town. It had long been a famed artists' retreat.

Page 31

1. **Welsh rabbit** (or "rarebit"), a common British dish, is toasted bread topped with a cheddar cheese sauce that typically includes beer or ale, Worcestershire sauce, cayenne, mustard, and paprika. Legend suggests that the name stems from poor Welsh peasants who, because of cost, substituted cheese in dishes that called for meat.

2. **Falafel** is a deep-fried ball or patty of ground chickpeas, fava beans, or both that is traditionally served in a pita pouch. It is a national dish in several Middle Eastern countries, and advocates in different countries claim credit for inventing it and vociferously reject all competing claims.

3. When Chief Justice John Roberts swore in **Barack Obama** as the new president on Jan. 20, 2009, he mistakenly switched around words in the oath, confusing Obama. To prevent any notion that

Obama's presidency might not be legal because he failed to state the constitutionally mandated oath, the swearing-in was repeated in private the following day.

4. The President's famed desk, called the **Resolute Desk** because it was built from wood of the British ship *Resolute,* was given by Queen Victoria to President Hayes in 1880. Franklin Roosevelt fitted the kneehole with a front panel, so the public would not see his wheelchair or leg braces. A famed photo shows John Kennedy's son ("John-John") peeking through the panel.

Page 32

1. **Bangers and mash** is a simple and popular British dish of sausages ("bangers") and mashed potatoes ("mash") covered with onion gravy. The term *bangers* supposedly arose during World War I, when meat shortages resulted in sausages made with fillers, especially water, that caused them to explode when heated.

2. Ukrainians and Russians have long argued over the origins of **chicken Kiev**. Stuffed with frozen herbal butter, the boneless chicken breast is rolled tight to keep the butter inside and then breaded and baked or fried. A similar dish, chicken cordon bleu, is stuffed with ham and cheese instead of butter.

3. **Saint Elmo's fire** is a weather phenomenon that occurs during storms when discharges of atmospheric electricity appear as a faint violet or bluish light on the extremities of pointed objects such as church towers, ship masts, or even airplane propellers. It is usually accompanied by a crackling or hissing sound. The name is a variant of St. Erasmus, patron saint of sailors.

4. The **Mariana Trench** in the floor of the Pacific Ocean is the deepest place on Earth. It is situated beneath U.S. dependencies (the Northern Mariana Islands and Guam) and was designated a U.S. national monument in 2009. In 2012, filmmaker James Cameron piloted a submersible in the trench to a depth of 35,756 feet, setting a new world record for a solo descent.

Page 34

1. While gazing at a painting by Leonardo da Vinci in Florence, Italy, in 1974, a pregnant young woman felt the child within her kick so fiercely that she decided to name her future son—actor **Leonardo DiCaprio**—after the great artist. DiCaprio was launched into international stardom for his role in *Titanic* (1997), one of the highest-grossing films ever.

2. Written by Michael Jackson and Lionel Richie and produced by Quincy Jones, the 1985 charity hit single "**We Are the World**" raised tens of millions of dollars to help the hungry of Africa. The song was sung by an historic assembly of the leading performers of the day, and it topped music charts worldwide.

3. **Lemmings,** found across the Northern Hemisphere, do not plunge into the sea in an act of mass suicide, as commonly believed. Their populations can grow very large, leading hordes of them to migrate. Some lemmings swim water barriers while others drown when they are pushed into the sea by the pressing momentum of the masses behind them.

4. The "funny bone" is actually the **ulnar nerve**. When hit around the elbow, the nerve bumps against the humerus (the long bone in the upper arm) and produces the strange, prickly, dull pain commonly associated with the "funny bone."

Page 35

1. **Marlon Brando** was the most celebrated of the method actors. He was famous for his visceral, brooding roles, and his slurred, mumbling delivery marked his rejection of classical dramatic training. Many of his performances—as in *A Streetcar Named Desire* (1951), *On the Waterfront* (1954), and *The Godfather* (1972)—rank among the greatest in film history.

2. For the Rolling Stones' concert at Altamont Speedway in Livermore, California, on Dec. 6, 1969, the **Hell's Angels** motorcycle gang was hired to work security. Trouble followed quickly and reached a climax when a man who had rushed the stage with a gun was stabbed to death in front of Mick Jagger. To some observers, the Stones' own aura of decadence somehow contributed to the tragedy.

3. **Mathew Brady** first photographed Abraham Lincoln on Feb. 27, 1860, when Lincoln addressed a large Republican audience at Cooper Union, a college in New York City. Lincoln's stirring speech (on why slavery should not be allowed to spread to the territories) received national attention, and Brady's photograph of him was widely reproduced. Lincoln later said he owed his presidency to the Cooper Union speech and photograph.

4. Abraham Lincoln had actually attended a previous play at Ford's Theatre in Washington, D.C., that starred his future killer, the popular actor **John Wilkes Booth**. Just five days after the South surrendered, ending the Civil War, the 26-year-old actor and rabid pro-slavery advocate shot Lincoln as he watched another performance at Ford's on April 14, 1865. Lincoln died the next morning.

Page 36

1. **George Carlin**, one of the greatest of stand-up comedians, was the host of the premiere episode of *Saturday Night Live* on Oct. 11, 1975. His famous routine, "Seven Words You Can Never Say on Television," led to a U.S. Supreme Court ruling that gave the Federal Communications Commission the right to censor radio and TV broadcasts.

2. *The Sound of Music* (1965) is one of the most commercially successful films in history. It tells the real-life story of the **von Trapp family,** professional singers who fled Nazi-dominated Austria in 1938 and eventually settled in the United States. The film, adopted from a Broadway musical, won five of its ten Academy Award nominations.

3. **Yogi Berra**, elected to the baseball Hall of Fame in 1972, held many of the records for catchers of his era. He hit the most home runs (313), had the most consecutive errorless games (148), and participated in the most World Series games (75). He is famous for his nonsensical maxims, such as "Baseball is 90 percent mental, the other half is physical."

4. **Joe DiMaggio**, one of baseball's best all-around players, set a record in 1941 that some believe will never be broken: he hit safely in 56 consecutive games. For his speed, grace, and range in the outfield, he was nicknamed the "Yankee Clipper" (reportedly after Pan American's popular flying boat). His 1954 marriage to film star Marilyn Monroe only added to his iconic status.

Page 37

1. *Reefer Madness* (1936) was a propaganda film about the dangers of marijuana. It is routinely called one of the worst films of all time. Unintentionally funny due to its horrible acting and rank exaggeration—smoking pot leads to delinquency, manslaughter,

suicide, sexual assault, and ultimately psychosis—the movie became a cult classic.

2. **Barry Sadler** was many things: a decorated member of the Green Berets who was wounded in Vietnam; a successful author of adventure novels; a gun-runner and village medic who served the Nicaraguan Contras in the 1980s; but, most famously, he was a singer-songwriter who rose to the top of the American music charts in 1966 with his patriotic hit single, "The Ballad of the Green Berets."

3. **Mesopotamia**, which means "land between the rivers" (in this case, the Tigris and Euphrates rivers, mainly in modern-day Iraq), was home to the earliest civilization some 5,000-6,000 years ago. Writing, as well as wine, first developed in Mesopotamia.

4. Socrates was the first of the three great Greek philosophers (the other two being Plato and Aristotle). In 399 BC, because of his questioning of established beliefs, he was accused of impiety and of corrupting youth and was sentenced to death. He carried out the sentence by swallowing a drink laced with poisonous **hemlock**.

Page 38

1. **Mary Todd Lincoln** was initially praised for her role as first lady during the early, difficult days of the Civil War, but she was later criticized for extravagant spending on her wardrobe and on White House furnishings. After her second son, Willie, died in 1862 of typhoid fever, her behavior became erratic. Supposedly she held séances in the White House to communicate with her dead son.

2. In the wake of the Watergate scandal, the perception of **Jimmy Carter** as a political outsider—he was a former peanut farmer and naval officer—helped him win the presidency in 1976. But his inability to free the American hostages in Iran, or to deal effectively with the economy or the "malaise" hovering over the country, doomed his reelection bid.

3. The Soviet Union's invasion of Afghanistan in December 1979 led to the largest boycott in Olympic history. Led by U.S. President Jimmy Carter, some 60 countries joined the United States in staying away from **Moscow**, the host city. Consequently, the Soviet Union and the communist countries of Eastern Europe swept the majority of medals at the Games.

4. Gale Sayers was the youngest player ever voted into the Pro Football Hall of Fame. His close friendship with fellow Chicago Bears halfback Brian Piccolo, who died of cancer in 1970, was depicted in the acclaimed 1971 television movie *Brian's Song*. As roommates while traveling to away games, they also defied racial taboos of their day (Sayers is black, Piccolo was white).

Page 39

1. **William Howard Taft** was the only man to serve as both U.S. president (1909-13) and Supreme Court chief justice (1921-30). He was also the heaviest president, weighing more than 300 lbs. Reportedly, he once even got stuck in the White House tub, a tale told by Taft's chief White House usher, Irwin "Ike" Hoover.

2. In 1877, **Rutherford B. Hayes** brought post-Civil War Reconstruction to an end in the South by withdrawing federal troops. His promise not to interfere with elections in the former Confederacy ensured a return there of traditional white Democratic supremacy. This was the beginning of the Jim Crow era of legally enforced racial segregation in the South.

3. **Ralph Lauren**'s designs—from his ties to his sport shirts—have long been characterized by a style that evokes the look of an old-money English or East Coast elite. His emblem is a player of that most exclusive of sports—polo. His style gained worldwide exposure when he dressed the actors in the films *The Great Gatsby* (1974) and *Annie Hall* (1977).

4. The dapper **John Dillinger** was one of America's leading outlaws whose daring bank robberies and escapes made national headlines. On July 22, 1934, Dillinger attended the Biograph Theatre in Chicago with his girlfriend and the "lady in red," the FBI informant whose orange skirt appeared red in the theater's outdoor lights. When Dillinger exited the theater with the women and noticed the FBI agents, he ran into a nearby alley, where he was shot and killed.

Page 40

1. **Dolley Madison**'s popularity as manager of the White House made that task a responsibility of every first lady who followed. She decorated the house so that it was both elegant and comfortable, though few Americans saw her improvements before the British burned the residence during the War of 1812. As the enemy approached, she directed the safe removal of many White House treasures.

2. Born in Illinois, President **Ronald Reagan** was noted for his affability and charm, superb communication skills, and fierce anticommunism. He is often credited with helping to bring down the "Iron Curtain" of communism in Eastern Europe and to end the Cold War. A former Hollywood star, he is the only entertainer ever to become president.

3. **Mustard** seeds are tiny but powerful in flavor. They were tossed on food in ancient Egypt and considered a symbol of good fortune, and they were found entombed with King Tut. Ancient Greeks used ground mustard as a paste to treat ailments, but ancient Romans mixed it with wine for use as a condiment.

4. When France refused to join the United States and its coalition in invading Iraq in March 2003, U.S. congressmen changed the name of French fries on the menus at governmental cafeterias to "**freedom fries**," while "French toast" became "freedom toast." Some restaurants countrywide followed suit in a gesture of scorn towards France and its position on the war.

Page 41

1. On July 2, 1881, after only four months in office, **James Garfield** was shot in the back at the railroad station in Washington, D.C. The assassin was a disappointed job seeker from the conservative ("Stalwart") wing of Garfield's own Republican Party. Garfield lingered for 80 days before dying, during which time the public and the media were transfixed by the drawn-out tragedy.

2. **Woodrow Wilson** is best remembered for his legislative accomplishments and high-minded idealism. He led the country in World War I, envisioned and advocated for the League of Nations, and won the 1919 Nobel Peace Prize. Approved during his tenure as president were the constitutional amendments that banned alcoholic beverages (1919) and gave women the right to vote (1920).

3. Seven colors make up a **rainbow**. They are, in order from outer edge to inner edge nearest the ground, red, orange, yellow, green, blue, indigo, and violet. A common acronym for remembering the colors in order is "ROY G BIV."

4. **Halley's Comet** was named for English astronomer Edmond Halley who, in 1705, discovered that the comet returned to view every 75-

76 years. Mark Twain was born in 1835, just days after the comet's visit, and he predicted that he would die when Halley next appeared. He died in 1910 on the day after the comet was sighted.

Page 42

1. The Norwegian-born American football coach **Knute Rockne** built the University of Notre Dame into a major power in college football. His pioneering use of the forward pass revolutionized the game, and he became intercollegiate football's first celebrity coach. His shocking death in a plane crash in 1931 prompted tributes from both the U.S. president and the king of Norway.

2. The **Indianapolis** 500-mile auto race, held annually from 1911 (except for the war years 1917–18 and 1942–45), draws crowds of several hundred thousand people. The race is widely cited as the world's best-attended single-day sporting event held at a single venue. The race is run on the weekend of America's Memorial Day holiday.

3. **Chuck Barris** worked on the set of Dick Clark's *American Bandstand* and wrote a hit song, "Palisades Park" (1962). He next created popular game shows, including *The Dating Game* (1965), *The Newlywed Game* (1966), and *The Gong Show* (1976). According to his autobiography, he was also a CIA assassin—something the CIA denies. This alleged "other life" was the focus of George Clooney's movie about Barris, *Confessions of a Dangerous Mind* (2002).

4. **Walter Cronkite** was a pioneer of TV news programming. His avuncular mien and journalistic integrity—exemplified by his sign-off line, "And that's the way it is"—endeared him to the public, and a 1972 poll named him "the most trusted man in America." As the longtime anchor of the *CBS Evening News* (1962–81), he reported on many of the historic events of the 20th century.

Page 43

1. Vlad III (Vlad Tepes), the 15th-century ruler of Walachia in the area of Transylvania, was also called Dracula, meaning "son of Dracul" (his father). He was later known as **Vlad the Impaler** for his cruel methods of killing enemies. Scholars have long suspected that he was the inspiration for Bram Stoker's fictional vampire in *Dracula* (1897).

2. **Charles Atlas** built a multimillion-dollar mail-order empire around his bodybuilding regimen. His famous advertising campaign, launched in 1928, showed a "97-pound weakling" who, after having sand kicked in his face by a bully at the beach, buys Atlas's program, builds a herculean physique, and then returns to challenge the bully. Atlas was often photographed wearing leopard-patterned trunks while flexing his muscles.

3. **The Three Tenors** was the name given to the Spanish opera singers Plácido Domingo and José Carreras and the Italian singer Luciano Pavarotti. They performed before enormous crowds in the 1990s and early 2000s, helping to spread opera's popularity to new audiences. Their televised performances were often held on the eve of World Cup (soccer) events, when a global audience could be expected.

4. **Bill Robinson** ("Bojangles"), well-known for his dancing roles with Shirley Temple in her films of the 1930s, was arguably the best tap dancer in history. His routines and innovative steps, such as his famous "stair dance," were widely copied by other performers. He also had a unique ability to run backward—almost as fast as other men could run forward.

Page 44

1. **Fusion cuisine,** the combination of different ethnic dishes and ingredients, grew in popularity beginning in the 1980s. It can refer to a restaurant that offers multiple ethnic cuisines (such as Thai and Indian) or to a dish prepared with nontraditional ingredients (such as Korean tacos with kimchi, or pot roast with Japanese wasabi).

2. **Fugu** (puffer fish) contains a poison called tetrodotoxin; a single fish, in fact, may contain enough toxicity to kill 30 people. As a result, to make the fish safe to eat, it must be carefully cleaned and prepared by a specially trained chef. A single serving may sell for hundreds of dollars.

3. **Zachary Taylor** won the presidential election of 1848 largely on his reputation as a hero of the Mexican-American War. He died, however, after only 16 months in office. His physician said he died of cholera, likely from drinking contaminated water or unpasteurized milk; others point to gastroenteritis caused by digesting contaminated cherries; still others have suggested he was poisoned.

4. **William Henry Harrison** was the oldest man (age 67) ever elected president up to that time, the last president born under British rule, and the first to die in office—after only one month's service. He had given his inaugural address (the longest in history) outside in the cold, without coat or hat, which led to the pneumonia that killed him on April 4, 1841.

Page 45

1. Few kings have been more reviled than **Richard III** (1452-85). He usurped the throne of England and for the next 500 years was portrayed as evil incarnate, a wickedness supposedly reflected in his physical deformity (he suffered from scoliosis, a curvature of the spine). He was not, however, a hunchback, as often asserted, and his bones were definitively identified in 2013.

2. The French-born urban designer Pierre Charles L'Enfant (1754-1825) was hired by George Washington to design the basic plan for **Washington, D.C.** Although he was ultimately fired, L'Enfant's plan for the city—focusing attention on the Capitol and the presidential mansion while creating squares, circles, and triangles where monuments and fountains could be featured—was followed nonetheless.

3. **Affogato** is an Italian dessert in which vanilla ice cream or gelato is doused with a hot shot of espresso. A mocha affogato simply uses chocolate ice cream instead of vanilla. A shot of liqueur may also be added.

4. Anglo-Irish writer and wit Jonathan Swift is best known for *Gulliver's Travels* (1726) and "A Modest Proposal" (1729). The latter was a brilliant work of satire, presented as a serious economic treatise, in which Swift suggested poverty in Ireland be ameliorated by butchering poor **children** and selling them as food to wealthy English landlords.

BRITANNICA BRAINBUSTERS

Criss Cross

The answers will fit in the rows below.
All letters from the letter box will be used only once.
Answers will not have a space between words.

FAMOUS & INFAMOUS

1 Nothing was more famous
and more ballyhooed,

Nothing was more tragic
than how I debuted.

2 My effects were cataclysmic,
unique in history,

I left a civilization, well-preserved,
under me.

LITERATURE & THE ARTS

3 I said "A thing of beauty
is a joy for ever,"

Its tie to the living
no man could ever sever.

4 Charlotte's spider web was large,
as was Stuart's loving heart,

My characters were precious
and enduring works of art.

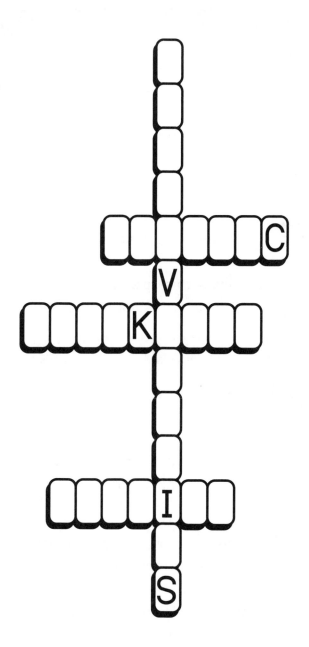

U J I M I N E I S T V B T O A T N
U S K H W A E N U H T S O V C E

53

Criss Cross

The answers will fit in the rows below.
All letters from the letter box will be used only once.
Answers will not have a space between words.

SCIENCE, SPACE & TECHNOLOGY

1 My telescopic views
   caused the Church strife,

And they nearly also
   cost me my life.

2 When the Moon is at its
   closest and also ultra-bright,

It claims this special name
   and gives astronomers delight.

LITERATURE & THE ARTS

3 Those who hail me as the
   world's greatest statue are legion,

Though controversy has shadowed
   my genital region.

4 Beware of Johnny and my canine,
   as well as my car,

I am Maine's most famous writer
   and scariest by far.

A I N O L K P E D M D G L S V
O R E I O P G N H S T A U N

54

BRITANNICA BRAINBUSTERS

Criss Cross

The answers will fit in the rows below.
All letters from the letter box will be used only once.
Answers will not have a space between words.

THE SPORTING LIFE

1 Invented for businessmen
who found basketball too vigorous,

I'm a net sport that requires
activity less rigorous.

2 Like no other woman
I brought muscle to my sport,

Displaying athleticism
unseen on the court.

LITERATURE & THE ARTS

3 The factory I founded
had no assembly line,

Just artists and drag queens
and supposed friends of mine.

4 I was forever "the woman"
at 221B,

The only gal to beat Sherlock,
the sole woman was me.

L E R L D R D O I R O A R E N N L E A L B
N Y M Y L A A L I E I H W V A S L S L E

Criss Cross

The answers will fit in the rows below.
All letters from the letter box will be used only once.
Answers will not have a space between words.

THE SPORTING LIFE

1 In every kind of racing
to victory did I steer,

In three different decades
was I driver of the year.

2 To control a goat carcass,
that is the aim,

Of this rugged equestrian
Afghan game.

SCIENCE, SPACE & TECHNOLOGY

3 I'm gassy and colorful
with very bad weather,

And I'm bigger than all of
my peers put together.

4 I computerized my high school's
schedule of classes,

Which increased my contact
with interesting lasses.

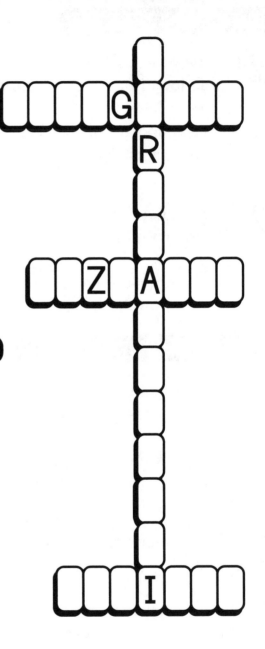

```
I L B P R R U S A E A I T J L U N
I S T K E T O M B D G H I Z T R E
```

Criss Cross

TThe answers will fit in the rows below.
All letters from the letter box will be used only once.
Answers will not have a space between words.

THE SPORTING LIFE

1 A sultan was I,
    the greatest of my day,

    I was sold nonetheless
      for a Broadway play.

2 My nickname was "The Great One,"
    my record hardly disappoints,

    Earning more assists alone than
      any other player's points.

FOOD & DRINK

3 My salty arms were crossed,
    and crossed in a special way,

    For children who could say
      all their prayers without delay.

4 No, I'm not really nuts,
    despite my name,

    I'm really legumes,
      despite what some claim.

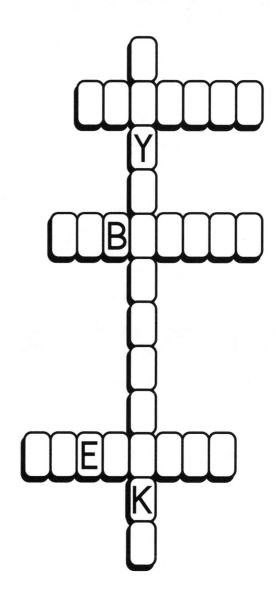

P R R Z T K B S E A T T Y Y E E
U P E N R W B H T A L N G U E S

Criss Cross

The answers will fit in the rows below.
All letters from the letter box will be used only once.
Answers will not have a space between words.

THE SPORTING LIFE

1 The Olympic run was
      for more than mere gold,

   As this film about it
      so beautifully told.

2 White, at this event,
      is strictly enforced,

   No colors, no off-whites,
      will be endorsed.

POP CULTURE & ENTERTAINMENT

3 With rings on my fingers
      I beat out the best,

   And ended on top when
      I drummed out the rest.

4 A python and a tower
      can both be tied to me,

   I'm one of England's silliest
      kings of comedy.

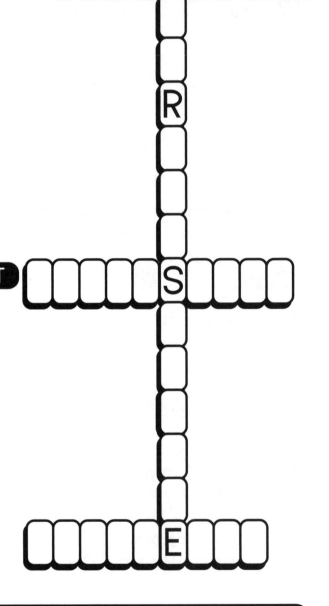

S N G R H T I M E O O O A E R B E W S
O H N E R F D I O I J L C N R A R T I F L

BRITANNICA
BRAINBUSTERS

Mind Lines

Try to get from the top line of categories to the bottom in the fewest moves. Check off each box (or mark initials in the box if playing opponents) after each correct answer to a riddle. Once a player "owns" a box, an opponent must find another path.

Fam - FAMOUS & INFAMOUS
Sci - SCIENCE, SPACE & TECHNOLOGY
Lit - LITERATURE & THE ARTS
Pres - U.S. PRESIDENCY & FIRST LADIES
Pop - POP CULTURE & ENTERTAINMENT
Sprt - THE SPORTING LIFE
F&D - FOOD & DRINK

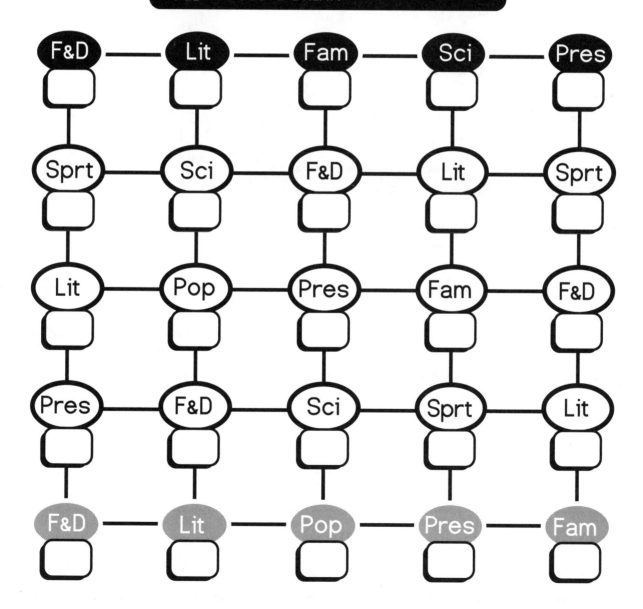

Criss Cross

The answers will fit in the rows below.
All letters from the letter box will be used only once.
Answers will not have a space between words.

THE SPORTING LIFE

1 714 is not tops,
not 762,

My record of 868
is the best, thank you.

2 At my sport did I excel
but was hounded by the hater,

Self-control was my chief goal
as I played the innovator.

U.S. PRESIDENCY & FIRST LADIES

3 Upon a president's death
did I start my presidency,

Which is why my many critics
called me "Your Accidency."

4 When asked how he would spend
his post-presidential day,

Pierce's answer had a candor
very rare today.

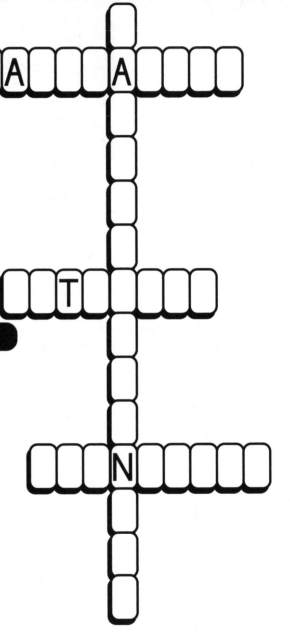

O I I U E T J A N L T N R J S E D O E
H D K N H G S R C O O R U A H Y A B K

Criss Cross

The answers will fit in the rows below.
All letters from the letter box will be used only once.
Answers will not have a space between words.

LITERATURE & THE ARTS

1 School I hate and
all "sivilizing" forces,

My story has been banned
in English courses.

2 In my house in Paris
draped in vines,

Lived 12 little girls
in two straight lines.

FOOD & DRINK

3 First boil in a stomach some
heart, lung, and liver,

And a dish you'll create
that leaves some folks ashiver.

4 "Americans will eat garbage,"
Henry James was confident,

Just "sprinkle it liberally" with this
pervasive condiment.

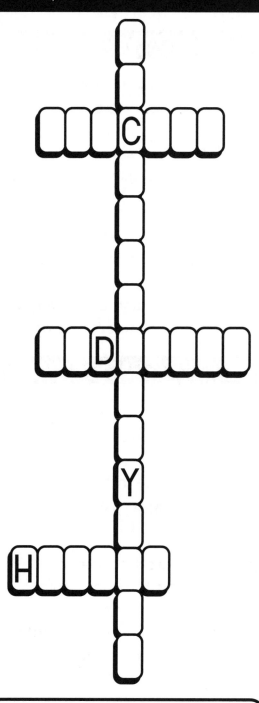

Letter box:

K G H T R C I N E Y E L H E N U A
N F G A I R M L E B D U K H P S

Criss Cross

The answers will fit in the rows below.
All letters from the letter box will be used only once.
Answers will not have a space between words.

LITERATURE & THE ARTS

1 My magical story came
to me on a train,

Though my search for a pen
to write with was in vain.

2 My drawings were as wonderful
as my numerous tales,

And Peter and J. Puddle-Duck
continue to spur sales.

SCIENCE, SPACE & TECHNOLOGY

3 I altered how we live and
how we travel there and back,

And I came in any color,
as long as you liked black.

4 I democratized travel,
added to urban strife,

Then spent years promoting
an old-fashioned, rural life.

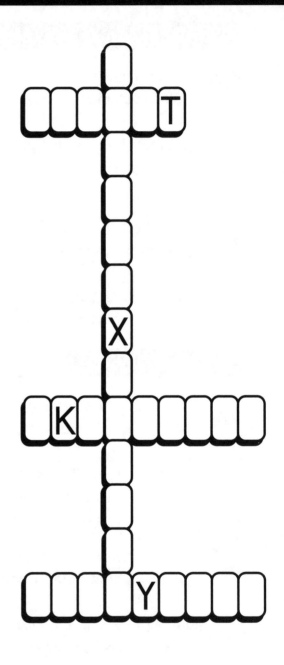

W B T E L I Y R N R L T E O O E R
I R T K H M F D J O A X T N G P D

Criss Cross

The answers will fit in the rows below.
All letters from the letter box will be used only once.
Answers will not have a space between words.

LITERATURE & THE ARTS

1 In Florence did
    I get my start,

The whole world now
    adores my art.

2 My face is very famous,
    with its understated smile,

When even on a magnet,
    I reflect my master's style.

POP CULTURE & ENTERTAINMENT

3 I was a titan's dying word,
    quite symbolic of his woe,

A reminder of his childhood
    that he would not let go.

4 She had lost that loving feeling,
    I told a woman in a bar,

But did I lose something, too,
    when my religious views went too far?

M A C I L U O M N L M E S A O U I
R H A G D E O I T R S B O S N E

Criss Cross

The answers will fit in the rows below.
All letters from the letter box will be used only once.
Answers will not have a space between words.

POP CULTURE & ENTERTAINMENT

1 My Spider-Man was quite novel,
while still only in his teens,

He became a superhero in
my comic magazines.

2 I was a playboy inventor,
quite footloose and free,

Till I tailored a suit from
which criminals can't flee.

FAMOUS & INFAMOUS

3 We were greater than four
but were fewer than six,

By spying for the Soviets
we got our kicks.

4 I trained and tried to be an artist,
that was my grand scheme,

How the world may have differed
had I accomplished my dream.

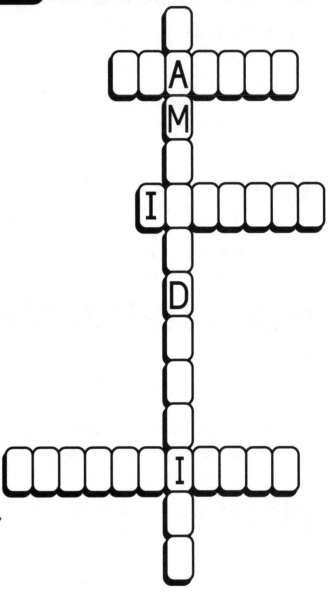

C V O L E D E A T S I R A B F E T D
F N N A R M G E O L H E I M L I N

BRITANNICA
BRAINBUSTERS

Mind
Lines

Try to get from the top line of categories to the bottom
in the fewest moves. Check off each box (or mark initials
in the box if playing opponents) after each correct answer to a riddle.
Once a player "owns" a box, an opponent must find another path.

Fam - FAMOUS & INFAMOUS
Sci - SCIENCE, SPACE & TECHNOLOGY
Lit - LITERATURE & THE ARTS
Pres - U.S. PRESIDENCY & FIRST LADIES
Pop - POP CULTURE & ENTERTAINMENT
Sprt - THE SPORTING LIFE
F&D - FOOD & DRINK

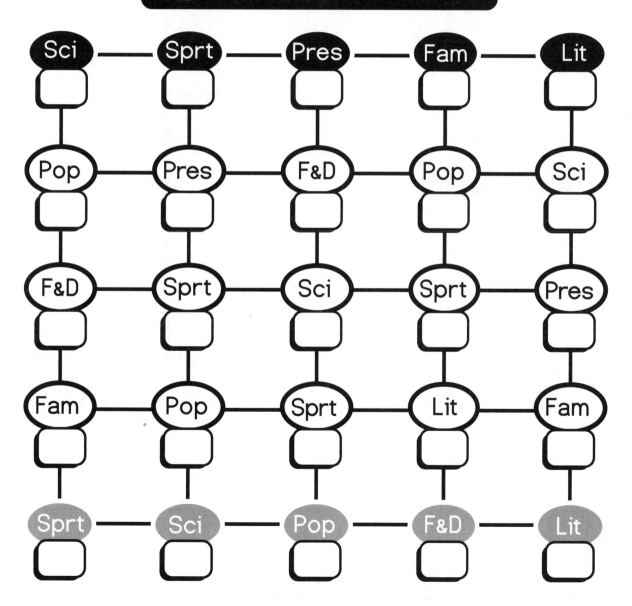

Criss Cross

The answers will fit in the rows below.
All letters from the letter box will be used only once.
Answers will not have a space between words.

FAMOUS & INFAMOUS

1 Two Kennedys I snared
with my zaftig, sexy shape,

And gentlemen all over
would ogle me and gape.

2 Men, armies, and empire
did I once rule,

I died, said the Bard,
by the "venomous fool."

THE SPORTING LIFE

3 Evolved from religious ritual,
my sport absolved sin,

With clean souls to the victors
who rolled to a win.

4 Only 16 goose feathers,
not those of a huge flock,

Were necessary to invent
my sport's shuttlecock.

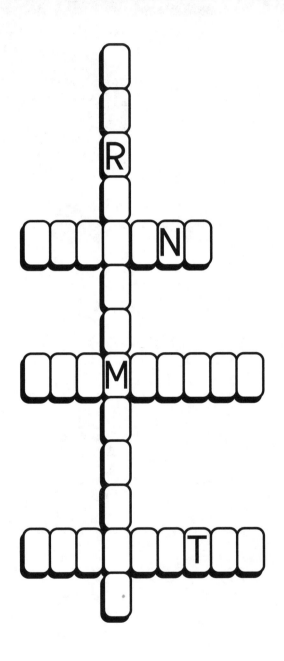

B B R A E T R A I A M L D A T G L
W I N Y O O P C N N I N M N O O E R

BRITANNICA
BRAINBUSTERS

Criss Cross

The answers will fit in the rows below.
All letters from the letter box will be used only once.
Answers will not have a space between words.

U.S. PRESIDENCY & FIRST LADIES

1 Barack Obama is a fan of mine,
leading some critics to question,

What reading comics might just say
about a man in his position.

2 "Handsome Frank" they called me,
I had especially nice hair,

And mourners at my coffin
even noted my fine care.

FOOD & DRINK

3 The undead really hate me,
I'm called "the stinking rose,"

I'm a culinary staple,
pungent to the nose.

4 I'm crisp, dry, and "steely,"
renowned on the wine map,

But when plastered on jugs
my name got a bad rap.

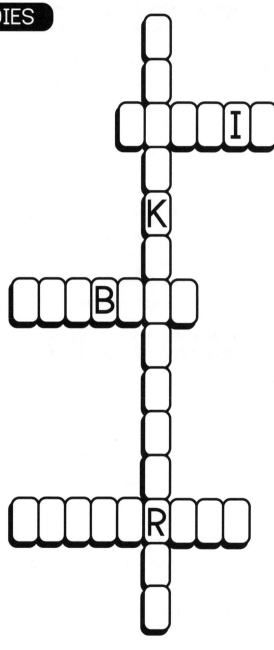

D N A C F A E I L R L K B R C M H
A C S S I I N P E G P L N E R I

67

Criss Cross

The answers will fit in the rows below.
All letters from the letter box will be used only once.
Answers will not have a space between words.

U.S. PRESIDENCY & FIRST LADIES

1 Harry Truman sent the order,
    my eagle's head was turned,

The olive branch of peace would now
    be welcomed and not spurned.

2 I'm the "Mother of Presidents,"
    birthplace of eight,

And the 49 others
    cannot beat my rate.

FAMOUS & INFAMOUS

3 I was the largest goose
    that ever flew,

But not in time to help
    win World War II.

4 Setting yourself on fire is
    not something I encourage,

But I understand and praise
    the self-immolators' courage.

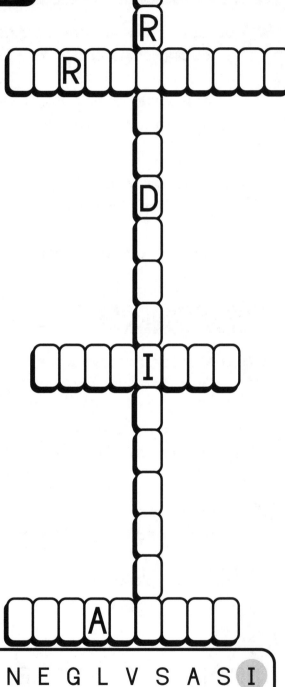

Letter box:

R A N A D L I C G P I N E G L V S A S I
P E S A A S I E A O U A R T E O I L R D M

BRITANNICA
BRAINBUSTERS

Criss Cross

The answers will fit in the rows below.
All letters from the letter box will be used only once.
Answers will not have a space between words.

U.S. PRESIDENCY & FIRST LADIES

1 No corners do I have,
but I'm not round,

A room this strangely shaped
is seldom found.

2 I was the only chief born on
Independence Day,

Though I seldom discussed it,
so little did I say.

SCIENCE, SPACE & TECHNOLOGY

3 I was the top number-cruncher
of antiquity,

I am often called the
"Father of Geometry."

4 Although critics often panned me
and my pop mystique,

Through TV and my books
I made astronomy chic.

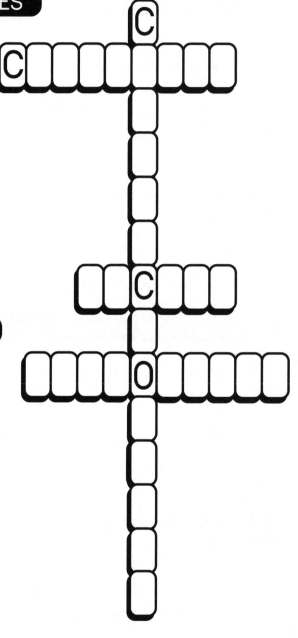

D I E E I L L S C F C A O L V L I G
C V N U O E O A R C A D N F G I L A

Criss Cross

The answers will fit in the rows below.
All letters from the letter box will be used only once.
Answers will not have a space between words.

U.S. PRESIDENCY & FIRST LADIES

1 This presidential edict
     was made very clear,

Telling Europe "Hands off!"
     the Western hemisphere.

2 I offer the same luxury,
     I'm the same as the president's,

But this is what we call it,
     whenever used by vice presidents.

LITERATURE & THE ARTS

3 Wartime flying and spying,
     I dabbled in each,

Willy Wonka I knew well and
     James's large peach.

4 I praised Adolf and Benito
     and was branded berserk,

While in custody I wrote some
     of my most famous work.

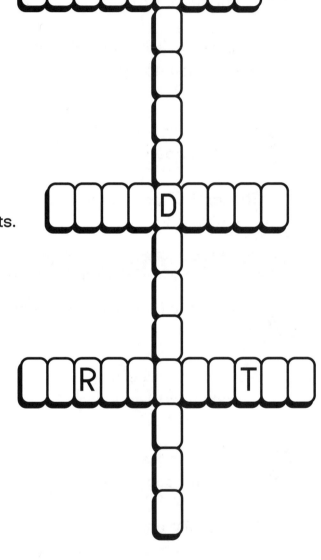

M O D N W R E D P T R A L R O R C O L E
C N E I E N O R U A A F A O O T H Z I D

BRITANNICA
BRAINBUSTERS

Mind Lines

Try to get from the top line of categories to the bottom in the fewest moves. Check off each box (or mark initials in the box if playing opponents) after each correct answer to a riddle. Once a player "owns" a box, an opponent must find another path.

Fam - FAMOUS & INFAMOUS
Sci - SCIENCE, SPACE & TECHNOLOGY
Lit - LITERATURE & THE ARTS
Pres - U.S. PRESIDENCY & FIRST LADIES
Pop - POP CULTURE & ENTERTAINMENT
Sprt - THE SPORTING LIFE
F&D - FOOD & DRINK

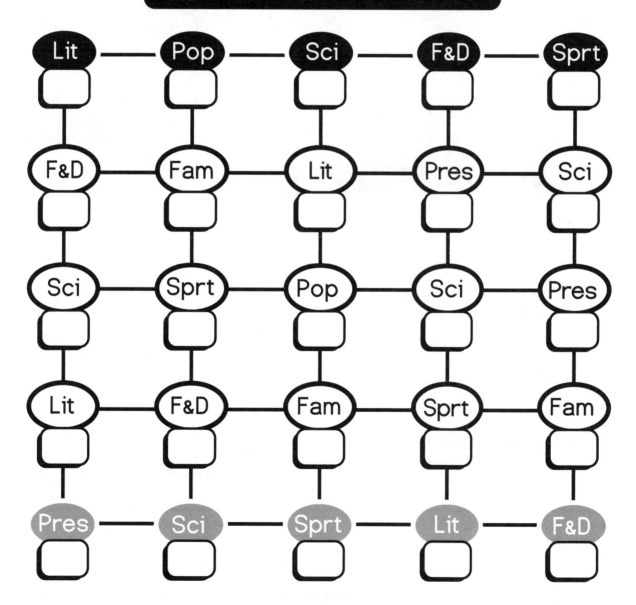

Criss Cross

The answers will fit in the rows below.
All letters from the letter box will be used only once.
Answers will not have a space between words.

U.S. PRESIDENCY & FIRST LADIES

1 I was the first "first lady"
to carry the name,

And an Easter egg roll on
our lawn brought me fame.

2 I paved the way for civil war,
some say that this is fact,

When I decided to enforce
the Fugitive Slave Act.

POP CULTURE & ENTERTAINMENT

3 Graffiti made me famous,
Indiana brought us thrills,

But my landmark space saga
is what really showed my skills.

4 I rose to the top in
a studded brassiere,

Music records I broke
in each hemisphere.

L R S N D F L O G L E R A R A U E I M S
Y L C C I N G M A L U Y H A E L M O O

72

Criss Cross

The answers will fit in the rows below.
All letters from the letter box will be used only once.
Answers will not have a space between words.

FOOD & DRINK

1 A president showcased this
chewy, sweet candy,

They kept him from smoking
and were always handy.

2 I'm a fruit dessert
that's served in a flame,

In New Orleans did I
garner my fame.

U.S. PRESIDENCY & FIRST LADIES

3 I lobbied for woman's suffrage,
smoked, and drove a car,

Among U.S. first ladies
I was a progressive star.

4 Western regions for the country
were acquired by me,

Though few chapters do
I fill in the books of history.

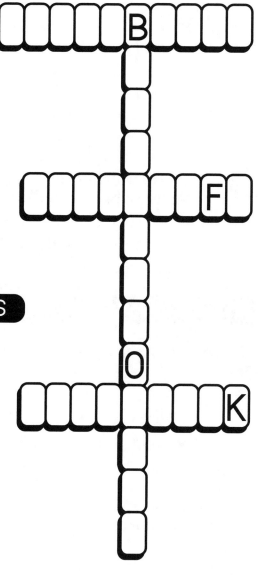

E L L O T N S L A A N L J E F N T J P E
R O S M H E B A A A A A E F E T S Y K

Criss Cross

The answers will fit in the rows below.
All letters from the letter box will be used only once.
Answers will not have a space between words.

FOOD & DRINK

1 I'm an inside-out creation,
a kind of sushi roll,

I have sticky rice not seaweed
encompassing my whole.

2 I'm a national emblem,
with furry pouch and tail,

And against my consumption
do activists now rail.

LITERATURE & THE ARTS

3 I'm a bold and flashy gypsy,
the sexiest around,

From bullfighters to soldiers,
my hungry suitors abound.

4 I am the most famous
graffiti artist in the world,

And around my identity
controversy has swirled.

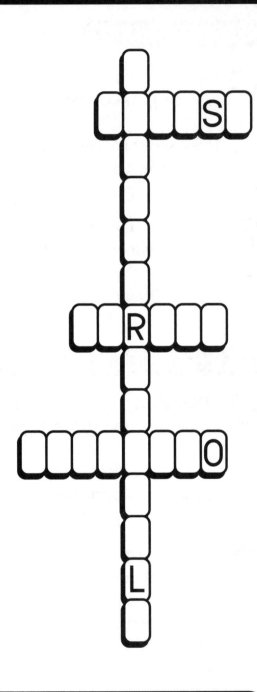

A B R M O I C I N L S A A O N C
R K G E N N L R F O O A K L Y

Criss Cross

The answers will fit in the rows below.
All letters from the letter box will be used only once.
Answers will not have a space between words.

SCIENCE, SPACE & TECHNOLOGY

1 My vaccine would make me famous
and an international star,

Saving thousands from the paralysis
that crippled FDR.

2 I'm nature's hardest substance,
I am in the record book,

But most folks only care about
how good I make them look.

LITERATURE & THE ARTS

3 I said candy is dandy,
but liquor is quicker,

And my young Jabez Dawes
would mock Santa and snicker.

4 An Abstract Expressionist,
that would be me,

Weird things could be found
in my splattery spree.

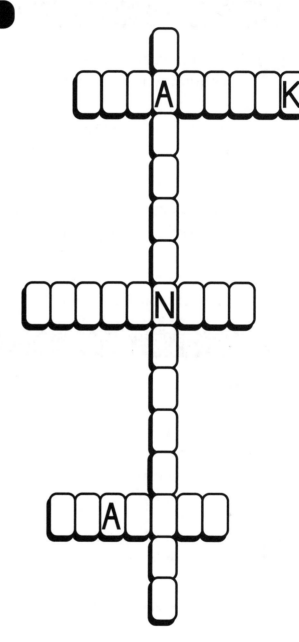

O A N D J O S D I S N P A G L L O C N
J A D E O L K K C S N A S H M K O

Criss Cross

The answers will fit in the rows below.
All letters from the letter box will be used only once.
Answers will not have a space between words.

LITERATURE & THE ARTS

1 I'm an operatic staple,
frequently performed,

After AIDS developed,
I was cleverly transformed.

2 My large artwork was created
with drills and dynamite,

If falling from my faces
60 feet would be your flight.

POP CULTURE & ENTERTAINMENT

3 My rise to fame
was meteoric,

My animation
quite historic.

4 I'm voted the scariest
film ever made,

Some viewers passed out
and were in need of first aid.

L O A H B E M H S H E R R O E T R O X
E U Y E T M N S I S R T C U Y O M T

76

BRITANNICA BRAINBUSTERS

Mind Lines

Try to get from the top line of categories to the bottom in the fewest moves. Check off each box (or mark initials in the box if playing opponents) after each correct answer to a riddle. Once a player "owns" a box, an opponent must find another path.

Fam - FAMOUS & INFAMOUS
Sci - SCIENCE, SPACE & TECHNOLOGY
Lit - LITERATURE & THE ARTS
Pres - U.S. PRESIDENCY & FIRST LADIES
Pop - POP CULTURE & ENTERTAINMENT
Sprt - THE SPORTING LIFE
F&D - FOOD & DRINK

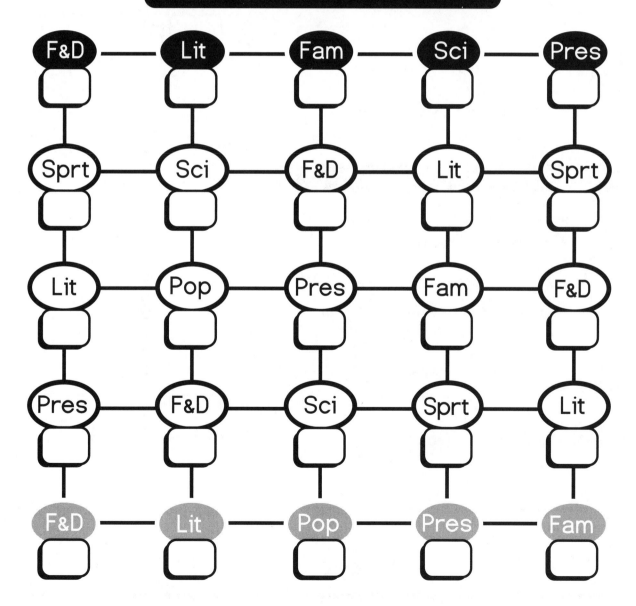

Criss Cross

The answers will fit in the rows below.
All letters from the letter box will be used only once.
Answers will not have a space between words.

SCIENCE, SPACE & TECHNOLOGY

1 In nearly all subjects
my knowledge was vast,

My staggering influence
would not be surpassed.

2 I'm called "hurricane" in one place,
in another place "cyclone,"

But by this name in the Pacific
would I be better known.

POP CULTURE & ENTERTAINMENT

3 Ancient Romans on the screen
I could easily handle,

But much harder to control
was my off-screen sex scandal.

4 To live as a pharmacist
I could not conform,

My "flexible greasepaint"
took Hollywood by storm.

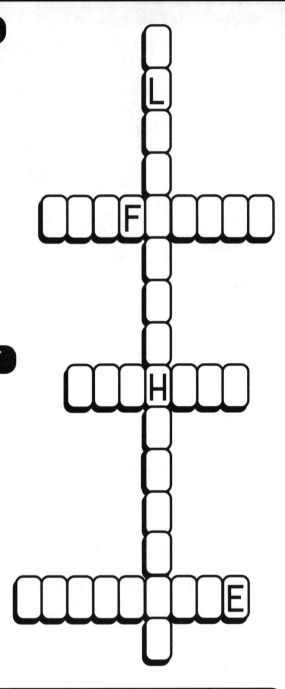

R O T R H B E T I A T E O X L T I T Y
Y A P T A A S Z O E N M C O F L L R

Criss Cross

The answers will fit in the rows below.
All letters from the letter box will be used only once.
Answers will not have a space between words.

POP CULTURE & ENTERTAINMENT

1 From royalty I came,
   I could rap a hip rhyme,

   With black shades and some gym trunks
   I hit the big time.

2 The monster I created
   is synonymous with fright,

   And people seem incapable
   of getting my name right.

FAMOUS & INFAMOUS

3 I'm where Napoleon
   met defeat,

   Now I'm shorthand
   for a rout complete.

4 My reign was unimportant,
   and it brought me little fame,

   But my style of departure
   was anything but lame!

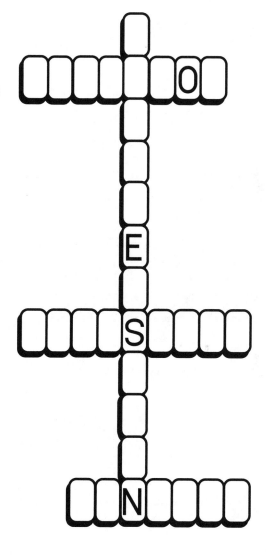

L K I I T L N S O N T T H K A I F
W N M E E R L E T I G T W O A U

79

Criss Cross

The answers will fit in the rows below.
All letters from the letter box will be used only once.
Answers will not have a space between words.

U.S. PRESIDENCY & FIRST LADIES

1 What really is "is"
   and had I really inhaled?

Both were part of what
   my presidency entailed.

2 Down the leg of my guard
   did I once pee,

"It's my prerogative,"
   I said with glee.

THE SPORTING LIFE

3 In light of the craze
   over UFO matters,

Mass production began
   on these "Pluto Platters."

4 My game inspired baseball,
   from me the sport derived,

Since the 18th century,
   I somehow have survived.

B B E N S F O N Y R N N U E J N O H
D L C I D I S N L O L S O I T O E R R

Criss Cross

The answers will fit in the rows below.
All letters from the letter box will be used only once.
Answers will not have a space between words.

FAMOUS & INFAMOUS

1 In Raphael's famous painting *School of Athens,*

Aristotle points down but I to the heavens.

2 I broadcast from Tokyo after war broke out,

America jailed me, though my crimes many doubt.

U.S. PRESIDENCY & FIRST LADIES

3 Before becoming president, an office I didn't win,

I was a model on the cover of *Cosmopolitan.*

4 I was serious and cerebral and could even seem grim,

I began each morning nude, in the Potomac, for a swim.

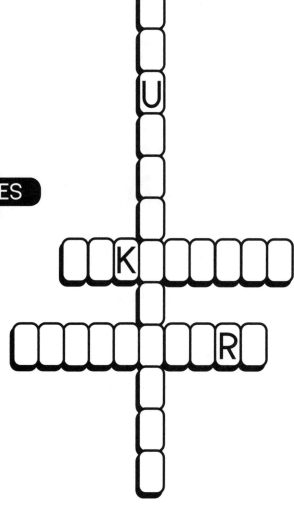

L H Q Y U S D C J A F L A E S R N N
O R A D R T A T O P O E G O K I O M

Criss Cross

The answers will fit in the rows below.
All letters from the letter box will be used only once.
Answers will not have a space between words.

THE SPORTING LIFE

1 I'm played with balls and wickets
 on a flat and grassy court,

 And wooden stakes are needed
 for this common backyard sport.

2 My sport covered the five skills
 a man would need,

 To survive in battle
 and in war succeed.

SCIENCE, SPACE & TECHNOLOGY

3 I pioneered scuba gear
 during World War II,

 And in the *Calypso* explored
 the ocean blue.

4 I am a major transmitter
 of disease,

 No creature has caused
 more human deaths than me.

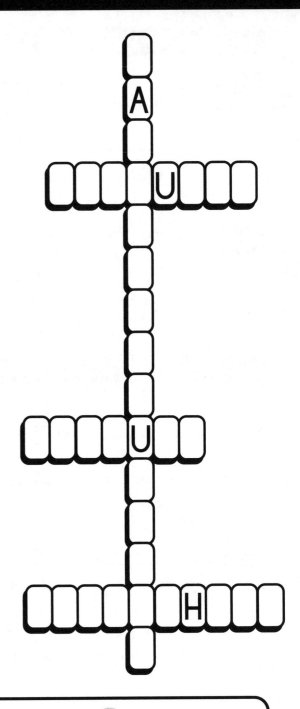

R M L Q C U T J T C U N S U S N O O
Q E O T A P E S A T E U H O E C I O T

BRITANNICA
BRAINBUSTERS

Criss Cross

The answers will fit in the rows below.
All letters from the letter box will be used only once.
Answers will not have a space between words.

SCIENCE, SPACE & TECHNOLOGY

1 I'm faster than a speeding bullet,
　　I soon become aflame,

　　If I survive my fiery plunge
　　　then this becomes my name.

2 I'm the method of explaining
　　a hot pepper's heat,

　　By measuring what it takes
　　　for the heat to deplete.

FAMOUS & INFAMOUS

3 I inspired movies
　　with my killing campaigns,

　　And decorated my house
　　　with human remains.

4 I freed damsels from corsets
　　　that caused them distress,

　　And gave them that staple
　　called the "little black dress."

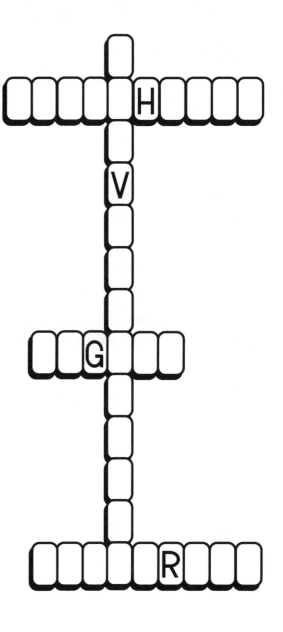

E S O D I C C E I H L A N R I E A N
V C E S E O L C M O O T G L T E L

83

Criss Cross

The answers will fit in the rows below.
All letters from the letter box will be used only once.
Answers will not have a space between words.

THE SPORTING LIFE

1 I said forget polite games
    with balls and courts,

Only life-risking pastimes
are truly sports.

2 We were shot at and killed,
    the sport was messy and mean,

In only one Olympics
was this cruelty seen.

LITERATURE & THE ARTS

3 I'm the barber of Seville,
    which brought me great fame,

And I famously adored
repeating my name.

4 Someone who's never seen me
    would be hard to find,

I'm a painting of the angst
of modern mankind.

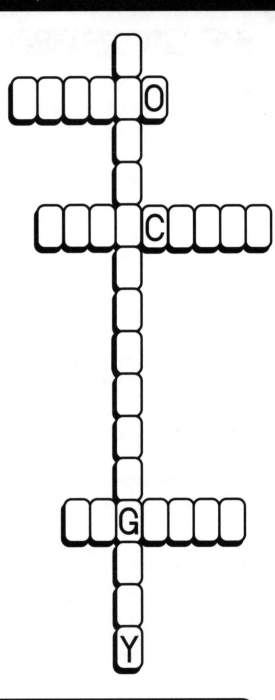

R E T I P E F I G Y S O E T E N M N
A H M O I C S E W A E G H N R A

Think about each riddle's answer.

BRITANNICA BRAINBUSTERS

Criss Cross

The answers will fit in the rows below.
All letters from the letter box will be used only once.
Answers will not have a space between words.

THE SPORTING LIFE

1 Government banned me
    as a danger to the nation,

Archery, it said,
    was the needed avocation.

2 Tom Hanks was our manager,
    as portrayed on the screen,

In the film about our skirt-wearing,
    hitting machine.

FOOD & DRINK

3 I am eaten the world over,
    I come from milk,

I am mildly sour
    but as smooth as silk.

4 For Christopher Columbus I fought scurvy,
    to Cleopatra I gave beauty,

And George Washington
    had a collection of 400 of me.

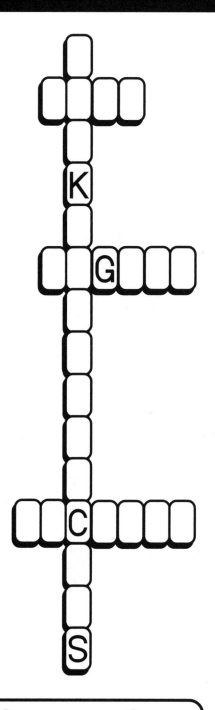

O C Y R H L K P D K E U S P
R C F G R T A E G E O F L I S

Criss Cross

The answers will fit in the rows below.
All letters from the letter box will be used only once.
Answers will not have a space between words.

POP CULTURE & ENTERTAINMENT

1 My age is more than 50,
    and still I cause debate,

About my plastic figure
    and if it's crude or great.

2 I am the only thing that can hurt
    the man of steel,

His powers and abilities
    I can swiftly steal.

THE SPORTING LIFE

3 I beat the hero
    of the Aryan race,

Who then came to my aid
    in a touch of grace.

4 After the attacks of 9/11,
    when loyalty was strong,

Baseball started a new tradition
    with this 7th-inning song.

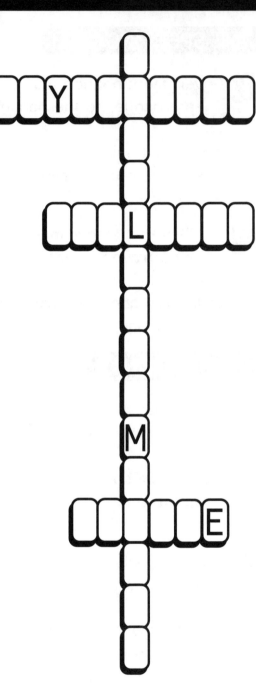

B T I O E I A A L R E Y S P E R J A
M B D O K E N E B T I I S O U C G S

Criss Cross

The answers will fit in the rows below.
All letters from the letter box will be used only once.
Answers will not have a space between words.

FOOD & DRINK

1 I'm single-celled fungi
   and culinarily divine,

   I'm crucial to the production of
   beer, bread, and wine.

2 These French pancakes are made
   from very thin batters,

   And then frequently served
   with very sweet matters.

FAMOUS & INFAMOUS

3 The war to find my weapons
   left my country a wreck,

   In a hole I took refuge
   and soon swung from my neck.

4 In Fulton was my meaning
   and significance unfurled,

   I was a famous barrier
   that divided the world.

Y S C T O A P E A E C I S D A U
I S R N S T H I R R S E D N M N

Criss Cross

The answers will fit in the rows below.
All letters from the letter box will be used only once.
Answers will not have a space between words.

THE SPORTING LIFE

1 I beat up men
and women, too,

And even chewed
an ear or two.

2 I began as a weapon
for slaying a foe,

But became something common
for athletes to throw.

FAMOUS & INFAMOUS

3 I was a dancer, seductress,
courtesan—but spy?

The French said "Oui"
and by firing squad I would die.

4 Denounced and discredited,
I lived on as an "-ism,"

In the study of hysteria
I am a prime prism.

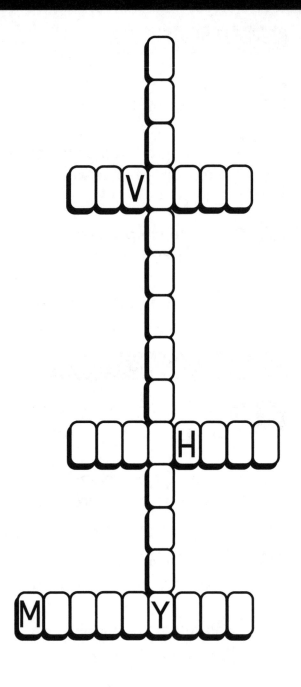

M A Y N M S A N I J I V O T C P M
A L C R J A E T E R T O H I S H K H

88

Criss Cross

The answers will fit in the rows below.
All letters from the letter box will be used only once.
Answers will not have a space between words.

LITERATURE & THE ARTS

1 My affairs made world headlines,
   a diva I was branded,

   The operatic limelight
   for decades I commanded.

2 With bold dabs of my brush
   I showed artistry,

   With a slice of my ear
   I made history.

FOOD & DRINK

3 I might be the most famous
   Greek dish around,

   And loud shouts of "Opa!"
   around me abound.

4 I come in various shapes,
   I'm baked for teatime,

   To dislike me in England
   is nearly a crime.

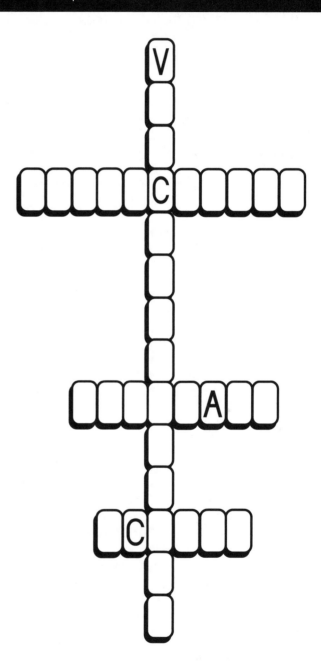

R L N O C S V T A A H K V N G E N I
L A A S A G C S A I G I M N S A N E

CRISS CROSS
Answer Key

Page 53

1. Few tragedies are better known than that of the *Titanic*, the British luxury liner that sank on its maiden voyage on April 14–15, 1912, just south of Newfoundland, while en route from Southampton, England, to New York City, killing some 1,500 people.

2. Pompeii, southeast of Naples, Italy, vanished on Aug. 24-25, AD 79, when nearby **Mount Vesuvius** exploded and buried it under 19-23 feet of volcanic debris. The city's burial served to protect it for the next 17 centuries from vandalism, looting, and destructive weather. Excavations have since uncovered the city, revealing life as it was lived the moment disaster struck.

3. English Romantic poet **John Keats** (1795-1821) devoted his short life—he died of tuberculosis at age 25—to the perfection of a poetry marked by great imagery and passion. His poetry inspired much of the Romantic verse that followed in the Victorian Age. "A thing of beauty is a joy for ever" is the first line of his poem *Endymion* (1818).

4. Writer **E.B. White** possessed a rare and eloquent style that appealed to readers of all ages. While writing witty essays for *The New Yorker*, White wrote such classic children's tales as *Stuart Little* (1945, film 1999), about a caring mouse, and *Charlotte's Web* (1952, film 1973 and 2006), about a community of barnyard animals centered around the spider Charlotte.

Page 54

1. **Galileo** (1564-1642) revolutionized astronomy with his discoveries with the telescope and helped prove the Copernican (Sun-centered) conception of the universe. The Inquisition, the judicial arm of the Church that had pronounced the Copernican cosmology heretical, harassed and censored Galileo for his views and ultimately condemned him to life imprisonment (in a kind of house arrest).

2. When the Moon is at perigee (the closest point to Earth in its orbit), it is called a **supermoon**. The Moon at this point is roughly 12 percent (about 27,000 miles) closer to Earth and about 25 percent brighter than when at apogee (its furthest point from Earth).

3. Michelangelo's *David* (1504) is considered a masterpiece of art and beauty, depicting an ideal human form. The statue's nudity, however, has caused controversy through the centuries, leading some (such as England's Queen Victoria) to affix a fig leaf to copies of the statue.

4. **Stephen King** of Maine helped revive the horror genre in fiction in the late 20th century. Many of his famous works—including *Carrie* (1974), *The Shining* (1977), *Cujo* (1981, about a killer dog), and *Christine* (1983, about a killer car)—were made into hit films. In the movie version of *The Shining*, Jack Nicholson utters the film's signature line, "Here's Johnny!"

Page 55

1. Invented in Holyoke, Massachusetts, in 1895 by a director of the YMCA, **volleyball** was designed for businessmen in need of an indoor sport less vigorous than basketball.

2. Tennis star **Serena Williams** revolutionized women's tennis with her powerful style of play, becoming one of the game's most dominant players in the early 21st century. She completed a career Grand Slam (winning all four of the component tournaments) in 2003.

3. Artist **Andy Warhol** (1928-87) was famous for his silkscreen reproductions of consumer brands (such as Campbell Soup cans) and celebrities (such as Marilyn Monroe). He attracted a following of underground film and rock stars and assorted hangers-on at his New York studio called the Factory, where in 1968 he was shot and nearly killed by a radical feminist writer.

4. **Irene Adler**, a major character in the Sherlock Holmes tale "A Scandal in Bohemia" (1891) by Sir Arthur Conan Doyle, is famous as the only woman to ever outwit the great detective housed at 221B Baker Street in London. Thereafter Holmes reverently referred to her as "*the* woman."

Page 56

1. The Italian-born American **Mario Andretti** was the first driver to win the premier races in three different types of racing: the Indianapolis 500 (IndyCar), Daytona 500 (NASCAR), and Formula One World Championship. He won American Driver of the Year honors in three decades (1967, 1978, and 1984).

2. **Buzkashi** is a rugged Afghan equestrian game in which riders compete to control a decapitated, dehoofed, and sometimes gutted goat or calf carcass weighing 40-100 lbs. The game can be rough, requiring superb riding skills. The winner is the one who rides free and clear with the carcass.

3. **Jupiter**, the fifth planet from the Sun and the largest of the eight, is bigger than all of the other planets put together. It's composed mainly of gases; its colorful bands reflect weather patterns; and its famous Great Red Spot is actually a huge storm large enough to engulf Earth.

4. When Microsoft cofounder **Bill Gates** (b. 1955) was given his school's class schedules to computerize, something strange happened. "By the time I was done," he recalled, "I found that I had no classes at all on Fridays. And even better, there was a disproportionate number of interesting girls in all my classes."

Page 57

1. In order to finance a Broadway play, the owner of the Boston Red Sox sold baseball icon **Babe Ruth** (the "Sultan of Swat," the "Bambino") to the New York Yankees in 1920. This resulted in the so-called "Curse of the Bambino," which supposedly explained why Boston failed to win a World Series for the next 84 years.

2. Canadian **Wayne Gretzky**, called "the Great One," is widely considered the greatest hockey player in history. His finesse and speed revolutionized a sport long known for its rough and physical play. Incredibly, Gretzky's 20-year career totals (he retired in 1999) include more assists than any other player's total points.

3. Legend holds that **pretzels** were created by a medieval Italian monk as a treat for kids who had memorized their Bible verses and prayers. The dough was woven to resemble crossed arms in prayer, with the resulting three holes in the pretzel symbolic of the holy Trinity.

4. Botanically defined, nuts typically come one to a shell, while legumes, such as **peanuts**, contain multiple seeds in their pods. The distinction explains why some people allergic to nuts can nonetheless safely eat peanuts, while those with peanut allergies can still eat certain nuts.

Page 58

1. ***Chariots of Fire*** (Best Picture Oscar, 1981) tells the stories of two British runners, one a Scottish Christian who refused to compete on the Sabbath and the other an English Jew, who brought glory to their country in the 1924 Olympics. The movie's theme song is one of the most famous in film history.

2. **Wimbledon**—one of the four "Grand Slam" tournaments of tennis, established in 1877 and held annually in London in late June and early July—enforces a strict code of white-only tennis apparel. Visible color trims are measured and may not exceed one centimeter in width.

3. In 1962, **Ringo Starr** was asked to join to the Beatles, replacing the band's original drummer, Pete Best. The ousting was hard on Best, especially once the Beatles went on to become the most celebrated rock band in history. At one point Best even attempted suicide.

4. British comic **John Cleese** is best known for his television work on *Monty Python's Flying Circus* and *Fawlty Towers* and for films such as *A Fish Called Wanda* (1988) and *Die Another Day* (2002) in which he played the role of Q, James Bond's gadget master. His comedic style involves looking absolutely normal while doing or saying absurd things.

Page 60

1. Baseball star **Sadaharu Oh** played for the Tokyo Yomiuri Giants in the Japanese Central League for 22 years from 1959-80 and holds the record for most career home runs (868). By comparison, Barry Bonds holds the record for the most home runs in U.S. Major League Baseball (762). Babe Ruth hit 714 home runs.

2. On April 15, 1947, **Jackie Robinson** broke the color barrier in Major League Baseball when he appeared on the field for the Brooklyn Dodgers. It was an arduous challenge for Robinson, who had to endure rough play, ugly remarks, death threats, and Jim Crow laws that forbade blacks from staying in hotels or eating in restaurants with the rest of his team.

3. William Henry Harrison's death in April 1841 created a crisis: the Constitution was vague on whether the vice president became president, serving out the deceased leader's term, or only "acting president" until a special election could be held. Despite critics who called him "Your Accidency," **John Tyler** concluded he was president, moved into the White House, and thereby established the precedent of presidential succession.

4. When asked what he would do in his retirement years, President Franklin Pierce (term: 1853–57) replied with a candor unheard of in politicians today: "**Get drunk.**" And get drunk he did, freely and frequently, giving in to the temptation that had haunted him for so long.

Page 61

1. One of the most famous characters in all of literature is **Huckleberry Finn**, the young river-loving outcast of Mark Twain's famed 1884 novel. Despite the book's status as a classic—Ernest Hemingway called it the source from which "all American literature comes"—it has long been embroiled in controversy due to its use of the "n-word."

2. Ludwig Bemelmans (1898-1962) worked in the hotel industry in New York before gaining fame as a magazine illustrator and author of the **Madeline** series of children's books. Most of the tales begin with the line, "In an old house in Paris that was covered in vines, lived twelve little girls in two straight lines ..."

3. **Haggis**, a national dish of Scotland, is made of the heart, liver, and lungs of a sheep, mixed with beef or suet and seasoned, and then packed and boiled in a sheep's stomach (or in a sausage casing). The dish is traditionally served on New Year's Eve and on Burns' Night (Jan. 25), birthday of poet Robert Burns, who wrote "Ode to a Haggis."

4. This condemnation of **ketchup** has been attributed to novelist Henry James, a major literary figure at the turn of the 20th century. His common theme was the innocence of the New World in contrast to the corruption of the Old, as seen in such classics as *Daisy Miller* (1879), *The Portrait of a Lady* (1881), and *The Ambassadors* (1903).

Page 62

1. **J.K. Rowling**, creator of Harry Potter, got the inspiration for her character during a long, delayed train ride from Manchester to London in 1990. Without a working pen to begin writing with and too shy to borrow one, she sat in frustration. But the delay proved fortuitous, she later said: it gave her time to think through her story.

2. **Beatrix Potter** wrote and illustrated with watercolor drawings classic children's stories such as *The Tale of Peter Rabbit* (1901). The only daughter of heirs to cotton fortunes, she lived a comfortable but largely solitary existence during her childhood, often in Scotland and in the scenic and rustic Lake District of northwest England. This background stimulated her love of animals and inspired her tales.

3. The iconic **Model T**, built by Henry Ford and his assembly-line method of production, was the first practical, affordable transportation for the common man. Mass production allowed its price to be lowered from $850 in 1908 to less than $300 in 1925. Called the "Tin Lizzie" or the "flivver," the car came, said Ford, in any color, "so long as it is black."

4. American industrialist **Henry Ford** revolutionized factory production with his assembly-line methods in the creation of the first affordable car, the Model T (1908-27). The transportation revolution he spurred permanently changed the economic and social character of the United States, which ironically left him longing for the simple rural life that existed before mass transportation.

Page 63

1. A prototype of the "Renaissance man," **Michelangelo** (1475-1564) produced paintings, sculptures, and architectural works that rank among the most famous in the world, including the *David* and *Pietà* in sculpture, the Laurentian Library in architecture, and the remarkable painted ceiling of the Sistine Chapel.

2. The ***Mona Lisa***, arguably the world's most famous painting and image, used in merchandising the world over, was painted by Leonardo da Vinci between 1503 and 1506. It hangs in the Louvre museum in Paris. The harmony of sitter and landscape achieved by Leonardo set the standard for portraits that followed.

3. *Citizen Kane* (1941), directed, produced, and co-written by Orson Welles, who also starred in the lead role, has often been voted the best film ever made. The mystery in the film surrounds the word

"**Rosebud**," which turns out to be the name of the beloved sled from the main character's childhood, a symbolic reminder of his lost innocence.

4. **Tom Cruise** emerged in the 1980s as one of Hollywood's most popular leading men, starring in numerous hit films including *Top Gun* (1986), in which he famously sang "You've Lost That Loving Feeling." His outspoken support of Scientology, however, proved controversial, and in 2013 he admitted that his religion had a played a role in the breakup of his marriage to actress Katie Holmes.

Page 64

1. In 1962, when writer **Stan Lee** and artist Steve Ditko introduced Peter Parker, the sickly and financially strapped orphan who transforms into "The Amazing Spider-Man," they broke established conventions of the comic-book superhero by creating a teenage character who was not relegated to sidekick status beside an older, more-experienced crime-fighter. Critics thought the character would never last.

2. The American comic-book superhero **Iron Man** is a mainstay of Marvel Comics who first appeared in 1963. The character and his alter ego, Tony Stark, became enormously popular when transformed into the live-action star of the film franchise starring Robert Downey, Jr., beginning with *Iron Man* in 2008.

3. The **Cambridge Five** were five young men from the British elite who were recruited as Soviet spies during their days at Cambridge University. Operating from the 1930s to early 50s, they used their high-level government posts and social connections to pass on vital information to the Soviets during World War II and the Cold War.

4. One of the common "What If?" games played by historians concerns how the 20th century might have evolved differently had **Adolf Hitler** achieved his dream of becoming an artist. After the Academy of Fine Arts twice rejected his admissions application, the young Hitler's anger and personality disorders only grew worse.

Page 66

1. Few people are more widely recognizable in the world than sex symbol and actress **Marilyn Monroe**, who reportedly had affairs with both John and Robert Kennedy. Her death on Aug. 5, 1962, by an overdose of sleeping pills, was ruled a "probable suicide," though conspiracy theories abound.

2. **Cleopatra** (c. 70-30 BC) ruled Egypt as queen for 22 years, during which she charmed the leading men of her day. Thinking (wrongly) she was dead, Marc Antony fell on his sword, whereupon Cleopatra also killed herself, reportedly by the bite of a poisonous snake, as dramatized by Shakespeare (the "Bard") in *Antony and Cleopatra* (1606/7).

3. Modern **bowling** evolved from a 3rd- or 4th-century German ritual in the cloisters of churches in which parishioners would prop up their *kegel* (a stake-like pin or club used for sport and self-protection) and roll a stone at it. Those toppling the *kegel*, the symbolic heathen, were deemed cleansed of their sins. "Kegler" remains a common name for a bowler.

4. With roots in antiquity, the game of **badminton** was named after the country estate of the dukes of Beaufort in Gloucestershire, England, where it was first played about 1873. The shuttlecock, or birdie, was originally composed of 16 goose feathers attached to a cork hemisphere.

Page 67

1. President Barak Obama's fondness for **Spider-Man** and Conan the Barbarian comics led to much tongue-in-cheek analysis when he ran for president in 2008. After he won the election, Marvel Comics depicted him on the cover of a March 2009 edition of *The Amazing Spider-Man,* in a story entitled, "Spidey Meets the President."

2. As one newspaper noted, when **Franklin Pierce** died in 1869, mourners passing his open coffin frequently noted the former president's fine "mass of curly black hair, somewhat tinged by age, but which was still combed on a deep slant over his wide forehead."

3. **Garlic**, called the "the stinking rose" for its odorous properties, is a bulb whose medicinal and culinary benefits have been known for centuries. According to legend, garlic even repels vampires, as Bram Stoker described in his famed novel *Dracula* (1897).

4. Official **Chablis** wines are made from the Chardonnay grape and grown in a designated area surrounding the French town of Chablis. But in recent decades, when the name was applied to jugs of inexpensive white wine that had nothing to do with the Chablis region of France, the wine's reputation suffered.

Page 68

1. The **Presidential Seal**, the official symbol of the office of the U.S. president, formerly had the eagle facing the arrows on the seal. Truman, in an effort to emphasize peace and not war, ordered that the eagle be changed to face the olive branch instead.

2. **Virginia** is the birthplace of more presidents than any other U.S. state. Four of the first five presidents, in fact, hailed from Virginia. The eight presidents are: Washington, Jefferson, Madison, Monroe, Harrison, Tyler, Taylor, and Wilson.

3. The *Spruce Goose*, built by Howard Hughes, was the largest aircraft in history, designed to carry 750 passengers, specifically troops during World War II. Due to wartime restrictions on building material, the plane was built entirely of wood. It was flown only once—a distance of one mile—in 1947, silencing skeptics who thought the behemoth could never fly.

4. The **Dalai Lama**, the spiritual leader of Tibet who was sent into exile in 1959, said he disapproves of the self-immolations that Tibetans have engaged in for decades as a form of protest against Chinese control of Tibet but understands and praises the courage of their convictions.

Page 69

1. The **Oval Office**, built in 1909, is the official office of the U.S. president, located in the West Wing of the White House. The decor of the office, and the large oval-shaped carpet that takes up most of the floor, is typically changed by each president.

2. **Calvin Coolidge**, who became president when President Harding died in 1923, was a man of few words. So-called "Silent Cal," however, was witty. When a woman seated next to him at a White House dinner said, "You must talk to me, Mr. President. I made a bet today that I could get more than two words out of you," Coolidge replied, "You lose."

3. **Euclid**, born in Alexandria, Egypt, c. 300 BC, was the most significant mathematician of Greco-Roman antiquity. His famous treatise on geometry, *Elements*, has been called the most influential textbook ever written and the second most reprinted book in the world, behind only the Bible.

4. **Carl Sagan**, at the height of his popularity in the 1980s, was America's most famous scientist, and his TV series and book (*Cosmos*) were enormous hits. But his critics were also legion, including Christians who denounced him as an atheist, conservatives who abhorred his criticisms of Ronald Reagan, and scientists who (jealously) looked askance at his popular success.

Page 70

1. The **Monroe Doctrine**, announced by President James Monroe in 1823 and a cornerstone of U.S. foreign policy, told the countries of Europe to stay out of the affairs of the Americas, now a U.S. sphere of influence. The U.S., in turn, promised not to interfere with the affairs of Europe.

2. *Air Force One* is the common name for (and official radio call signal of) any airplane carrying the U.S. president. The president's specially designed Air Force planes are also available to the vice president, but the plane is then called *Air Force Two*. The first president to fly was Franklin Delano Roosevelt.

3. British writer **Roald Dahl** was a fighter pilot and spy during World War II, but he is best known for his children's stories that became hit films and stage productions, including *James and the Giant Peach* (1961), *Charlie and the Chocolate Factory* (1964), and *Matilda* (1988). He also wrote the screenplay for the James Bond film *You Only Live Twice* (1967).

4. Poet and critic **Ezra Pound** was a leader of the Modernist movement in English and American literature who, while writing his own work, helped shape the work of such masters as James Joyce, Ernest Hemingway, Robert Frost, and T.S. Eliot. His pro-fascist broadcasts during World War II led to his postwar arrest and confinement until 1958.

Page 72

1. **Lucy Hayes** is associated with several "firsts." She was the first first lady to earn a college degree; the first widely called the "First Lady"; and the one who began the Easter tradition for children of egg-rolling on the White House lawn. Her critics dubbed her "Lemonade Lucy," due to her ban on serving alcoholic beverages at the White House.

2. By enforcing the Fugitive Slave Act of 1850, which allowed slave owners to capture runaway slaves, **Millard Fillmore** further antagonized both sides in the slavery debate: he spurred the North toward complete abolitionism, which the South would never tolerate, and encouraged Southern recalcitrance.

3. American film director, producer, and screenwriter **George Lucas** has produced some of the most popular films in history, including *American Graffiti* (1973), the *Star Wars* saga (beginning in 1977), and the *Indiana Jones* series (beginning in 1981). In 2012, his Lucasfilm's network of properties, studios, and subsidiary companies were bought by the Walt Disney Company for $4 billion.

4. American singer, songwriter, actress, and entrepreneur **Madonna** (b. 1958) is frequently cited as the best-selling female recording artist in history. Bold and brassy, she achieved levels of power and control unprecedented for a woman in the entertainment industry.

Page 73

1. Ronald Reagan's association with **jelly beans** began when he ate them as a substitute for pipe smoking during his run for governor of California in 1966. When Reagan became president in 1981, more than three tons of jelly beans were supposedly delivered to Washington, D.C., for the various inauguration festivities.

2. **Bananas Foster** is a dessert made of ice cream and bananas with a rum and brown sugar sauce that is flambéed at the table before serving. It was created in the early 1950s at Brennan's Restaurant in New Orleans, then a major port of entry for bananas from Central and South America. "Foster" was the name of a local civic leader.

3. **Helen Taft** was an independent-minded and progressive first lady (1909-13) by the standards of her day. She lobbied for woman's suffrage, hired minorities for White House positions previously reserved for whites, served alcohol at functions despite the outrage of prohibitionists, smoked and played cards for money with the men, and changed the presidential mode of transportation from horse-drawn carriages to motorcars.

4. **James Polk** is a little-remembered president, but he was popular and successful. Whether through conquest (the Mexican-American War) or purchase, the country during his term (1845-49) expanded dramatically in size, adding the areas associated with Utah, Nevada, Arizona, New Mexico, California, Texas, and western Colorado.

Page 74

1. A **California roll**, a staple of fusion cuisine, is a kind of inside-out sushi roll (uramaki) in which vinegared rice (rather than nori, an edible seaweed) forms the outside roll. It was invented in California in the 1960s to appeal to Americans turned off by sushi's traditional seaweed wrap, and it usually contains cucumber, crab, and avocado.

2. **Kangaroo** meat used to be widely eaten in Australia, though it is less popular and acceptable today. Some observers have credited the change to "the Skippy factor," so-called after a popular 1960s TV show, *Skippy the Bush Kangaroo,* that deepened affection for the animal, the country's national symbol. Animal rights activists have also fought the selling of kangaroo meat.

3. **Carmen** is the fiery and seductive gypsy protagonist of Georges Bizet's famed 1875 opera of the same name. Her entrance aria, "Habanera," and the "Toréador Song" are among the most famous arias in all opera.

4. "**Banksy**" is the pseudonymous name for the satirical graffiti artist and filmmaker whose artwork began appearing on buildings in England in the 1990s. He carefully conceals his identity, and he uses stencils to expedite his work and escape detection. His documentary, *Exit Through the Gift Shop* (2010), was nominated for an Academy Award, but he was denied permission to attend the ceremony in disguise due to fears that multiple imposters would crash the event.

Page 75

1. American physician and medical researcher **Jonas Salk** developed the first safe and effective vaccine for polio. After its release in the United States in 1955, the vaccine dramatically reduced the incidence of the disease that had struck hundreds of thousands of children every year.

2. **Diamond** is a mineral composed of pure carbon. Diamonds are the hardest naturally occurring substance known—and the most popular gemstone. Because of their extreme hardness and high thermal conductivity, diamonds have a wide variety of industrial applications. They are used in saws, drill bits, and heat sinks (cooling agents for electronics).

3. **Ogden Nash**, famous for humorous poetry and biting verse, is known for such lines as "Candy is dandy, but liquor is quicker" and for irreverent tales such as "The Boy Who Laughed at Santa Claus"

(1942). In the latter, a naughty boy named Jabez Dawes mocks Santa Claus and is turned into an ugly toy by St. Nick.

4. Painter **Jackson Pollock**, famous for his poured and "drip" techniques, was one of America's most influential artists and a leader in the Abstract Expressionist movement; random objects, including keys, coins, and cigarette butts, helped layer some of his dense works. Ed Harris, in the acclaimed film *Pollock* (2000), portrayed the mercurial artist who died in an alcohol-related car crash in 1956.

Page 76

1. In 1996, 100 years after the premier of Giocomo Puccini's opera *La Bohème*, the hit musical *Rent* opened in New York. The musical was loosely based on the Puccini classic. Whereas consumption (tuberculosis) was the disease that shadowed the Parisian artists of the 1830s in *La Bohème,* AIDS was the disease that plagued the New York artists in the award-winning *Rent*.

2. To build **Mount Rushmore** into the granite rock of the Black Hills in South Dakota, it took sculptor Gutzon Borglum and his son 14 years (1927-41) of drilling, blasting, and carving. Borglum wanted to reflect the first 150 years of American history with his carved portraits of presidents George Washington, Thomas Jefferson, Abraham Lincoln, and Theodore Roosevelt.

3. *Toy Story* (1995), by Pixar Animation Studios, was the first entirely computer-animated feature-length film. It was an instant classic, earning both critical acclaim and commercial success. The film spawned a highly lucrative cottage industry of spin-off products, from toys, clothing, and games to attractions at theme parks.

4. *The Exorcist* (1973) has often been called the scariest movie of all time. It was highly controversial due to the disturbing special effects and the graphic nature of the script for the then-13-year-old actress Linda Blair, who plays the demon-possessed character in need of the exorcist. The film was banned in some places, and in others paramedics were present to aid viewers who fainted or became emotionally distraught.

Page 78

1. Greek philosopher and scientist **Aristotle** (384-322 BC) was one of the greatest intellectual figures in history. Many of his philosophical and scientific notions survived the Renaissance, Reformation, and Enlightenment and remain embedded in Western thinking today.

2. **Typhoon**s, cyclones, and hurricanes are all regionally used names for the same extreme weather condition. In the Atlantic and Northeast Pacific oceans, off the coasts of North America, the name "hurricane" is used; the same storm in the Northwest Pacific Ocean is a "typhoon"; "cyclones" occur in the South Pacific and Indian oceans.

3. Few actresses stirred up more tabloid scandal than **Elizabeth Taylor**. She was married eight times, and her extramarital affair with costar Richard Burton during the filming of *Cleopatra* (1963) garnered headlines as well as a rebuke from the Vatican, which condemned her "erotic vagrancy."

4. **Max Factor**, the Polish-born pharmacist-turned-makeup designer, was a pioneer in developing makeup for motion picture film. Unlike stage makeup, his concoction did not cake or crack, and for his achievements he received a special award from the motion picture academy in 1928. His "flexible greasepaint" was the forerunner of today's foundation cream and sparked the cosmetic empire that continues in his name.

Page 79

1. **Will Smith**'s charm, clean-cut good looks, and quick wit helped him transition from rap music in the 1980s to acting in the 1990s. After gaining fame in his popular TV sitcom *The Fresh Prince of Bel-Air* (1990-96), he starred in such movies as *Independence Day* (1996), *Men in Black* (1997), and *Ali* (2001). For his portrayal of boxer Muhammad Ali, he earned an Academy Award nomination.

2. **Frankenstein**, the title character of Mary Wollstonecraft Shelley's 1818 novel, is the prototypical "mad scientist" who interferes with nature and creates a monster by which he is eventually killed. Frankenstein's monster, however, is popularly (and mistakenly) called by the doctor's name. The creature is the most famous monster in movie history.

3. **Waterloo**, about nine miles south of Brussels, Belgium, was the site of Napoleon's final defeat. The battle pitted the 72,000 troops of Napoleon against the Duke of Wellington's Allied army of 68,000 (British, Dutch, Belgian, and German units) and about 45,000 Prussians. "Waterloo" became a synonym for any decisive loss or defeat.

4. **King Tut** (short for "Tutankhamen") was a teenage pharaoh of ancient Egypt whose reign was of little consequence. But his renown was secured in 1922 when British archaeologist Howard Carter discovered his magnificent tomb. The king's mummy lay within a nest of three coffins, the innermost of solid gold. Other assorted treasures filled the tomb.

Page 80

1. President **Bill Clinton** presided (1993-2001) over the country's longest peacetime economic expansion, but controversy and scandal were his constant companions. Often the controversies were compounded by his evasive answers, as when he said he smoked marijuana but didn't inhale and suggested, during inquiry into his extramarital affairs, that "it depends on what the meaning of the word *is* is."

2. **Lyndon Johnson** became president upon the assassination of John Kennedy on Nov. 22, 1963. He was notorious for his rather crude mannerisms. He reportedly once urinated down the leg of a Secret Service agent. When the agent questioned him about it, the president reputedly quipped, "It's my prerogative."

3. Flinging pans from the Frisbie Pie Company of Bridgeport, Connecticut, was a popular pastime with New England college students in the late 19th century. Similar discs were produced as a toy during the UFO craze of the late 1940s and early '50s. First called "Flying Saucers" and then "Pluto Platters," the plastic discs were renamed "**Frisbees**" in 1957.

4. Baseball developed from the older English bat-and-ball game of **rounders**. Around since at least the 18th century, rounders is still popular with English schoolchildren. Wanting to establish a native origin for the "national pastime," an American commission in 1907 concluded erroneously that Abner Doubleday invented baseball at Cooperstown, New York, in 1839.

Page 81

1. In Raphael's famous painting *School of Athens* (1508-11), two different philosophies are represented. While **Plato** points upward (in a gesture to the eternal, higher reality of ideas such as truth, beauty, and justice), his student Aristotle holds his hand down (toward the human reality of lived experience).

2. The women who conducted radio broadcasts of Japanese propaganda in English during World War II were collectively called "**Tokyo Rose**" by American servicemen. The most prominent one was Iva Toguri, an American caught in Japan after the war broke out and forced to work for Japan as an enemy alien. After the war she served six years in a U.S. prison for treason. In 1977, President Gerald Ford pardoned her.

3. **Gerald Ford** was the only president and vice president elected to neither post. He was named vice president when Spiro Agnew resigned in 1973 and then became president when Richard Nixon resigned the following year. He worked as a model in the 1940s, appearing on the cover of *Cosmopolitan* magazine.

4. **John Quincy Adams,** son of President John Adams, was known for many things: his grim reserve, his pet alligator, his fondness for skinny-dipping, his brilliant service as U.S. secretary of state (he wrote the Monroe Doctrine), his election as sixth U.S. president (1825-29), and his celebrated career in the U.S. House of Representatives (1831-48). Adams collapsed on the House floor and died two days later.

Page 82

1. **Croquet** is a popular garden sport. It evolved from the French mallet-and-ball game of "pall-mall"—a game at least as old as the 13th century—and developed into the slightly more complicated sport involving a series of six or more hoops (wickets), laid out in a pattern, through which balls are driven with mallets.

2. When designed for the Olympic Games in 1912, the new **pentathlon** was modeled on the five skills that Baron Pierre de Coubertin, founder of the modern Games, saw as emblematic of the ideal soldier. These were fencing, shooting, swimming, running, and horseback riding. Only in 2000 was the modern pentathlon offered as a women's event, too.

3. **Jacques Cousteau** was a French naval officer and World War II hero who co-invented the first fully automatic scuba equipment. His book, *The Silent World* (1953; filmed 1956), and American television series, *The Undersea World of Jacques Cousteau* (1968-76), made him famous.

4. The **mosquito** has caused more human deaths than any other creature. Through the bloodsucking of the females, mosquitoes transmit such serious diseases as yellow fever, malaria, and West Nile virus.

Page 83

1. A meteoroid (a stony or metallic natural object from interplanetary space) that survives its fiery plunge through Earth's atmosphere and lands on the surface is called a **meteorite**. Meteoroids travel many times faster than a speeding bullet, and the vast majority of them burn up in the upper atmosphere before ever reaching land.

2. The **Scoville Scale**, invented in 1912 and named for its inventor, pharmacist Wilbur Scoville, measures the amount of water needed to neutralize a pepper's heat. For example, a poblano pepper's Scoville Heat Unit (SHU) of 1,500 means 1,500 cups of water would have to be added to neutralize the heat of one cup of the ground pepper. The hottest peppers top one million SHU.

3. When killer and grave robber **Ed Gein** was arrested in Plainfield, Wisconsin, in 1957, police found his house and furniture decorated with human body parts and organs. With his ghoulish ways, including the wearing of skin flayed off dead women, he was the

inspiration for assorted fictional and film villains including Norman Bates in *Psycho* and Buffalo Bill in *The Silence of the Lambs.*

4. **Coco Chanel** (1883-1971) ruled over Parisian haute couture for almost six decades. Her elegantly casual designs inspired women to abandon complicated, uncomfortable clothes such as petticoats and corsets. She gave them instead her now-classic innovations: the Chanel suit, costume jewelry, and the "little black dress."

Page 84

1. "There are only three sports: bullfighting, motor racing, and mountaineering; all the rest are merely games." This quote is often attributed to **Ernest Hemingway**. The novelist's virile prose and adventurous personal life often mirrored this conception of sport. He was an avid big-game hunter, an accomplished amateur boxer, and wrote extensively—both fiction and nonfiction—on bullfighting.

2. Pigeon shooting was an Olympic "sport" only once, at the Games of 1900. The objective was simple: shoot and kill as many **pigeons** as possible. Some 300 birds died during the single event, leaving the grounds a bloody mess of feathers, carcasses, and injured birds.

3. **Figaro** is the main character of Pierre-Augustin de Beaumarchais's classic comedy plays *The Barber of Seville* (1775) and *The Marriage de Figaro* (1784). In the 1816 operatic version of the former by Gioachino Rossini, Figaro makes his entrance singing the classic aria "Largo al factotum" in which he famously repeats his name: "Figaro! Figaro! Figaro!"

4. Norwegian painter Edvard Munch dealt with psychological themes, built upon the tenets of 19th-century Symbolism, and greatly influenced Expressionism in the early 20th century. His painting *The Scream*, or *The Cry* (1893) is one of the most recognized paintings in the world. It is widely seen as a symbol of modern spiritual angst.

Page 85

1. The game of **golf** was likely invented by the Dutch. The popular notion that it originated in Scotland, where the game was popularized and refined, is based on 15th-century references in Scottish Acts of Parliament that condemned and outlawed the sport. The resolutions encouraged the Scots to practice archery instead, a skill that could aid in the country's national defense.

2. The All-American Girls Professional Baseball League grew from a stopgap wartime entertainment to a professional showcase for women baseball players. The **Rockford** (Illinois) **Peaches** was one of the two teams that played all 12 years of the league's existence (1943-54), and its history was the focus of the film *A League of Their Own* (1992), starring Tom Hanks as the team's manager.

3. **Yogurt** is a semifluid fermented milk food that has a smooth texture and mildly sour flavor due to its lactic acid. It is made from the milk of various animals, including cows, sheep, goats, and water buffaloes.

4. Some believe **pickles** originated in Mesopotamia, with cucumbers from India, some 4,400 years ago. It is said that Cleopatra ate pickles as a beauty aid; Christopher Columbus served them to his crew to prevent scurvy; and George Washington collected more than 400 varieties of them.

Page 86

1. Since **Barbie**'s inception in 1959, the doll has incited controversy. She was criticized in the 1950s for having "too much of a figure"; in the 1970s she was branded materialistic; and in the 1990s researchers concluded that a real woman with her measurements would not have enough body fat to menstruate. However, some women have praised Barbie for remaining single and pursuing a career.

2. **Kryptonite** is the element from Superman's home planet of Krypton that can drain the "Man of Steel" of his powers. Although it can come in many forms, kryptonite most often appears as a green, glowing substance.

3. The 1938 boxing match between Germany's Max Schmeling and American heavyweight champion **Joe Louis** was portrayed by American media as a battle between Nazism and democracy. Louis's knockout victory in the first round made him a national hero and arguably the first black American widely admired by whites. In later years Schmeling helped Louis financially and even paid for part of his funeral in 1981, at which Schmeling was a pallbearer.

4. After the terror attacks of 9/11, Major League Baseball decided to honor the victims and to show American unity by having "**God Bless America**" sung at the start of the seventh-inning stretch. It is still played during Sunday games and on holidays. At least one team, the New York Yankees, plays it every game.

Page 87

1. **Yeast** is a single-celled fungus used for leavening and fermenting certain foods and drinks, such as beer, bread, and wine. The fungi feed on sugars, producing alcohol and carbon dioxide, though the alcohol produced in bread-making is eliminated when the dough is baked.

2. **Crepes** are French pancakes made from a thin batter containing flour, eggs, melted butter, salt, milk, water, and perhaps sugar. For crepes suzette, the pancakes are folded in four, soaked in a syrup flavored with orange liqueur, and then flambéed.

3. **Saddam Hussein** was the president of Iraq (1979-2003) whose brutal rule was marked by costly and unsuccessful wars against neighboring countries. His supposed possession of weapons of mass destruction spurred the American-led invasion of Iraq in 2003. American soldiers found Hussein hiding in a hole in December 2003. He was tried in 2005-6 and executed by hanging in 2006.

4. The **Iron Curtain** was the political, military, and ideological barrier erected by the Soviet Union after World War II to seal off itself and Eastern Europe from contact with the West. It was defined in a March 5, 1946, speech in Fulton, Missouri, by former British Prime Minister Winston Churchill. Soviet-dominated countries were called Iron Curtain countries during the Cold War.

Page 88

1. **Mike Tyson**, at age 20, became the youngest heavyweight boxing champion in history. Self-control, however, proved difficult for him. He was accused of abusing his wife, actress Robin Givens; was imprisoned for sexually assaulting another woman; and then lost his boxing license for biting Evander Holyfield's ears in a 1997 championship match.

2. The **javelin**, shorter and lighter than a spear, was a popular offensive weapon in antiquity. The javelin throw was included in the ancient Greek Olympic Games as one of five events comprising the pentathlon.

3. **Mata Hari** was the famed dancer and courtesan whose name has become a synonym for the seductive female spy. On Oct. 15, 1917, she was shot by a French firing squad on charges of spying for Germany during World War I. The nature and extent of her espionage activities remain uncertain, and her guilt is widely contested.

4. U.S. senator **Joseph McCarthy** dominated the early 1950s with his sensational but unproved charges of communist subversion in high government circles. His reckless accusations and innuendo, and the mass hysteria and distrust they caused, gave rise to the term McCarthyism.

Page 89

1. **Maria Callas** was the biggest opera star of the mid-20th century. Her soprano voice was not the purest, but her delivery and sense of the dramatic made her famous. She was just as famous off the stage, for her diva-like temperament, feuds with rivals, and well-publicized affair with shipping tycoon Aristotle Onassis, who eventually left her to marry Jacqueline Kennedy.

2. Perhaps no art story is more well-known than **Vincent van Gogh**'s severing of his left ear on Christmas Eve, 1888, and delivering it to a woman at a brothel. However, some recent scholars have suggested that it was Paul Gauguin, the famed painter who was staying with van Gogh at the time, who severed Vincent's ear.

3. **Saganaki** is perhaps the most frequently ordered Greek appetizer. It typically consists of Kasseri cheese that is breaded with flour, pan-fried in butter or olive oil, and then, at the table, doused with brandy and flambéed to shouts of "Opa," an utterance that serves as a general exclamation of joy.

4. **Scones**, an English single-serving quick bread, are a common component of England's famed teatime. There are many variations. Most scones are round, others are triangular or square, and clotted cream may be applied to the scone first or after assorted jams.

Fill in the Blanks

Fill in the blanks with letters from the letter box below. All letters will be used only once in answering the riddles.

FAMOUS & INFAMOUS

1 "CROATOAN" on a post and "CRO" on a tree,
That's all that was left of this missing colony.

R _ _ _ _ E   _ _ _ _ _ D

2 My supporters hailed from a town in Missouri,
Lindbergh I landed in Paris to much flurry.

P _ _ _ _   _ _   T   _ _ _ S

THE SPORTING LIFE

3 I was famous at the hustle and was heavy on the scale,
I really hit the big time when Jackie Gleason told my tale.

_ _ _ _ _ _ _ _ A   F _ _ _

4 I marshaled a faithful army, on battlefields of green,
Winning numerous victories and spurring crowds unseen.

_ _ _ _ _ D   _ _ _ _ _ R

R F L K A E N A P N O R T A M L L E T E
S O M O I P S S I D T N D A L S
R I I S O A A O S N F U T I O N R

Fill in the Blanks

Fill in the blanks with letters from the letter box below. All letters will be used only once in answering the riddles.

FAMOUS & INFAMOUS

1 My airborne feat made headlines, it was widely ballyhooed,
But nothing like the way the press would cover what ensued.

2 I was a radical and saboteur for social change,
From prisoner to president did my career arc range.

FOOD & DRINK

3 I led to hunger, migration, and widespread calamity,
All of it caused by this emerald land's vegetable malady.

4 Banana with some peanut butter was my foodie vice,
For a life of adoration I paid a deadly price.

E E O N L R P R E L O D H H B T N N I V P
F I O R A A G S N L M E A E E N S H
D A A S R L I I T S E I L S M Y L C E

98

Fill in the Blanks

Fill in the blanks with letters from the letter box below. All letters will be used only once in answering the riddles.

FAMOUS & INFAMOUS

1 I told countrymen and friends, "lend me your ears,"
And thus did I undermine Rome's mutineers.

2 Seven easy pieces are all that women need,
With four simple letters do I wildly succeed.

U.S. PRESIDENCY & FIRST LADIES

3 My portraits of American leaders brought me goodwill,
And my half-done Washington was used on the dollar bill.

4 As the youngest first lady I became a celebrity,
Advertisers used my image and kids were named after me.

```
R R A N D N K V T A S R R A T B D
L C N E N I A L N R S L A A C M
K A E O O T U N F Y T E G A E N
```

Fill in the Blanks

Fill in the blanks with letters from the letter box below. All letters will be used only once in answering the riddles.

FAMOUS & INFAMOUS

1 Fans and critics of my fashions were widespread,
And a crazed serial killer shot me dead.

`[ ][ ][ ][ ][ I ]` `[ ][ ][ ][ ][ C ]`

2 What I founded was red, in the Caribbean Sea,
But were there really 600 attempts to kill me?

`[ ][ D ][ ][ ]` `[ ][ ][ ][ R ]`

POP CULTURE & ENTERTAINMENT

3 When I emerged from the sea I turned male heads indeed,
I was the first of the Bond girls who followed my lead.

`[ U ][ ][ ][ ][ ][ ]` `[ ][ ][ ][ ][ S ][ ]`

4 I played headstrong girls, and in trousers I dressed,
But Oscar still loved me, and fans were impressed.

`[ ][ ][ ][ ][ ][ R ][ ][ ]` `[ ][ ][ ][ B ][ ][ ]`

```
N I N R N V N U A D O H E T R S F
A N B I A E E R S D I S E U A R R T
L K G E A R S A H U S C E A I P L C
```

Fill in the Blanks

Fill in the blanks with letters from the letter box below. All letters will be used only once in answering the riddles.

SCIENCE, SPACE & TECHNOLOGY

1 Self-cleaning glass and sunscreens that are clear,
Both novelties from this new tech frontier.

		N		T									Y

2 Water, carbon dioxide, and sunlight,
All help me keep plants (and humans) upright.

		O										S

FAMOUS & INFAMOUS

3 Power, riches, and subjects did I compel,
Severing the church and pretty heads as well.

			R			I		

4 Not for pepper but for salt did I protest and walk,
For reform without violence did I march and talk.

				M		G					

N O Y P H I O T N T C H A E H Y G Y H
T N V S I E A O N L E O H S G S
A R I H M D T O A N A N I M I

Fill in the Blanks

Fill in the blanks with letters from the letter box below. All letters will be used only once in answering the riddles.

SCIENCE, SPACE & TECHNOLOGY

1 I shocked Victorian society with my bold suggestion
About the origins of species, which I called into question.

2 I was 23 days late to be first in space,
But among all Americans I hold first place.

LITERATURE & THE ARTS

3 Creatures in formaldehyde and diamonds on a skull,
Whether worshipped or deplored, my art is seldom dull.

4 I'm the oldest continuously published and revised English work to date,
First published in Edinburgh, Scotland, in 1768.

H A N A A N Y P N R D R I D N W D N
M S H O E S E L I A I L I A C A N A T A
A H E P E B I C A E T R S R R C L I D C

BRITANNICA BRAINBUSTERS

Mind Lines

Try to get from the top line of categories to the bottom in the fewest moves. Check off each box (or mark initials in the box if playing opponents) after each correct answer to a riddle. Once a player "owns" a box, an opponent must find another path.

Fam - FAMOUS & INFAMOUS
Sci - SCIENCE, SPACE & TECHNOLOGY
Lit - LITERATURE & THE ARTS
Pres - U.S. PRESIDENCY & FIRST LADIES
Pop - POP CULTURE & ENTERTAINMENT
Sprt - THE SPORTING LIFE
F&D - FOOD & DRINK

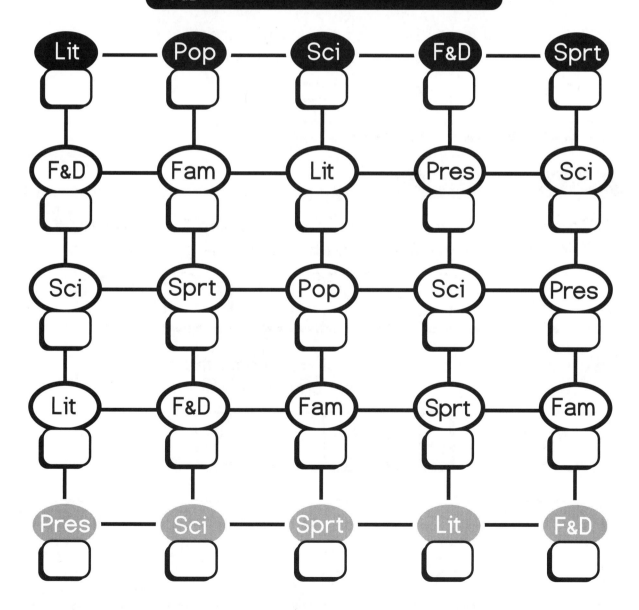

Fill in the Blanks

Fill in the blanks with letters from the letter box below. All letters will be used only once in answering the riddles.

SCIENCE, SPACE & TECHNOLOGY

1 I'm numerically sound, there are no overlaps,
You'd follow my rules for tiling without gaps.

[ ][ ][ ][ ][ ][L][ ][ ][ ][N][ ][ ]

2 The vistas from above took away my breath,
I pioneered in space and even in death.

[S][ ][ ][ ][ ] [ ][ ][E]

THE SPORTING LIFE

3 Poor pay for women athletes is something I long fought,
My "Battle of the Sexes" did by no means go for naught.

[ ][ ][L][ ][ ][ ] [J][ ][ ][ ] [ ][ ][N][ ]

4 I cracked my head, but I still took home the gold,
While keeping a secret that long went untold.

[ ][ ][E][ ] [ ][ ][ ][ ][ ][ ][N][ ]

T G L L L I K J E G E S A E D
I B E G L N I S S L L U E T N N
Y L I S A I A E R O A I N R O G

104

BRITANNICA
BRAINBUSTERS

Fill in the Blanks

Fill in the blanks with letters from the letter box below. All letters will be used only once in answering the riddles.

SCIENCE, SPACE & TECHNOLOGY

1 Both my husband and my daughter each won what I won twice,
And for that which made me famous I paid a deadly price.

| A | | | | | | U | | | |

2 Eat turkey by day and drink warm milk at night,
And from both you'll soon feel the sleep I incite.

| | | | P | | | H | | |

FOOD & DRINK

3 "If you're afraid of butter," said this spy and chef extraordinaire,
Then simply "use cream!" she uttered with her characteristic flair.

| | | L | | | | | | L | |

4 Synonymous with the games at Wimbledon, I'm a court-side snack,
I'm a marriage of fruit and dairy that goes five centuries back.

| | | | | | B | | | | | | | N | | | | | | M |

S	W	E	I	H	L	M	T	R	D	S	A	J	A	I	B	T	T
D	R	A	A	C	C	I	I	E	P	L	M	E	H	E	U
R	R	R	C	A	R	Y	E	I	U	R	A	O	P	N	N

Fill in the Blanks

Fill in the blanks with letters from the letter box below. All letters will be used only once in answering the riddles.

FOOD & DRINK

1 I'm harvested from excrement, I'm the dearest in the world,
Around my high-priced beans a certain controversy has swirled.

[ ][ ][P] [ ][U][ ][ ][ ]

2 Visiting Paris, said I, is like a lifelong treat,
Memories will follow you like a moveable feast.

[ ][ ][N][ ][ ][ ] [H][ ][ ][ ][ ][ ][ ][ ][ ]

U.S. PRESIDENCY & FIRST LADIES

3 The sole bigamist among first ladies was I,
Before even reaching the White House I would die.

[ ][ ][ ][ ][ ][L][ ] [ ][ ][ ][K][ ][ ][ ]

4 Although my faith said not to gamble, and to abstain,
Poker earned me the funds needed for my first campaign.

[ ][ ][ ][H][ ][ ][ ][ ] [ ][ ][ ][ ][N]

R A N I K I O W A C H E J A H X E
U S A R S I A M C W K L N E R
C D N G N O H P T K I R L E O N Y

Fill in the Blanks

Fill in the blanks with letters from the letter box below. All letters will be used only once in answering the riddles.

FOOD & DRINK

1 "Poor" is a matter of perspective, this Danish tale reveals,
All taught amid the courses of the most luscious of film meals.

2 I'm wrapped in sausage, then breaded and fried,
I'm a British pub food famous worldwide.

POP CULTURE & ENTERTAINMENT

3 A sex scandal and extortion campaign,
Both played a part in my long late-night reign.

4 I was a long way from home, kids came to my aid,
And to see how I glowed many millions were paid.

E A S D O T B C T E T G C E L E T T N T
T M H E E V R R S X A B E R E A H
I E T L A G E I T E D A A F R T R S S

Fill in the Blanks

Fill in the blanks with letters from the letter box below. All letters will be used only once in answering the riddles.

FOOD & DRINK

1 My candies and golden tickets left kids obsessed,
But it really was all a morality test.

W □ □ □ □   □ □ □ K □

2 The Brit who played cards while eating meat,
Soon gave his name to this common treat.

□ A □ □ □ □ □ H

FAMOUS & INFAMOUS

3 Forget egos, superegos, and ids, oh my!
A cigar may only be a cigar, said I.

□ □ G □ □ □ □ □   □ R □ □ □

4 So horribly I stuttered, public speaking was a fright,
Then suddenly I found myself in the public spotlight.

□ □ □ G   □ □ □ □ □ □ E □   □ □

W R S D I Y F S I E G O G H
K L D N G E U A N I K U G D
N N E I R C O L M W W I V A

BRITANNICA
BRAINBUSTERS

Mind Lines

Try to get from the top line of categories to the bottom in the fewest moves. Check off each box (or mark initials in the box if playing opponents) after each correct answer to a riddle. Once a player "owns" a box, an opponent must find another path.

Fam - FAMOUS & INFAMOUS
Sci - SCIENCE, SPACE & TECHNOLOGY
Lit - LITERATURE & THE ARTS
Pres - U.S. PRESIDENCY & FIRST LADIES
Pop - POP CULTURE & ENTERTAINMENT
Sprt - THE SPORTING LIFE
F&D - FOOD & DRINK

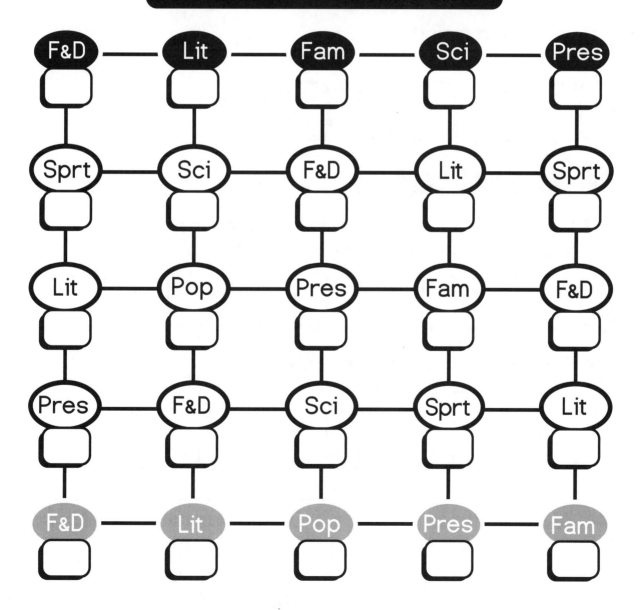

Fill in the Blanks

Fill in the blanks with letters from the letter box below. All letters will be used only once in answering the riddles.

FOOD & DRINK

1 Although a legendary figure, I existed in fact,
Spreading seeds wherever I went in this nature-friendly act.

[ ][ ][H][ ][ ][ ] [ ][P][ ][ ][ ][ ][ ][ ]

2 We are two food groups that should be never be blended,
If compliance with Jewish law is intended.

[ ][ ][A][ ] [ ][ ][D] [ ][ ][ ][K]

LITERATURE & THE ARTS

3 I choreographed not just in Europe and for ballet,
But for film and musical theater in the U.S.A.

[ ][ ][ ][ ][G][ ] [ ][ ][ ][ ][ ][C][ ][ ][ ][ ]

4 Evasive was I, the "Napoleon of Crime,"
I'm among the most dastardly villains, all-time.

[ ][ ][ ][F][ ][ ][ ][ ][ ] [M][ ][ ][ ][ ][ ][ ][ ]

O L L A T H Y I E C O Y A L S P R J N O
M N K H D F O A G E E A P B S N R T A
R E S I R I P N M E D N E G R E M A O E

Fill in the Blanks

Fill in the blanks with letters from the letter box below. All letters will be used only once in answering the riddles.

LITERATURE & THE ARTS

1 This central creation was based on innovation,
And included a zoo, three lakes, and police station.

`[ ][ ][ ][ ][R][ ]   [P][ ][ ][ ]`

2 "Today you are You," I proclaimed this is true,
"There's no one alive who is Youer than You."

`[ ][ ][ ][ ][ ][D][ ][ ]   [ ][ ][ ][ ][S][ ]   [ ][ ][ ][S][ ][ ]`

FAMOUS & INFAMOUS

3 I designed a "New Look" for women after the war,
And I made Paris the fashion capital once more.

`[ ][ ][ ][ ][ ][S][ ][ ][ ][ ][ ]   [ ][ ][O][ ]`

4 Among Soviets and sinners as a leader I shined,
And my realm without borders was religiously defined.

`[ ][ ][ ][N][ ]   [ ][ ][ ][L][ ]   [ ][ ]`

`[ E  I  O  T  L  R  R  N  A  H  S  O  O  O  O  T  C  I  C ]`
`[ H  I  H  U  S  N  A  R  E  R  G  A  L  T  I  E  R ]`
`[ J  N  P  U  S  D  E  S  P  D  I  I  S  K  E  A  L ]`

111

Fill in the Blanks

Fill in the blanks with letters from the letter box below. All letters will be used only once in answering the riddles.

LITERATURE & THE ARTS

1 So moved by this music the king took to his feet,
Spawning a custom that still spurs folks from their seat.

2 I was killed by affectation,
In a scarf-based strangulation.

THE SPORTING LIFE

3 The Olympics used to like me, church picnics still do,
But my players have lost arms and had fingers cut through.

4 Wherever I played ball, I was used to first place,
And then to a disease I gave a human face.

A	M	A	D	H	N	O	U	G	U	F	T	N	N	E	A	C
H	R	C	W	N	A	R	C	O	U	J	O	H	O	D		
A	O	A	G	L	A	S	L	J	I	I	S	S	R	L	H	U

Fill in the Blanks

Fill in the blanks with letters from the letter box below. All letters will be used only once in answering the riddles.

LITERATURE & THE ARTS

1 My painting is sober, there's a pitchfork in hand,
And my meaning is one rural folks understand.

2 The DAR stifled my voice in 1939,
Inadvertently helping to bring down the color line.

SCIENCE, SPACE & TECHNOLOGY

3 We're sticky pools of asphalt, we're located in L.A.,
Prehistoric life-forms we trapped for studying today.

4 The Eiffel Tower was my rival, Chicago my debut,
And I garnered much attention with my stunning points of view.

M N T A I E A S M N A N E E L T H A I
R R G W I E R O A C P B L S F A
O E N R R H D A R E S R I A C I T

Fill in the Blanks

Fill in the blanks with letters from the letter box below. All letters will be used only once in answering the riddles.

LITERATURE & THE ARTS

1 I was killed in battle, I thought I'd never see,
A poem, or anything, lovely as a tree.

`| | | C | | | | | M | | |`

2 I epitomized a decade, the Jazz Age brought me fame,
I acted out the excesses I wrote in Gatsby's name.

`| | | | T | | | | | | Z | | | | | L |`

U.S. PRESIDENCY & FIRST LADIES

3 Trying to tackle Jim Thorpe ended my football career,
But my roles in war and peace I considered much more dear.

`| W | | | | | | | I | | | | | | W | | |`

4 The White House was barren, I hung wash in the East Room,
So much was still unfinished, the house seemed like a tomb.

`| | | G | | | | A | | | | |`

O D I L I I A K S T H R Y A J G I C
W D D D T T R A E A R I I W S E C T
B E F M N G S F E Z E L G O E H A O M L

BRITANNICA
BRAINBUSTERS

Mind Lines

Try to get from the top line of categories to the bottom in the fewest moves. Check off each box (or mark initials in the box if playing opponents) after each correct answer to a riddle. Once a player "owns" a box, an opponent must find another path.

Fam - FAMOUS & INFAMOUS
Sci - SCIENCE, SPACE & TECHNOLOGY
Lit - LITERATURE & THE ARTS
Pres - U.S. PRESIDENCY & FIRST LADIES
Pop - POP CULTURE & ENTERTAINMENT
Sprt - THE SPORTING LIFE
F&D - FOOD & DRINK

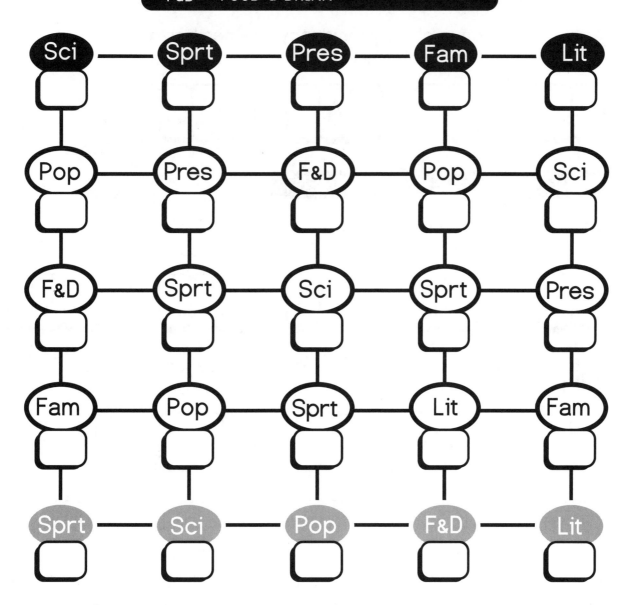

Fill in the Blanks

Fill in the blanks with letters from the letter box below. All letters will be used only once in answering the riddles.

U.S. PRESIDENCY & FIRST LADIES

1 Presidents Arthur and Carter tried to spell my doom,
But still I'm played when the president enters a room.

[ ][ ][ ][L] [ ][ ] [ ][H][ ] [ ][ ][ ][E][ ]

2 The best days of my presidency I remember well,
The day that I took office and the day I said farewell.

[ ][ ][ ][T][ ][ ] [ ][A][ ] [ ][ ][ ][ ][ ][N]

POP CULTURE & ENTERTAINMENT

3 I made an actor and soundtrack international stars,
My music, dance moves, and white suit would now dominate bars.

[ ][ ][ ][ ][ ][ ][D][ ][ ] [ ][I][ ][ ][ ] [ ][ ][V][ ][ ]

4 Some called me infestation, I caused a sensation,
It was a kind of "beetle" that sparked my migration.

[ ][ ][ ][ ][ ][S][ ] [ ][V][ ][ ][ ][ ][ ]

```
H A I T I S T U H V N B R G T I T A H A
F V D N O U R N M E A E S F E R I N E I I
H S H A A R I B Y E C I T V R L N T O N
```

BRITANNICA BRAINBUSTERS

Fill in the Blanks

Fill in the blanks with letters from the letter box below. All letters will be used only once in answering the riddles.

U.S. PRESIDENCY & FIRST LADIES

1 From Napoleon did Jefferson finagle this deal,
The greatest bargain in history, this was quite a steal.

2 I tenderly kissed his foot then leg and thigh and chest and face,
My final moments with my husband I would handle with grace.

FOOD & DRINK

3 I look like cigarette lighters, but I'm sold in the candy shop,
I was invented first for smokers who really wanted to stop.

4 Pounding garlic and pine nuts, cheese, and basil quite green,
Creates this staple of Northern Italian cuisine.

```
O E U N E S H P T L P U E N Z
P I N U K C E A E A Q A D
L I A E J O C S R I S E N Y
```

117

Fill in the Blanks

Fill in the blanks with letters from the letter box below. All letters will be used only once in answering the riddles.

U.S. PRESIDENCY & FIRST LADIES

1 The presidency did I detest,
The Supreme Court was what I loved best.

`_ _ _ _ _ I _ _ _ _ _ _ _ D _ _ F _`

2 For speeding with my horse I had to pay a meager fee,
For leading during wartime I won the presidency.

`_ _ _ _ _ _ S _ _ _ _ _ _ N _`

THE SPORTING LIFE

3 My nails, speed, and bodysuits brought me fame,
But charges of drug use tarnished my name.

`_ _ _ _ _ _ _ C _ _ _ _ Y _ _ _`

4 What began with grunge riders tricking in empty pools,
I transformed into a professional sport with rules.

`_ _ N _ _ A _ _`

```
I T E E I T L R N R A Y O L F A A F A
U W A H N S G Y C S O S R J E O
Y E L N L H T R D T S O W W M K N
```

118

Fill in the Blanks

Fill in the blanks with letters from the letter box below. All letters will be used only once in answering the riddles.

U.S. PRESIDENCY & FIRST LADIES

1 From Capitol Hill to the White House do I spread,
I'm frequented by presidents, alive or dead.

		N								V			

2 I tried to shake his hand, but his intentions I misread,
Two shots he fired in me, and in a week I would be dead.

					M		C					

SCIENCE, SPACE & TECHNOLOGY

3 We were husband and wife whose efforts were teamed,
Our discoveries proved that man was older than seemed.

		Y					U				K	

4 I won the Nobel, my theories were rare,
But famous, too, was my unruly hair.

		E					S			

E	E	N	T	B	L	S	T	L	S	M	N	E	N	E	R	N	L	R	S	I	K
N	E	M	I	Y	E	E	I	A	D	Y	A	I	L	V	O	A	L	N	U	E	Y
L	P	A	W	U	C	I	N	A	I	A	Y	N	V	L	A	I	A	M	K	E

Fill in the Blanks

ENCYCLOPÆDIA Britannica®

Fill in the blanks with letters from the letter box below. All letters will be used only once in answering the riddles.

THE SPORTING LIFE

1 To Uncle Sam I said no when the army came calling,
But I was brilliant as champ with my style of brawling.

				M	A				

2 Never missing games, I had enormous drive,
And I died as the luckiest man alive.

		U				R		

LITERATURE & THE ARTS

3 My famed "dit-dit-dit-dah" in musical lore,
Is the ominous rap of fate on the door.

			T					P				

4 I made structures that looked like the prairie plain,
My loved ones were killed by a servant insane.

				K					D				I		

F I E P Y Y L A A U I F N W H R I A T
Y K R G D S M H U O N M O G
T G H D O M M I L F H R H A L L

120

BRITANNICA BRAINBUSTERS

Mind Lines

Try to get from the top line of categories to the bottom in the fewest moves. Check off each box (or mark initials in the box if playing opponents) after each correct answer to a riddle. Once a player "owns" a box, an opponent must find another path.

Fam - FAMOUS & INFAMOUS
Sci - SCIENCE, SPACE & TECHNOLOGY
Lit - LITERATURE & THE ARTS
Pres- U.S. PRESIDENCY & FIRST LADIES
Pop - POP CULTURE & ENTERTAINMENT
Sprt - THE SPORTING LIFE
F&D - FOOD & DRINK

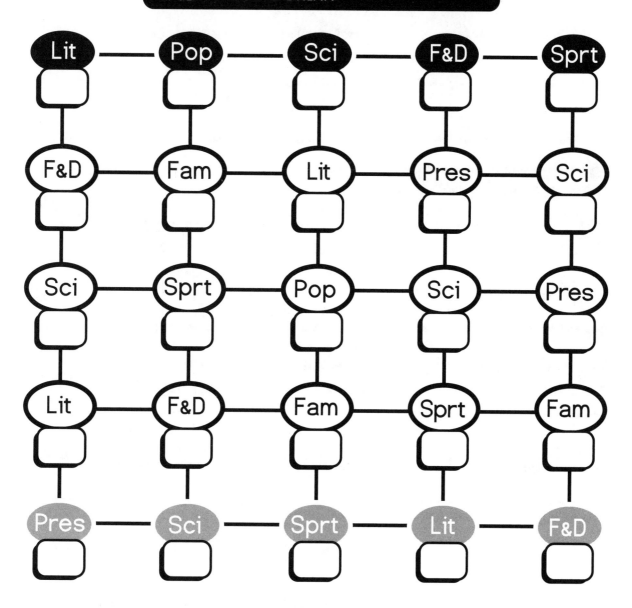

Fill in the Blanks

Fill in the blanks with letters from the letter box below. All letters will be used only once in answering the riddles.

THE SPORTING LIFE

1 I was the greatest athlete, many did say,
And yet my gold medals were taken away.

⬜ I ⬜ ⬜ ⬜ ⬜ R ⬜ ⬜

2 I'm played with a stick and a puck but never ice,
As an Olympic sport I was never played twice.

⬜ ⬜ L ⬜ ⬜ ⬜ H ⬜ ⬜ ⬜ ⬜

FAMOUS & INFAMOUS

3 I rid the king of one wife, found another instead,
But when my matchmaking went wrong, it cost me my head.

⬜ ⬜ ⬜ M ⬜ ⬜ ⬜ ⬜ ⬜ ⬜ W ⬜ ⬜ ⬜

4 I made pant suits and tuxedos for chic women to enjoy,
Nonwhite models for the runaway did I daringly employ.

V ⬜ ⬜ ⬜ A ⬜ ⬜ ⬜ ⬜ ⬜ U ⬜ ⬜ ⬜ ⬜

O H H L T E L R R E I Y S Y S E T R O
E R C K T V E W H R L I S M M A
E L C O A N N T M O L O U A J P

Fill in the Blanks

Fill in the blanks with letters from the letter box below. All letters will be used only once in answering the riddles.

THE SPORTING LIFE

1 The run to this city after Persia's disgrace,
Spawned a competition and now world-famous race.

2 From slugger to war hero, no one was better than me,
And I was frozen cryonically for eternity.

FOOD & DRINK

3 Cary Grant held the tray, a bright light glowed in me,
It was Hitchcockian cinematography.

4 "Everything you see," said this Roman beauty,
"I owe to" one thing, and that is "spaghetti!"

Fill in the Blanks

Fill in the blanks with letters from the letter box below. All letters will be used only once in answering the riddles.

LITERATURE & THE ARTS

1 Thrown objects and punches, but even a duel?
Just part of the lore of this balletic jewel.

T _ _   _ _ _ E   _ _   _ _ _ _ N

2 Go to heaven for weather that's always swell,
But for good company, I said go to hell.

_ A _ _   _ _ A _ _

POP CULTURE & ENTERTAINMENT

3 I ranked among the creepiest villains ever screened,
I ranged from handsome cowboy to cutthroat, grinning fiend.

_ _ _ T   L _ _ _ _ _

4 Although a former leach, I was debonair,
And my good looks and accent gave me a flair.

_ _ R _   _ _ _ _ T

T	N	P	R	C	L	R	S	F	E	E	W	G	K	T
T	E	Y	I	T	G	I	A	E	A	T	R	D	H	R
A	I	H	M	H	G	E	R	R	N	A	A	O	N	

BRITANNICA
BRAINBUSTERS

Fill in the Blanks

Fill in the blanks with letters from the letter box below. All letters will be used only once in answering the riddles.

U.S. PRESIDENCY & FIRST LADIES

1 The youngest president ever elected was not me,
But I still was the youngest president in history.

2 Despite its name it had nothing to do with tea,
But it put a dark stain on a presidency.

POP CULTURE & ENTERTAINMENT

3 I was released at the apex of the British Invasion,
I captured Beatlemania, becoming a sensation.

4 I am a classic flick about a devilish gestation,
That mingles Satanism with New York sophistication.

H Y O R O A I T O R O E C M E A S T R Y A E
A E A S A N H O B S T O D T D E D R Y
O D B N T E L S A D S G H A V M E P R L

Fill in the Blanks

Fill in the blanks with letters from the letter box below. All letters will be used only once in answering the riddles.

LITERATURE & THE ARTS

1 During the Russian Revolution, Lara I adored,
And my publication was one the Soviets abhorred.

2 I'm the embodiment of winter, I'm morally cold,
But I warmed up to redemption as Dickens so well told.

SCIENCE, SPACE & TECHNOLOGY

3 I earned the Nobel for my three-letter discovery,
But ended my career in a race-based controversy.

4 No muscle is stronger than I based on weight,
I leave your food in a digestible state.

```
O T H A R E N Z E B S S S W R E M
O S N O O R T C I E M C G A J
E E Z O E R V A E T S A O D G
```

Fill in the Blanks

Fill in the blanks with letters from the letter box below. All letters will be used only once in answering the riddles.

FAMOUS & INFAMOUS

1 I went from hero to zero with my treasonous plan,
Betraying my general and the country he soon ran.

2 Young, pretty, and popular, I bore heirs to the throne,
And there were protests for me when a flag was not flown.

LITERATURE & THE ARTS

3 My statues looked real, so realistic in fact,
Some charged me with using real bodies as a cast.

4 I was so short in stature an actor played me on his knees,
And I obsessed over women who like to sing, dance, and tease.

```
E N T B D A A G U E U R D S U O I
T I O R I D A D R N N S E E P O T C
E R T C A U L N C I S L O E S N U A L
```

Fill in the Blanks

Fill in the blanks with letters from the letter box below. All letters will be used only once in answering the riddles.

U.S. PRESIDENCY & FIRST LADIES

1 I was the last president before the civil fray,
And the first one in the office to be gay, some say.

				S						H				

2 My beard was the first that a president dared sport,
All due to a little girl's letter of support.

					H								L	

POP CULTURE & ENTERTAINMENT

3 As "Good Morning to All" I am not renowned,
But by this other name my tune knows no bound.

		P								D		

4 Of the Best Director Oscars from the Academy,
Only one went to a woman, the one that went to me.

K									G				

```
A L Y A B C E Y N U B A D O I J A R H
H R H P A K I W S A G I Y M C E A
H A H N A M L T B R N B L N P T O N
```

Fill in the Blanks

Fill in the blanks with letters from the letter box below. All letters will be used only once in answering the riddles.

SCIENCE, SPACE & TECHNOLOGY

1 With money from our print shop and bikes we would repair,
We funded our invention that famously took air.

				H			R						

2 When I said, "Watson—come here," by phone,
I changed the world with this milestone.

						D			G									L

POP CULTURE & ENTERTAINMENT

3 Famed Motown I established, both the company and sound,
The singers I discovered are incredibly renowned.

				Y				D	

4 I'm sexy and smart, a serial killer I played,
And my mother killed my dad in a real-life tirade.

						Z							N	

```
W A E L R I H T H A G A H C G E Z A
R G O E D T T L M O R L L R B E E Y R E
A H O N X R N B Y E R H R R D I B R S
```

Fill in the Blanks

Fill in the blanks with letters from the letter box below. All letters will be used only once in answering the riddles.

LITERATURE & THE ARTS

1 Despite my musical name, I do not deal with keys,
I build for the public, its masses I try to please.

⬜⬜⬜[Z]⬜ ⬜⬜⬜[N]⬜

2 Crumpled ships and shavings on top of a cake,
Such thoughts come to mind from the buildings I make.

⬜⬜⬜⬜[K] ⬜⬜[H]⬜

FOOD & DRINK

3 I was loved by the Marx Brothers, and Shirley Temple too,
And especially by children who are fond of the zoo.

⬜⬜⬜⬜⬜[L] ⬜⬜⬜[C]⬜⬜⬜

4 For accompanying pasta, fish, meat red or white,
Turn to me for selecting a wine to delight.

⬜⬜⬜[M]⬜⬜[E]⬜

E F R L P E M O S N I A L A A E
O C N S I K Y N C H K I M
A A G R R R R E R M Z E O R N

130

BRITANNICA BRAINBUSTERS

Fill in the Blanks

Fill in the blanks with letters from the letter box below. All letters will be used only once in answering the riddles.

FAMOUS & INFAMOUS

1 Women criminologists loathed me and viewed me with alarm,
For the way the media fawned over my good looks and charm.

2 My watery damage has lingered for years,
Millions of victims were left dead or in tears.

THE SPORTING LIFE

3 My double McTwists sail quite high,
Proving that even fruit can fly.

4 When I caught the Bambino it changed my life,
But the chase and my race would cause me great strife.

E O R U N N A I S Y A U N W N B
H E S T A N D N C H T E I H I
M N N D A A T I A U A O K D

Fill in the Blanks

Fill in the blanks with letters from the letter box below. All letters will be used only once in answering the riddles.

LITERATURE & THE ARTS

1 The famous *Mona Lisa* I really didn't swipe,
My jumbled geometrics helped spur a new art type.

☐ ☐ B ☐ ☐ ☐ ☐ ☐ ☐ S ☐ ☐

2 I fought for freedom from the British throne,
Then promoted a language all our own.

☐ ☐ ☐ H ☐ ☐ ☐ ☐ S ☐ ☐ ☐

POP CULTURE & ENTERTAINMENT

3 Sam would never have played this song,
Had Ingrid kept her tresses long.

☐ ☐ T ☐ ☐ ☐ G ☐ ☐ ☐ ☐ ☐

4 My friends were fuzzy and portly and even green,
Child-friendly and unlike what most folks had seen.

☐ I ☐ ☐ ☐ ☐ S ☐ ☐

A	T	N	M	I	E	E	O	E	S	S	E	Y	S	B
A	B	S	I	W	N	R	J	H	B	O	O	G	L	
A	E	M	O	C	S	I	N	A	P	S	P	T	H	O

Fill in the Blanks

Fill in the blanks with letters from the letter box below. All letters will be used only once in answering the riddles.

FAMOUS & INFAMOUS

1 I am nasty and I'm vile and the king of sinful sots,
And my heart's a dead tomato squashed with moldy purple spots.

_ _ E _ _ R _ _ _ _

2 I was the first from the south, the first from the west,
And my washing of girls' feet left many distressed.

_ _ _ E _ _ R _ _ _ _ _ _

SCIENCE, SPACE & TECHNOLOGY

3 According to a legend, I was lounging 'neath a tree,
And from a falling fruit I learned the laws of gravity.

_ _ _ A _ _ _ _ _ T _ _

4 I messed up my line as I took my famous step,
But made history despite my verbal misstep.

_ _ _ I _ _ _ _ _ _ _ _ _ _ G

N I E A A E E O P C S F C M I O
L A W G H R T N T R C I I A
I T R N N O N E G S S R P N H

FILL IN THE BLANKS
Answer Key

Page 97

1. When John White, leader of the early English settlement of **Roanoke Island**, off the coast of North Carolina, retuned with supplies in 1590 after an absence of more than two years, he found that the colony had disappeared. All that was left of the community were the words "CROATOAN" on a post and "CRO" on a tree. The mystery has never been solved.

2. Flying the ***Spirit of St. Louis***, Charles Lindbergh made the first nonstop solo flight from New York to Paris (May 20-21, 1927). The plane, now on display at the Smithsonian Institution, was named to honor the men from St. Louis who sponsored the flight.

3. Rudolf Wanderone, Jr., was the prototypical, fast-talking pool hustler who was thought to be the inspiration for "**Minnesota Fats**" in the movie *The Hustler* (1961) and in the book of the same name. After the film became a hit, Rudolf dropped his other monikers, including "New York Fats," and adopted "Minnesota." His larger-than-life personality matched his corpulent frame of some 300 lbs.

4. **Arnold Palmer**, a golfing icon and a pioneer in sports marketing, was the first to win the Masters Tournament four times and the first to earn $1 million in prize money. During his professional career (1954-75) he won 92 tournaments and 7 Majors. A fan favorite, he attracted unprecedented crowds on the golf course, a vast following dubbed "Arnie's Army."

Page 98

1. Aviator **Charles Lindbergh** became a worldwide celebrity after making the first nonstop solo flight across the Atlantic Ocean in 1927. But tragedy followed in 1932 when Lindbergh's 20-month-old son was kidnapped, held for ransom, and killed. The trial of German carpenter and burglar Bruno Hauptmann for the crime was dubbed the "trial of the century."

2. **Nelson Mandela** was an anti-apartheid revolutionary and saboteur in South Africa before serving 27 years in prison. Released in 1990, he joined negotiations with President F.W. de Klerk to abolish apartheid and establish multiracial elections. For their efforts, de Klerk and Mandela were awarded the Nobel Peace Prize in 1993. Mandela then served as South Africa's first black president (1994-99).

3. The **Irish Potato Famine** of 1845-49, spurred by a fungal blight that destroyed the crop, caused some one million people to starve to death and led to the emigration of some two million others, many of whom came to the United States. The famine was the worst to hit Europe in the 19th century.

4. **Elvis Presley**, the "King of Rock and Roll" and one of the top entertainers from the 1950s until his death in 1977, had assorted eccentricities that made headlines, including his love for certain foods, his struggles with his fame, and his fatal addiction to prescription medicine that contributed to his death at age 42.

Page 99

1. **Mark Antony** was Julius Caesar's ally. His stirring eulogy at Caesar's funeral, as dramatized by Shakespeare, was a masterpiece of irony, beginning, "Friends, Romans, countrymen, lend me your ears; I come to bury Caesar, not to praise him." Masked as an oration justifying the assassination of Caesar, Antony cleverly transforms Caesar into a martyr and the assassins into villains.

2. **Donna Karan** took the fashion world by storm with her Seven Easy Pieces collection (DKNY: Donna Karan New York) in 1985. All women needed, said Karan, was a foundation of seven interchangeable, black-based items (such as leggings and a blazer) to move from the board room to a dinner party with style. She "mainstreamed the concept of black," said the *New York Times*.

3. **Gilbert Stuart** is renowned for his portraits of America's Founding Fathers. His famous unfinished painting of George Washington, begun in 1796, became iconic once reproduced on the dollar bill beginning in 1869. It was also used on generations of postage stamps.

4. **Frances Cleveland** was only 21 years old when she married President Grover Cleveland in the Blue Room of the White House on June 2, 1886. Her status as the youngest first lady captivated the country. Advertisers began using her image in illustrations and seeking her endorsement of their products; parents even began naming their daughters after her.

Page 100

1. **Gianni Versace** was famous for his daring fashions and glamorous lifestyle. He moved in a world of international celebrities, including the "supermodels" who wore his designs. According to some, Versace was at his creative peak in 1997 when he was shot to death on the front steps of his Miami Beach home by serial killer Andrew Cunanan.

2. **Fidel Castro** has been the face of Cuba since 1959, when he founded the first communist government in the Western Hemisphere. He was at the center of major conflicts during the Cold War, such as the Bay of Pigs invasion of 1961 and the Cuban Missile Crisis of 1962. The number of attempts to kill him supposedly number in the hundreds.

3. Swiss-born actress **Ursula Andress** was the first "Bond Girl," the beautiful love interest of the secret agent in the James Bond series of films. Her emergence from the sea in a white bikini in *Dr. No* (1962) is one of the most famous scenes in film history, one that Halle Barry recreated in the Bond film *Die Another Day* (2002).

4. **Katharine Hepburn** (1907-2003), winner of four Academy Awards for Best Actress, introduced into her roles a strength of character previously considered unladylike in Hollywood. Iconoclastic, she did as she pleased, refusing to grant interviews, wearing casual clothes at a time when actresses were expected to exude glamor, and often clashing with more experienced film associates.

Page 101

1. **Nanotechnology** operates on the scale of atoms. Stain-resistant clothing, for example, results from microscopic "nanowhiskers" that have been molecularly hooked onto fibers. Antimicrobial bandages, self-cleaning glass, deflation-resistant tennis balls, scratch-resistant car surfaces—all are now possible due to nanotechnology.

2. **Photosynthesis** is the process by which plants create food for survival and growth. In fact, it is a key process for all life on Earth, because the plants themselves are a principal food source for both humans and the animals that humans consume, and they produce the oxygen needed for animals to survive.

3. **Henry VIII** famously ruled over England from 1509-47, broke from Rome and the Catholic Church, and established the Anglican Church. He was also a notorious glutton with a seemingly insatiable appetite for both meals and marriages. Of his six wives, two he divorced, one died of natural causes, and two were beheaded. The sixth one survived him.

4. **Mahatma Gandhi**, leader of the Indian nationalist movement against British rule, is internationally esteemed for his use of nonviolent protest to achieve political and social progress. His Salt March in 1930—protesting the heavily taxed, imported British salt that India's poor could not afford to buy—was the first act in his larger campaign of civil disobedience. It garnered him worldwide attention.

Page 102

1. The theory of evolution by natural selection that **Charles Darwin** propounded in *The Origins of Species* (1859) shocked Victorian society by suggesting that animals and humans shared a common ancestry. When Thomas Huxley defended Darwin in public and in print, Bishop Samuel Wilberforce famously inquired whether Huxley's ancestral apes were on his grandmother's or grandfather's side.

2. The 15-minute suborbital flight in the *Freedom 7* spacecraft by **Alan Shepard** on May 5, 1961, came 23 days after Soviet cosmonaut Yury Gagarin became the first human in space, but Shepard's flight energized the U.S. space initiative and made him a national hero. He commanded the *Apollo 14* lunar mission in 1971, famously hitting golf balls on the moon.

3. **Damien Hirst**, one of the YBAs (Young British Artists) who came to fame in the late 1980s, shocked the public with his displays of animals in formaldehyde, his installations of maggots feeding on a severed cow head, and his diamond-studded skull that arguably is the most expensive piece of art ever created. He reputedly became Britain's richest living artist.

4. *Encyclopædia Britannica*, first published in Edinburgh, Scotland, in 1768, is the oldest continuously published and revised work in English. In 2012, it was announced that only digital versions of the famed encyclopedia would continue to be published; the last print edition was published in 2010.

Page 104

1. **Tessellation** is the use of certain shapes and angles for tiling a flat surface without overlaps or gaps. It is also a branch of mathematics that studies shapes and angles, in a variety of dimensions. The artist M. C. Escher is famous for his clever tessellations using irregular interlocking shapes.

2. Astronaut **Sally Ride** became the first American woman, and the youngest American (age 32), in space when she flew into orbit aboard the space shuttle *Challenger* on June 18, 1983. When her homosexuality was revealed in her obituary in 2012, she also was acknowledged as America's first known gay astronaut in space.

3. **Billie Jean King**, winner of 39 Gram Slam titles in tennis, fought tirelessly for equal prize money for women athletes. Her famed 1973 "Battle of the Sexes" match against former tennis champion Bobby Riggs, who claimed that the women's game was inferior, was played before a worldwide TV audience of some 50 million. King won in three sets.

4. When diver **Greg Louganis** hit his head on the platform at the 1988 Olympics and required stitches, he decided not tell the doctor treating him, or the public, that he was HIV positive. Although there was little risk of infecting others by his bleeding into a chlorine-treated pool, some concluded he should at least have told the doctor who treated his wound without protective gloves.

Page 105

1. Polish-born French physicist **Marie Curie** was famous for her work on radioactivity—work that led to the leukemia that ultimately killed her. She was the first woman to win a Nobel Prize and the only woman to win the award in two different fields (physics, 1903; chemistry, 1911). Her daughter and her husband were also Nobel laureates.

2. Turkey and milk both have an amino acid called **tryptophan** that helps the body produce niacin, which in turn produces the sleep-inducing chemical serotonin. But most post-Thanksgiving-dinner sleepiness is caused by the heavy carbohydrate meal in combination with alcohol.

3. Before becoming a famed chef and TV personality, **Julia Child** (1912-2004) worked for America's spy agency, the Office of Strategic Services, during World War II, serving in Ceylon (Sri Lanka) and China. Working at first with documents control, she eventually reported directly to OSS Director William Donovan.

4. Wimbledon is Britain's most prestigious tennis tournament and the oldest in the world, played annually in London since 1877. Its many traditions include grass courts, an all-white dress code for the athletes, and its signature refreshment dating back to the Tudors some 500 years ago: **strawberries and cream**.

Page 106

1. **Kopi luwak** is civet coffee, a drink based on the coffee beans digested by, and fermented within, the Indonesian wild Asian palm civet. After the excrement is dried, the coffee beans are recovered, processed, and sold for $100 per pound or more. Animal activists have condemned the conditions that caged civets endure on the farms of some unscrupulous coffee suppliers.

2. *A Moveable Feast* (1964) was **Ernest Hemingway's** posthumously published memoir of Paris during the 1920s. The title came from something he reputedly told his friend and biographer A.E. Hotchner: "If you are lucky enough to have lived in Paris as a young man, then wherever you go for the rest of your life, it stays with you, for Paris is a moveable feast."

3. Upon hearing (incorrectly) that her estranged husband had divorced her, Rachel Robards married Andrew Jackson in 1791. Because she wasn't actually divorced, her marriage to Jackson made her guilty of adultery and bigamy. Her husband then divorced her on those grounds, forcing Andrew and **Rachel Jackson** to wed a second time. Rachel died just months before Jackson's inauguration.

4. Raised a Quaker, **Richard Nixon** was taught not to gamble. Nonetheless, Nixon became an avid poker player, and a very astute one to boot. In fact, his first political campaign—for a seat in the U.S. House of Representatives in 1946—was largely funded by his poker winnings.

Page 107

1. *Babette's Feast* (1987), winner of the Academy Award for Best Foreign Language Film, is often credited with depicting the most luscious meal in film history. Babette is a French refugee who, in a small 19th-century Danish village, teaches her hosts a lesson about life through the elaborate meal she prepares for them.

2. A London department store claims to have invented the **Scotch egg**—a hard-boiled egg wrapped in sausage meat and then breaded and fried—in 1738 for wealthy travelers needing a portable treat for long carriage rides. Others claim it was invented by Scottish farmers as an inexpensive dish. It is now commonly served with dipping sauces.

3. **David Letterman**, one of the longtime kings of late-night American TV, became famous for his deadpan humor and silly skits, but a scandal arose in 2009 when Letterman revealed that a TV producer had attempted to extort $2 million from him to keep quiet about Letterman's affairs with interns on the show.

4. *E.T. the Extra-Terrestrial* (1982), the classic science fiction tale about a group of children who befriend and hide a lost alien until they can manage to arrange for his return home, surpassed *Star Wars* as the highest-grossing film of all time. Signaling emotion and love, the alien's heart and finger glow in the film's climatic final scenes.

Page 108

1. In Roald Dahl's classic children's novel *Charlie and the Chocolate Factory* (1964), chocolatier **Willy Wonka** entices children to his factory with golden tickets and the promise of a lifetime supply of candy. His true purpose is to put the kids to a test in the hope of finding an honest heir.

2. Although this means of eating meat and bread must be as old as the food items themselves, the name "**sandwich**" was adopted in the 18th century for John Montagu, 4th Earl of Sandwich, who had meat placed between slices of bread and brought to him at the gaming table. By doing so, he could eat his meal and continue his game without getting his cards greasy.

3. **Sigmund Freud**, the founder of psychoanalysis, is one of history's most influential figures. Although a major crux of psychoanalysis is the interpretation of symbols, especially in dreams, Freud (an incessant cigar-smoker) reportedly conceded that "a cigar is sometimes just a cigar," meaning not everything is reflective of a deeper or psychosexual meaning.

4. **King George VI** reigned over the United Kingdom from 1936 to 1952. He assumed the throne on Dec. 11, 1936, the day after his brother Edward VIII shockingly abdicated to marry the American divorcee Wallis Warfield Simpson. King George struggled with a severe stammer, which was the focus of the Academy Award-winning film *The King's Speech* (2010).

Page 110

1. **Johnny Appleseed**, one of America's most famous (and eccentric) folk heroes, was based on frontier nurseryman John Chapman (1774-1845). Chapman traveled the countryside on foot, distributed and sold apple seeds, and planted orchards throughout the American Midwest. He's the subject of countless stories and works of art.

2. One of the dietary laws of Judaism requires that **meat and milk** not be blended or cooked and eaten together; there must even be separate utensils for cooking each food group. *Kosher* is the name applied to foods prepared and consumed according to these dietary laws.

3. Born in St. Petersburg, Russia, in 1904, **George Balanchine** came to the United States in 1933, co-founding the New York City Ballet in the late 1940s. Called "Mr. B" in the ballet world, Balanchine transformed the look of contemporary ballet and spurred modern dance and choreography for film and musical theater.

4. **Professor Moriarty** was Sherlock Holmes's chief nemesis. In fact, the famed detective was ostensibly killed during his struggle with Moriarty in *The Final Problem* (1893), but the public outcry over the fictional character's death was so intense that Doyle resurrected the character in 1903.

Page 111

1. Famed landscape architect Frederick Law Olmsted is best known for designing outstanding public parks, especially **Central Park** (1876) in New York City. Less well remembered is that, between 1852 and 1855, he reported weekly on the effect of slavery on the American South for the *New York Times,* stories later published as *The Cotton Kingdom* (1861).

2. American writer and illustrator **Theodor Seuss Geisel**, more popularly known by his pseudonym "Dr. Seuss," produced some of the most popular children's books ever published, including *How the Grinch Stole Christmas* (1957), *The Cat in the Hat* (1957), *Green Eggs and Ham* (1960), and *The Lorax* (1971).

3. **Christian Dior** reestablished Paris as the world's fashion center after World War II. He did so with his sensational "New Look" in 1947. Accustomed to the simple short skirts of the war years, when fabric was limited and rationed, women initially balked at Dior's longer hemlines. But the New Look caught on and established Dior's reputation worldwide.

4. St. **John Paul II** was the head of the Roman Catholic Church (1978-2005), the first non-Italian pope in 455 years, and the first ever from a Slavic country. His unabashed Polish nationalism aided the Solidarity movement in communist Poland in the 1980s and ultimately contributed to the peaceful dissolution of the Soviet Union in 1991.

Page 112

1. According to lore, at the London premiere of Handel's *Messiah* on March 23, 1743, King George II was so moved by the "**Hallelujah Chorus**" that he rose from his seat. This caused everyone in attendance to stand as well. Standing for the iconic chorus has been a tradition ever since.

2. **Isadora Duncan** was a pioneer of modern dance. She died tragically on Sept. 14, 1927, in Nice, France, when her signature long scarf became entangled in the rear wheel of the open car she was riding in, pulling her from the vehicle and breaking her neck. The bizarre accident led Gertrude Stein to quip, "Affectations can be dangerous."

3. The common children's game of **tug-of-war** was actually a team Olympic sport from 1900 to 1920. The pastime has ancient roots and remains a part of the Scottish Highland Games and other large outdoor social gatherings. Tragically, participants have lost limbs and fingers after wrapping the rope around their hands and arms to gain better leverage and from the whipping force of snapped ropes.

4. Basketball star Earvin **"Magic" Johnson** led his high school to a state championship (1977), Michigan State University to a national championship (1979), and then the Los Angeles Lakers to five NBA championships (between 1980 and 1988). In 1991, he made headlines when he announced that he was HIV-positive. As an HIV/AIDS activist, he helped inform the public about the disease.

1. Grant Wood's 1930 painting of a plain and sober rural couple, the man holding a pitchfork, is one of the best-known icons of American art. Its title—***American Gothic***—refers to the Carpenter Gothic window on the house in the background. The Iowa-born painter was one of the chief exponents of the Midwestern Regionalism movement in art that flourished during the 1930s.

2. The Daughters of the American Revolution (DAR) provoked outrage in 1939 when they blocked African American contralto **Marian Anderson** from singing at their hall in Washington D.C. First Lady Eleanor Roosevelt helped to arrange for Anderson to perform at the Lincoln Memorial instead. Drawing a crowd of 75,000, the Easter Sunday event became a watershed moment in civil rights history.

3. **La Brea Tar Pits** are thick pools of viscous asphalt (the lowest grade of crude oil) that have oozed to the surface from a large petroleum reservoir. Located in Los Angeles, they have yielded the fossilized skulls and bones of trapped prehistoric animals, such as a mastodon and a sabre-toothed cat, as well as one partial human skeleton and many human artifacts.

4. The Chicago organizers of the World's Columbian Exposition (World's Fair) of 1893 wanted to showcase American ingenuity by topping the engineering feat of Gustave Eiffel, whose tower had had been a star of the Paris Exposition of 1889. Bridge-builder George Ferris had the answer: a giant circle of entertainment forever known as the ***Ferris wheel***.

1. Although a prolific writer, American poet **Joyce Kilmer** is mainly famous for one poem: his 12-line verse "Trees" (1913), which states "I think that I shall never see / A poem lovely as a tree." In 1918, he was killed in action during World War I, and he was posthumously awarded the Croix de Guerre for bravery.

2. **F. Scott Fitzgerald** was famous for his tales of the Jazz Age of the 1920s. His most brilliant novel, *The Great Gatsby* (1925), depicts the moral abyss created by a crass and meretricious society. Fitzgerald's personal life, with his wife Zelda, reflected the profligacy of the period and became almost as celebrated as his novels.

3. **Dwight D. Eisenhower** was the 34th U.S. president (1953-61) and the supreme commander of the Allied forces in Western Europe during World War II. He was a superb football player while at the U.S. military academy at West Point, but his football career was cut short when he injured his knee while trying to tackle Jim Thorpe, arguably the greatest athlete of the 20th century.

4. **Abigail Adams** was the country's second first lady but the first to reside at the newly built, though still unfinished, White House. Arriving there in November 1800, she lived there for only four months. She famously hung her family's laundry in the barren East Room to dry.

1. "**Hail to the Chief**," the presidential anthem, was first tied to the U.S. presidency in 1815, when it was played to honor the late George Washington and the end of the War of 1812. President Chester Arthur replaced the song with another, but the replacement never stuck, and when President Carter banned any song from being played, public outrage forced him to reinstate the tune.

2. **Martin Van Buren**, eighth president of the United States (1837–41), was one of the founders of the Democratic Party. Known as the "Little Magician" in recognition of his cunning, he faced many problems during his presidency, including a bad economy, a war with Native Americans, and controversy over the annexation of Texas.

3. The film ***Saturday Night Fever*** (1977) mainstreamed and epitomized the disco phenomenon. It made actor John Travolta and the music of the Bee Gees internationally famous. Travolta won rave reviews for his acting and dancing, and he was nominated for an Academy Award for Best Actor. His wardrobe in the film, especially his famed white suit, influenced fashion worldwide.

4. The **British Invasion** was the large movement of British rock-and-roll bands to the United States in the mid-1960s. What sparked this "second British Invasion" was the Beatles' triumphant arrival in New York City on Feb. 7, 1964. British acts, such as Peter and Gordon, the Animals, Herman's Hermits, and, most significantly, the Rolling Stones, soon dominated the American musical scene.

1. The **Louisiana Purchase**, secured by Thomas Jefferson from France in 1803, brought the area west of the Mississippi to the Rocky Mountains under American control, doubling the size of the United States. It strengthened the country materially and strategically and spawned a sense of manifest destiny.

2. **Jacqueline Kennedy** refused to leave the emergency room where John Kennedy was taken after the shooting in Dallas on Nov. 22, 1963. While the president lie dead and covered with a sheet, onlookers stood in silence as the blood-stained first lady kissed one of her husband's exposed feet and then worked her way up to a final kiss on his lips.

3. **PEZ** candies, invented in Vienna in 1927, were originally developed as a breath mint for smokers, and the name PEZ derives from the German word for peppermint ("PfeffErminZ"). Their famed dispensers, invented in 1948, were designed to look like cigarette lighters to appeal to smokers who wanted to quit.

4. Originating in the area of Genoa in northern Italy, **pesto** is a blend of basil, garlic, cheeses, pine nuts, and olive oil. Derived from the Italian verb "to pound," pesto is traditionally made in a marble mortar with a wooden pestle. It is often served over pasta and as a base for pizza.

1. **William Howard Taft**, 27th U.S president (1909-13) and 10th chief justice of the United States (1921-30), hated being president and said "politics make me sick." However, he cherished his position as chief justice.

2. **Ulysses S. Grant** was the commander of the Union armies during the late years (1864-65) of the American Civil War and the 18th U.S. president (1869-77). He loved to ride fast and sometimes even challenged other riders to a race. On one occasion, early in his presidency, the D.C. police pulled him over for recklessly driving his horse-drawn carriage. He was fined five dollars.

3. Runner **Florence Joyner**, known as "Flo Jo," won a silver medal at the 1984 Olympics and became a media celebrity with her 6-inch decorated fingernails and eye-catching racing suits. By 1988, she had improved her times dramatically, and she captured three gold medals and a silver at the 1988 Olympics, spurring accusations of steroid use, though drug tests revealed no banned substances.

4. **Tony Hawk** is the seminal figure in the history of skateboarding. Through his technical innovations, successful equipment and apparel companies, and tireless promotional work, he helped the sport of skateboarding enter the mainstream at the end of the 20th century.

Page 119

1. **Pennsylvania Avenue** in Washington, D.C., is one of the most famous streets in the world. It connects Capitol Hill to the White House (the address of which is 1600 Pennsylvania Ave., NW), and it's a common venue for the inaugural parades of new presidents, the funeral processions of dead presidents, and protest marches.

2. During **William McKinley**'s presidency, the country won a war against Spain in 1898 and thereby acquired a global empire, including Puerto Rico, Guam, and the Philippines. On Sept. 6, 1901, while shaking hands with well-wishers at the Pan-American Exposition in Buffalo, New York, he was shot by an anarchist. McKinley died a week later, whereupon Theodore Roosevelt became president.

3. Archaeologists **Mary and Louis Leakey**, working in East Africa between the 1930s and 1970s, were a remarkable team. Their fossil finds showed that humans were far older than had previously been thought and that human evolution was centered in Africa, not Asia.

4. Perhaps no intellectual will ever be more famous than physicist **Albert Einstein**, recipient of the Nobel Prize for Physics in 1921. His silhouette, with his wild hair, is one of the most recognizable in the world.

Page 120

1. **Muhammad Ali** was the first boxer to win the world heavyweight championship on three occasions. In 1967, citing his religious beliefs, Ali refused induction into the U.S. Army, saying "I ain't got no quarrel with them Vietcong." Ali was stripped of his championship and banned from fighting for three and a half years.

2. **Lou Gehrig** was one of baseball's greatest players. His career batting average was .340 (.361 in seven World Series), and he appeared in 2,130 consecutive games. In 1939, he was diagnosed with amyotrophic lateral sclerosis (ALS), now widely known as Lou Gehrig's disease. In his famous speech at Yankee Stadium on July 4, 1939, Gehrig called himself "the luckiest man on the face of the earth."

3. The **Fifth Symphony** (No. 5 in C Minor, Op. 67) by Ludwig van Beethoven, which premiered in Vienna in 1808, is widely recognized for its ominous four-note opening—short, short, short, long. The motif, known the world over, has long been interpreted as the musical manifestation of "fate knocking at the door."

4. **Frank Lloyd Wright** was one of America's greatest architects, noted for his "Prairie style." He suffered a grisly tragedy on Aug. 20, 1914. On that day an insane houseman at Wright's residence called Taliesin near Spring Green, Wisconsin, set the place on fire and then axed to death seven residents and visitors, including Wright's mistress and her children, as they tried to escape.

Page 122

1. **Jim Thorpe**, a Native American, was one of the greatest athletes in history. He excelled at football, baseball, basketball, swimming, boxing, lacrosse, hockey, and track and field. Because he had played semiprofessional baseball, he was deemed in violation of the Olympics' amateur status requirement and was stripped of the gold medals he earned at the 1912 Games. The medals were restored to his family in 1983.

2. **Roller hockey** appeared as an Olympic sport only once, at the 1992 Olympic Games in Barcelona. The game followed the rules of hockey, except that the skates were roller skates. The sport, typically using inline skates, is popular in many countries.

3. **Thomas Cromwell** was the principal adviser (1532-40) to England's Henry VIII. After the death of Henry's wife Jane Seymour, Cromwell attempted to forge an English-German Protestant alliance by having Henry marry German princess Anne of Cleves. The marriage was a disaster. Henry blamed Cromwell for the mismatch and had him executed for treason.

4. French fashion designer **Yves Saint Laurent** (1936-2008) was noted for his popularization of trousers and tuxedos for women. He also shocked haute couture with his ready-to-wear lines, drew inspiration from non-Western cultures, and opened up the runway to nonwhite models.

Page 123

1. The **marathon,** a footrace now covering 26.2 miles, was first held at the revival of the Olympic Games in Athens in 1896. It commemorates the legendary feat of a Greek soldier who, in 490 BC, supposedly ran from Marathon to Athens, a distance of about 25 miles, to bring news of the Athenian victory over the Persians. Upon completing the run, he died.

2. **Ted Williams**, arguably the best baseball hitter ever, flew some three dozen combat missions during the Korean War. He was the last player to hit .400 in Major League Baseball (.406 in 1941). After he died in 2002, his head was separated from his body and both were preserved in liquid nitrogen at a cryonics facility in Arizona.

3. One of Alfred Hitchcock's most memorable scenes occurs in *Suspicion* (1941), as Cary Grant walks up stairs to give his wife a **glass of milk**. Grant's wife fears poisoning, and to heighten the suspicion, Hitchcock cleverly hid a light in the glass, making the milk glow eerily in the dark.

4. Italian film actress **Sophia Loren**, universally hailed as one of Italy's most beautiful women and its most famous film star, won an Academy Award for Best Actress for *La ciociara* (1961; *Two Women*), in which she portrays the courageous mother of a teenage girl during World War II.

Page 124

1. Igor Stravinsky's ballet ***The Rite of Spring***, famous for its violent rhythms and shocking dissonances, was one of the first examples of Modernism in music. Its premiere in Paris on May 29, 1913, nearly caused a riot—punches were thrown among audience members and objects were tossed at the stage. The pulsating music, combined with Vaslav Nijinsky's jarring choreography, made for a tumultuous opening.

2. One of America's greatest writers and the leading humorist of his day, **Mark Twain** (1835-1910) could muster a witticism on nearly any subject. Having suffered through tragedy so often in his life—bad investments, bankruptcy, and the death of his wife and three of his four children—he saw "humor [as] the great thing, the saving thing."

3. **Heath Ledger** won critical acclaim for his role as a gay cowboy in *Brokeback Mountain* (2005), but his eerie and frenetic performance as the Joker in the Batman film *The Dark Knight* (2008), released some six months after his death, earned him an Academy Award for Best Supporting Actor.

4. Born in Bristol, England, in 1904, American film actor **Cary Grant** (original name: Archibald Alexander Leach) was famous for his good looks, debonair style, and flair for both romantic comedies and suspense thrillers. He was one of Hollywood's most popular and enduring stars.

Page 125

1. The youngest president ever elected was John F. Kennedy, who was 43 years old upon taking office. Vice President **Theodore Roosevelt**, however, ascended to the presidency at age 42 upon the assassination of President William McKinley in 1901.

2. The **Teapot Dome Scandal** of the early 1920s involved the granting of leases to oil reserves, including the Teapot Dome reserve in Wyoming, by the U.S secretary of interior in exchange for bribes. The scandal, and others involving cabinet members, took a serious toll on the health of President Warren Harding, who died during his third year in office (in 1923).

3. *A Hard Day's Night* (1964), starring the Beatles, traces the frenetic daily life of the band at the height of Beatlemania. Combining humor with the Beatles' hit songs, the film was a critical and commercial success. It employed pioneering techniques, including the extensive use of handheld cameras and jump-cut editing, and it is widely considered a classic.

4. *Rosemary's Baby* (1968) is Roman Polanski's landmark horror movie about an unsuspecting Manhattan woman whose husband has made a deal with Satanists for her to give birth to the devil's spawn. An enormous hit, the film offered audiences a novel, intelligent take on Satanism. The scene in which Rosemary is raped by the devil is ranked among the scariest movie moments.

Page 126

1. Boris Pasternak was awarded the Nobel Prize in Literature for *Doctor Zhivago* (1957), but he was compelled to decline the prize due to pressure from Soviet authorities, who banned the book. The book became an international best-seller, and the 1965 movie version—directed by David Lean and starring Omar Sharif and Julie Christie—won five Academy Awards.

2. **Ebenezer Scrooge** is the miserly protagonist of Charles Dickens's classic *A Christmas Carol* (1843). Although he is transformed at the end of the story—after visits from the ghosts of Christmas past, present, and future—the character is best remembered as the curmudgeon who dismisses Christmas with his catchphrase, "Bah, humbug!"

3. Geneticist **James Watson** played a critical role in the discovery of the double-helix structure of DNA, the basis of heredity. He shared the 1962 Nobel Prize for Physiology or Medicine. His suggestion in 2007 that the intelligence of Africans might be inferior to that of other groups caused great controversy and was immediately denounced as racist. He retired amid the controversy and then, in 2014, shockingly put up for auction his gold Nobel Prize medallion, which sold for $4.1 million.

4. The **masseter,** the main muscle of the jaw, is the strongest human muscle based on its weight. It is primarily used in chewing food. It can be felt at the side of the jaw when the teeth are clenched.

Page 127

1. **Benedict Arnold** was a brave officer who served George Washington and the cause of the American Revolution until 1779. It was then, feeling insufficiently rewarded for his military service, that he shifted his allegiance to the British. He escaped to London in 1781 and died there in 1801. His name lives on as an epithet for a traitor.

2. After news broke that **Princess Diana** had died in a car crash in Paris on Aug. 31, 1997, the British public expected to see a flag flying at half-mast above Buckingham Palace as a sign of royal mourning. The Queen refused to allow this for several days, reinforcing the perception that the royal family was heartless, indifferent, and "out of touch."

3. The sculptures of French artist **Auguste Rodin**, famous for *The Thinker* (1880) and *The Kiss* (1886), could be so realistic that some accused him of using casts from live persons.

4. Although obsessed with his stunted growth and hindered by alcoholism and mental illness, Henri de **Toulouse-Lautrec** famously captured in his art the bohemian life of the cafés and cabarets of Paris of the 1890s. To play him in the movie *Moulin Rouge* (1952), actor José Ferrer performed on his knees with special pads.

Page 128

1. **James Buchanan,** the 15th U.S. president (1857-61), was a moderate Democrat whose efforts to find a compromise in the conflict between the North and the South failed to avert the Civil War (1861–65). Buchanan was the only bachelor president, and his close relationship with Sen. William R. King of Alabama led to speculation that the men were gay.

2. **Abraham Lincoln** was the first bearded president. He was encouraged to grow his whiskers by 11-year-old Grace Bedell of Westfield, New York. In an Oct. 15, 1860, letter to Lincoln, she suggested that a beard might improve the presidential candidate's looks. Lincoln replied four days later and then, as President-elect, visited the girl in February 1861 to show her his beard.

3. "**Happy Birthday**" is the world's most recognized song in English. It is based on an 1893 melody called "Good Morning to All," widely attributed to two Americans, Patty and Mildred Hill. The women were sisters and kindergarten teachers, and they reportedly composed the tune for their students. The earliest publication of the tune with the lyrics "Happy Birthday to You" is 1912, though the song likely existed earlier.

4. As of 2014, **Kathryn Bigelow** was the only woman to have won an Academy Award for Best Director. Her film *The Hurt Locker* (2008) beat out the special-effects blockbuster *Avatar* to win the Academy Award for Best Picture and five others. Produced on a relatively meager budget, the film depicts a trio of American soldiers on a bomb-disposal squad in war-ravaged Iraq.

Page 129

1. Wilbur and Orville Wright used the money they earned from running a print shop and repairing bicycles to fund their aeronautical experiments. And the experiments paid off. On Dec. 17, 1903, just south of Kitty Hawk on the North Carolina coast, the **Wright brothers** achieved the first powered, sustained, and controlled airplane flight.

2. The Scottish-born American inventor and scientist **Alexander Graham Bell** is best known for his invention of the telephone (1876) and the refinement of the phonograph (1886), but he was also a noted teacher of the deaf and one of the founders of the National Geographic Society (1888).

3. **Berry Gordy**, Jr., founded Motown Record Corporation in 1959. It became the most successful black-owned American music company, and through it Gordy developed the "Motown sound" and many

of the great rhythm-and-blues performers of the 1960s and '70s, including Diana Ross and the Supremes, Smokey Robinson and the Miracles, Stevie Wonder, Marvin Gaye, and Michael Jackson and the Jackson Five.

4. The South African-born actress and model **Charlize Theron** won the Academy Award for Best Actress for her performance as a serial killer in *Monster* (2003). Tragically, at age 15, she witnessed her mother shoot and kill her father in self-defense after being attacked by him while drunk.

Page 130

1. Italian architect **Renzo Piano** has designed some of the most famous buildings in the world, including the Pompidou Centre in Paris, the Modern Wing of the Art Institute of Chicago, and the Shard in London. He won the prestigious Pritzker Architecture Prize in 1998.

2. **Frank Gehry** is the prototypical avant-garde "starchitect" whose "wow-factor architecture" has been coveted widely in recent decades. His iconic buildings include the glass-and-titanium Guggenheim Museum in Bilbao, Spain—a crumpled boat-like structure called, by some, the greatest building of our time—and the Pritzker Pavilion in Chicago's Millennium Park. The pavilion's curved steel shavings and metal trellis have become prime tourist attractions.

3. *Animal Crackers* was the name of a 1930 Marx Brothers movie, a hit song ("Animal Crackers in My Soup") sung by Shirley Temple in the 1935 film *Curly Top,* and of course the animal-shaped cookies packaged in a box resembling a circus wagon. The familiar string on the box was for hanging the container on a Christmas tree.

4. A **sommelier** is a waiter in a restaurant who is in charge of serving wine. He or she is the person to turn to for advice on which wine best accompanies a particular food.

Page 131

1. Serial killer **Ted Bundy**, who lured women to their death with his good looks and charm, raped and killed some 30 women and was executed for his crimes in 1989. Many observers were appalled by the media attention he garnered—including books and movies about his life—which transformed him, some thought, into a romantic figure of sorts.

2. After an undersea earthquake struck the Indonesian island of Sumatra on Dec. 26, 2004, a series of tsunamis (giant ocean waves, some 30 feet high) triggered by the quake spread across the Indian Ocean, devastating coastal regions along the whole of the ocean rim, from Asia to East Africa. The **Indian Ocean Tsunami** killed some 225,000 people.

3. Snowboarder **Shaun White** won Olympic gold medals in the halfpipe event in 2006 and 2010. At the 2006 Games in Turin, Italy, White's gregarious personality and thick mop of red hair—which earned him the nickname "the Flying Tomato"—made him a media darling and an international star. Although widely called a vegetable, the tomato is actually a fruit.

4. **Hank Aaron**, in his 23 years in Major League Baseball, broke the hitting records of many of the mightiest hitters in the game and endured racism along the way, from his days in the Negro leagues in the South in the 1950s. He received hate mail upon breaking Babe Ruth's career home-run record of 714 on April 8, 1974.

Page 132

1. When the famed *Mona Lisa* by Leonardo da Vinci was stolen from the Louvre in Paris in 1911, painter and sculptor **Pablo Picasso**—one of the founders of Cubism—was brought in for questioning. It seems Picasso owned two sculptures that, unbeknownst to him, had been previously pilfered from the museum. The real thief was discovered two years later, and the painting was returned.

2. **Noah Webster** (1758-1843), after serving briefly in the American Revolution, produced a speller and a dictionary that were instrumental in distinguishing American from British English. He strove to give the language of his budding new nation a dignity and vitality all its own.

3. **"As Time Goes By,"** the iconic song of the classic film *Casablanca* (1942), was nearly cut from the production in favor of an original song. The only thing that saved the tune was the fact that Ingrid Bergman had already cut her hair for her next film role, making re-takes with a new song impossible.

4. **Jim Henson** called his famed creations *Muppets,* a portmanteau of *marionettes* and *puppets.* His characters—including such familiar figures as Kermit the Frog, Miss Piggy, Big Bird, and the Cookie Monster—became popular after appearing on the hit children's show *Sesame Street,* beginning in 1969. Their own TV show and film series followed, gaining them and Henson world-wide fame.

Page 133

1. **The Grinch** is the notorious grump and holiday-hater at the heart of *How the Grinch Stole Christmas,* a children's story by Theodor "Dr. Seuss" Geisel that was made into a successful animated television special of the same name in 1966.

2. **Pope Francis I**, elected as leader of the Roman Catholic Church in 2013, was the first pope from South America—the first from anywhere in the Western Hemisphere. He quickly shocked church traditionalists when he included two girls in the Maundy Thursday reenactment of Jesus's washing of the feet of his disciples on the night of the Last Supper, a ritual usually reserved for only men.

3. **Isaac Newton** (1642-1727), a pioneering figure of the Scientific Revolution, laid the foundations of modern optics, physics, and calculus, and his three laws of motion resulted in the universal law of gravitation, a theory that came to him (according to lore) while sitting under a tree and watching an apple fall perpendicular to the ground.

4. When **Neil Armstrong** stepped off the Lunar Module on July 21, 1969, becoming the first person on the Moon, he mistakenly dropped the "a" from his famous epigram—"That's one small step for [a] man, one giant leap for mankind"—undercutting his meaning, since *man* in this usage is synonymous with *mankind.*

BRITANNICA
BRAINBUSTERS

Word Search

The answers are hidden in the grid of letters below. Answers may be read forwards, backwards, up, down, or diagonally. The answer key will provide the answer to a riddle without giving away the answer's location.

U.S. PRESIDENCY & FIRST LADIES

1 I was too honest for my own good in 1976,
When I suddenly admitted to my lusting after chicks.

2 To the Pledge of Allegiance was I added in,
Something critics denounced as a secular sin.

SCIENCE, SPACE & TECHNOLOGY

3 Lavoisier was the "Father of Modern Chemistry,"
And then his head was severed in this conflict's bloody spree.

4 In the ancient art of calligraphy, I really became astute,
And communications I transformed with technology named for fruit.

```
H Y B J T B N J Q Y J O G K Y F X N
Y H S H T G K L L R Q F Q D E X K K
G S F R E N C H R E V O L U T I O N
W P R Z I H Q J A E U D O F U N C S
I P C H D W Q L I T Q R M N Q G U T
Y Y J F R B B W Q M M D D E R G X E
F I P Y W B F Q F H M E R W L T W V
M N X U Y S L S V R R Y R K U B I E
E U E U Y L U J A G B V C U J O K J
N Q E Z P E B A O N N H P A W T I O
I L J C I I C D L B O H B O R H V B
P N E E Y E L Q L P Z H C Q Z T T S
K T Q K P R C T I C M S I U B T E D
E V F H O B P N F D T S F T G R E R
I T K B R H J B C R S V U T M V A K
```

Word Search

The answers are hidden in the grid of letters below. Answers may be read forwards, backwards, up, down, or diagonally. The answer key will provide the answer to a riddle without giving away the answer's location.

LITERATURE & THE ARTS

1 The boy who wouldn't grow up was my creation,
My horrible boyhood was my inspiration.

2 I painted and designed, even conceived of human flight,
And scholars did I frustrate by not writing left to right.

POP CULTURE & ENTERTAINMENT

3 My parents were murdered, I was molded by tragedy,
A disguise I then donned and fought crime as a remedy.

4 Among the pioneers in film history, I stood at the front,
But this hardly proved helpful during America's red hunt.

```
U Y G T J L J I T R W J Z S C L C E
O P U Z J E P V Q M W V I H K Y O H
E Y Y U J O E I R Q D K A P E U A I
G D U D N N K G O N H R D K B H R N
H H I K H A Y T N V L F M I Q C P J
L I M E W R M G P I E I R R A B M J
L V G Z N D A T E I V X L Q F Q H D
W W X Q H O F C A J E K I A T G B Z
I N V U R D H D K B S M H O N X C C
B T S Q O A X Z B L D F T Y U S Y G
B M R B P V U O I Y X U R E I L S A
B D K L C I O H L V N P U S X T W W
X E I B O N L Z B Q K Q U Z U O Q U
D N G R W C V S K Q I O Z I W K N C
L T W M F I H R J R V Q H C K W L T
```

BRITANNICA
BRAINBUSTERS

Word Search

The answers are hidden in the grid of letters below. Answers may be read forwards, backwards, up, down, or diagonally. The answer key will provide the answer to a riddle without giving away the answer's location.

SCIENCE, SPACE & TECHNOLOGY

1 The Earth goes 'round the Sun, said I, and not the other way,
And for that novel notion I'm still remembered today.

2 I led the first controlled chain reaction of fission,
Which led to a war-ending military mission.

POP CULTURE & ENTERTAINMENT

3 A top chairman was I who loved the saloon,
On stage or in film I caused young girls to swoon.

4 Skewered was I for my large mental region,
But my late-night fans for decades were legion.

```
K M I T B A W Q S F M O X X B S F M
K E M V C B B L J Z I Y H O J E L J
R R R A Q Z I C L G E B N K D A J B
S J E H R L D G H Y P E E N G W M F
S Z F P R T G B Y V L B K I O T N P
G L O X M X A L A Y U K B O U J I P
L N C R L C V N A Y M A O I H U P X
S Y I A T D G J I I N I J K C Y P F
Y B R Y W L U V I S H X X A M R E G
H A N R K X J G A Y K E T V A N S Y
G V E I G M Z X R F W N C V W R Q J
S U C I N R E P O C S U A L O C I N
W J E I U Y Y U J W A E E R O K E R
D Z R K S H S I H O W N R C F Y M L
Z T A F L W U D V P U P B N W Z U W
```

ENCYCLOPÆDIA
Britannica

Word Search

The answers are hidden in the grid of letters below. Answers may be read forwards, backwards, up, down, or diagonally. The answer key will provide the answer to a riddle without giving away the answer's location.

SCIENCE, SPACE & TECHNOLOGY

1 For studies in the jungle I was knighted as a dame,
My subjects got to know me well and with me grew quite tame.

2 Only rarely am I seen, according to a phase,
I'm the second full moon that occurs in 30 days.

U.S. PRESIDENCY & FIRST LADIES

3 "Remember the ladies" was my two cents,
As John assisted our independence.

4 No children I fathered but a father I became,
In both wartime and peacetime did I gather much fame.

```
W W L J A S M V I H I D H B J C E C
X G X X R B L X X U Y O H O E F G V
E B Z B T D I W C S H R T A E R A F
Y C N E R X O G J Q B I B G N B M B
Y G E O R G E W A S H I N G T O N S
C J D F K P Z B N I C U H V E Z X R
V M J M S R L O E N L V O M B S K R
X R C K M U P W G W X A N S Y U V Z
Q V U K E I N B O M W I D B D V L H
P Q Q M Y L A T O N F A H A R L X E
W H O D G Z R W D O H Q E T M E V Y
F O E B K U K C A A L N J S S S N D
N L K P H M T H L J E R A F A A X C
Q E J D H O A S L Y B Y K F H S M C
K C W F C W F K U C U I K V Q L U H
```

BRITANNICA
BRAINBUSTERS

Word Search

The answers are hidden in the grid of letters below. Answers may be read forwards, backwards, up, down, or diagonally. The answer key will provide the answer to a riddle without giving away the answer's location.

POP CULTURE & ENTERTAINMENT

1 I was the first summer blockbuster, set in the ocean blue,
And my mechanical mandible scared the life out of you.

2 In Boston I chased Diane and in Springfield I haunted Bart,
In Seattle I said "I'm listening" in another part.

U.S. PRESIDENCY & FIRST LADIES

3 When my husband collapsed and then suddenly died,
Some accused me, the first lady, of homicide.

4 I was the wife of a president, the mother of one too,
And some memoirs would be written from my doggies' point of view.

```
L X H P E Z F I D U G K A R Q T W G
O O X H Z F D W D B T E E J L O P N
D F P W R C H H T K B M Y W A C B I
O R Y O C W J Y H C M B Q H G W H D
G S U X Q B B L A A T M M B F K S R
Q K A I Y A B A R B A R A B U S H A
N F X V X N X G W E E T R G U U V H
T M L N C J Y A N G W N Y Y P C W E
R C I R N E K T G W R Y Y Y I N E C
M C V O S O Y B V S N G A S R D P N
C X N L U W T Q Y P L J G J O W D E
H I E E B G R X C H T J G H U O E R
S K R T Y S W X I Y D V I V M N O O
W A S J O I R N J B W T I P M H S L
W Y S M F M I Z C Y F Z H M O Y M F
```

145

Word Search

The answers are hidden in the grid of letters below. Answers may be read forwards, backwards, up, down, or diagonally. The answer key will provide the answer to a riddle without giving away the answer's location.

POP CULTURE & ENTERTAINMENT

1 "Only her hair is red," my husband declared,
When rumors that I was a leftist were aired.

2 Actors have long adored me, my gold-plated, 13-inch frame,
Bette Davis even claimed credit for my buttocks and name.

FAMOUS & INFAMOUS

3 The custody battle over me was wild,
Though I never, ever was any human's child.

4 My family would worship my wild-eyed fervor,
And dutifully carry out mayhem and murder.

```
V T X R L N N N M M H G A M H J C M
G D Y F L L O P K W O N V V P M J N
F T T D A X I S V X J V G X Q E X E
P O B T B Z U J N T J U H U T W P M
U D S U E V T O A A N Q M R A I B P
P O P A L Q B B K L M Q M Q H J S J
V U M I L F U J V W Q S N P A G N C
G A L Q I U H J N J U X E W G F B O
Y Z C X C N Q Y L G G Q I L V Q V J
J T F M U M I A V J W D J L R Y V N
E E N C L H S H M Y W H C R Y A Z P
I B Z B E A Y C Y Z M U A U Z Q H I
L O X V T T Y F F B G C Z Z W H L C
W E U X Z G U C K C S O H G U B S E
B V F W N Q H V K O A Z U W A S M U
```

BRITANNICA BRAINBUSTERS

Mind Lines

Try to get from the top line of categories to the bottom in the fewest moves. Check off each box (or mark initials in the box if playing opponents) after each correct answer to a riddle. Once a player "owns" a box, an opponent must find another path.

Fam - FAMOUS & INFAMOUS
Sci - SCIENCE, SPACE & TECHNOLOGY
Lit   - LITERATURE & THE ARTS
Pres- U.S. PRESIDENCY & FIRST LADIES
Pop - POP CULTURE & ENTERTAINMENT
Sprt - THE SPORTING LIFE
F&D - FOOD & DRINK

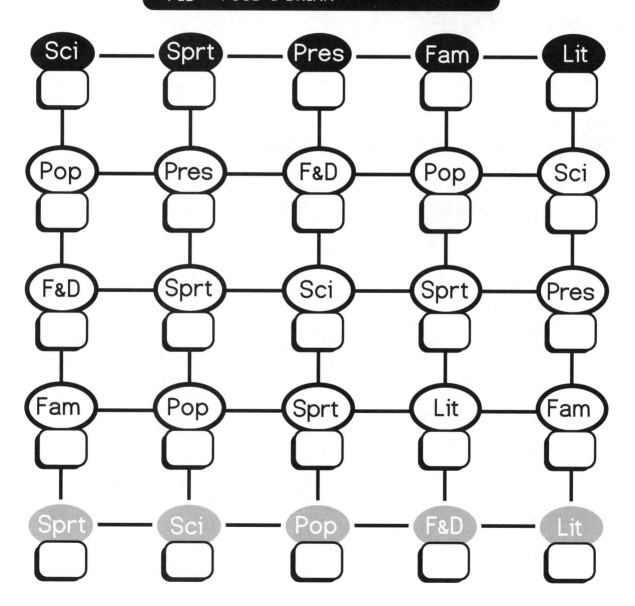

Word Search

The answers are hidden in the grid of letters below. Answers may be read forwards, backwards, up, down, or diagonally. The answer key will provide the answer to a riddle without giving away the answer's location.

FOOD & DRINK

1 Many a dessert and treat on me depend,
Just never, ever feed me to man's best friend.

2 "Cauliflower is nothing" was my humorous summation,
Nothing more than "cabbage with a college education."

THE SPORTING LIFE

3 As the most famous athlete in the world in my day,
I won cups in three decades, so well did I play.

4 I frequently won, I was used to first place,
And I famously mastered the master race.

```
U S N X O Q F S Q U R G U F B G Y S
Q V H D J F W X S M E H X X I L N Q
K J F R T M N V Y V A O R K P E M P
O O R W I Z O F Z W C R N G W S Z D
E I Z P M D P G W N L P K O H X S O
R S J N Q V G L T S M Z E T W H P M
F N C H O C O L A T E S L B W J R U
N U W V A P R D P J S P N K U A G L
G S M Y H E I R Y E R B E D T B I X
P S Q Y L L X W J L D T F S O A J N
Y K O W T E C S M E V V Z C G A H R
B R K R D M K A R O W S J F N J S Q
U O Z F A R S A S L Y F Q A K O C A
Z Y B H K J G A D R E I H D N C J K
G U S T O N P W P J M I U O W Z X C
```

148

Word Search

The answers are hidden in the grid of letters below. Answers may be read forwards, backwards, up, down, or diagonally. The answer key will provide the answer to a riddle without giving away the answer's location.

FOOD & DRINK

1 Drinking milk without me could engender great peril,
For microbes I'm killing for the drink to be sterile.

2 For teens and adults I am no big deal,
But for newborns I could be their last meal.

FAMOUS & INFAMOUS

3 I was the largest camp where so many were lost,
I became the chief symbol of the Holocaust.

4 Death-dealing inventions brought unwanted fame,
I donated prizes to redeem my name.

```
H W F L E B O N D E R F L A Y U A P
S N L Z T V Y E J R D N H E I O A P
D T C A R G E H A P W D Z V I S C X
N K L D I R N A E Z O N Y P T Y E T
O M Z A E A O O O T Z V Z E V K I Q
Y Q J Z J G H D E E Q Z U T J H B K
S U Z T T G S T U I N R I V J X Y B
I L Y Z C I U V K O I A D A L M C T
Q K F S V V W W K Z J M V O F C F L
N E N H Q M Z H A Z P Q M L I I R C
V O C I F Q E T C R Y Z S I H N M B
U I D E V I I O F S P K X B L T L Z
A J J M R O V O B K U Q H C B J N G
A S F U N L Y C S S N A Z C P L A H
N U V L E P E D I S D P O X I W Y Z
```

Word Search

The answers are hidden in the grid of letters below. Answers may be read forwards, backwards, up, down, or diagonally. The answer key will provide the answer to a riddle without giving away the answer's location.

THE SPORTING LIFE

1 I was a star, one of the best in the Majors,
What got me in trouble were margins and wagers.

2 It was hard to catch me, on the field or in court,
And never was I late at a gate of an airport.

FAMOUS & INFAMOUS

3 Universities and airlines were the focus of my crimes,
As explained in my long writings in the *Post* and to the *Times*.

4 The day of candy hearts was special to me,
And fatal to the hearts of my enemies.

```
P N X E T Z G S S E E U S B V C N O
O G P N D Y V J S X N S L Z M I J S
X G D O R L C C Z G Z U O X Y S O Y
G S A P D B W Q G F S Q S R I Y O W
D O L A P N N V J H X L H M E U Y A
B D A C Y Y S E S D D A P R Z T T T
H U A L M A W Q G U G S H O Q W E B
J V G A D B P H T B O G O H U W T P
C H L D T O L G D N T Y I J I S X E
N X A K O B N R Y R E B M O B A N U
C A X C U K W X F O N M X D E L M J
V Y Y C C Y P I Z J G Y G U A K P F
G X G S J F O Q F M F Q D E P L X R
M J D K F J B D O E I V I O C W J Q
Y T J E I W S Z B W N H B K P M P N
```

Word Search

The answers are hidden in the grid of letters below. Answers may be read forwards, backwards, up, down, or diagonally. The answer key will provide the answer to a riddle without giving away the answer's location.

THE SPORTING LIFE

1 I was 9, 12, 35, 45, and 23,
Few athletes could copy my competitive esprit.

2 In 16 months, with 16 won,
I set records at 1:59 and 31.

POP CULTURE & ENTERTAINMENT

3 Celebrity pairs like "Tomkat" get hybrids forthwith,
As did we, the stars who played Mr. and Mrs. Smith.

4 Girls, gadgets, and spying have brought me great fame,
And I always, I always repeat my name.

```
G B A C Z R G K W A E W Q C W M H S
Q P T N T R Z X M U Z H O U I L P G
M L A J I N X K W T R N S C O J A O
Y W X H C L R R C X B G H C R Y H Q
X N Z A D T E R K P U A I M A Z L I
V W U D N Z A G V O E B C Z G P Y X
Q C R B O I N T N L K D Y L M D M Y
N A X A B G C Y J A T Z J G X G F K
N E M O S O D O F J R I X Q M R V N
F V Y W E Y R C Z R X B Y U N H R G
V R Q G M D W N H V H Y F N Q E F U
E D B M A O K T A I R A T E R C E S
Z J Z N J G D E X Q B L M B O Y X V
W W Z H N W W B B B N P A N I G L U
B E H K R H C W J J U B I R X R Y H
```

Word Search

The answers are hidden in the grid of letters below. Answers may be read forwards, backwards, up, down, or diagonally. The answer key will provide the answer to a riddle without giving away the answer's location.

U.S. PRESIDENCY & FIRST LADIES

1 Beware of political parties and ties with a foreign nation,
Cautioned George Washington in this famous and final proclamation.

2 I said no to a period after the "S" in my name.
Since the letter stood for nothing, I said leave it all the same.

FOOD & DRINK

3 A frothy yogurt-based drink, I come sweet, spiced, or salted,
From India I hail, where I'm widely exalted.

4 A rat in a kitchen usually holds little charm,
But the public in this case certainly saw no harm.

```
Z F O F A I T G W A J J P C P F H O
W N Q R A R Y N Y T S V U E F Z A H
A E O R M R D A C Z U V V V L B R E
C T S F O L E F R B X D B D B A R O
O W D H Z G W W D Q P X W O T E Y W
Q Q B G W L V G E C M M U A G K S R
N U D L E C P D V L G J T N A C T K
P Y Z S E Z W O Q V L O Z R C W R A
M G V U I P X K S E U A U G E L U I
Y X V G O W G G M I Q D D O X W M Y
A B G K K T C M L P G J L D Z Z A U
H F I I S S A L W K E Z X W R O N K
Z J X I X L E S M N N K K W J E O V
P U R L F E G P I R X X L C D S S T
M W B D W M J Z J V G X C W A L Y S
```

BRITANNICA
BRAINBUSTERS

Mind Lines

Try to get from the top line of categories to the bottom in the fewest moves. Check off each box (or mark initials in the box if playing opponents) after each correct answer to a riddle. Once a player "owns" a box, an opponent must find another path.

Fam - FAMOUS & INFAMOUS
Sci - SCIENCE, SPACE & TECHNOLOGY
Lit - LITERATURE & THE ARTS
Pres - U.S. PRESIDENCY & FIRST LADIES
Pop - POP CULTURE & ENTERTAINMENT
Sprt - THE SPORTING LIFE
F&D - FOOD & DRINK

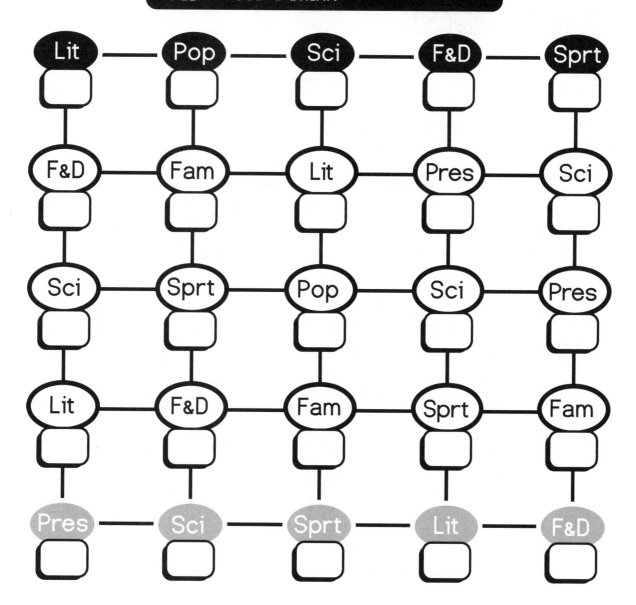

Word Search

The answers are hidden in the grid of letters below. Answers may be read forwards, backwards, up, down, or diagonally. The answer key will provide the answer to a riddle without giving away the answer's location.

LITERATURE & THE ARTS

1 I leaped and danced like no one else but hated Soviet constrictions,
So I defected, danced, and acted too, but now without restrictions.

2 My illustrated kids' books made me a star,
And I always knew where the wild things are.

THE SPORTING LIFE

3 My triumphs put me on the sporting map,
I was the Babe without the Yankees cap.

4 Countries compete fiercely to be my host,
Worldwide my cup is sought after the most.

```
E W I L A W S D T W G C Q J B H A O
B A V M W J K U Z M E K N D E P M P
J A G Z R Q A A L Y R V A U M S T L
Z K B N I G Y M K K X C A G A R B M
C D L E G Z P L M G X P T K U O Z L
T C B V D D L T K E W K S J R T Z G
M I K H A I L B A R Y S H N I K O V
Z T K S F G D U Q L S W Y K C S I X
B H O D V Y Y R R J O S X W E Q G D
F R S M O R A P I R U D E P S F X R
S E Z U T C Z K L K N P L X E H C H
M Q T K K M T D M L S I G K N P W Y
W J J U K B C H J R S O W D D N F A
L J B Z L U Y E E C G J N Z A D M F
I L Z Q P A Q Q C J E C Z F K B J E
```

Word Search

The answers are hidden in the grid of letters below. Answers may be read forwards, backwards, up, down, or diagonally. The answer key will provide the answer to a riddle without giving away the answer's location.

FAMOUS & INFAMOUS

1 My hair curls were pulled and my baby teeth checked,
Even the Vatican viewed me as suspect.

2 At Yalta I drank my Slavic tea,
And crimes Hitleresque are traced to me.

THE SPORTING LIFE

3 A phenom was I, a racing star,
More famous (some said) than FDR.

4 Scandinavians invented me,
For testing how well you shoot and ski.

```
Q M S N P Z W K G H H L L C L Z J J
N V H A G Z E C V S O V U F M G O D
F I I K W C Q U B Y N J Z N D S A J
W G R J K R Q H E O D O I J E T C H
V N L Z Q R N O T R X I L P O D Q L
F W E R T A I J V P W S H H A J T H
P Z Y G S R Y E Q P L S E R T N I A
R D T K Z W X D D A T Y F P Q A D O
R K E J V G K J E A V S Z R D B I I
Z A M F Z Z S E L H G R V K I E V B
P O P X C D U I X Y Z V Q B T O L U
C U L Y W R N G U A V I D X T M P G
H U E K I T F N T I U C S I B A E S
P A R K A B Y M U H V P M L L Y M V
Q G J R H G C B Y A C D V C V P K W
```

Word Search

The answers are hidden in the grid of letters below. Answers may be read forwards, backwards, up, down, or diagonally. The answer key will provide the answer to a riddle without giving away the answer's location.

FAMOUS & INFAMOUS

1 The Peoples Temple was my legacy and domain,
Where more than 900 of my followers were slain.

2 I have billions of children, which is not really a mystery,
When you remember I fathered three religions in history.

SCIENCE, SPACE & TECHNOLOGY

3 AC, not DC, was my winning position,
Edison lost in our shocking competition.

4 I studied big apes who had never been caged,
My life, was it taken by poachers enraged?

```
J W X E Q W D C C Z S N M G X E V J
K G D W J Q K U D H I E V S G R S N
G N E N L Y J E J K G K N G Z B Q R
A N E M V H W G O O O N E O B P W L
L K O Y M L D L W R N V L T J C A U
Z I C W G R A Z D O U T L W R M A M
G O S T Z T Y E S S O F N A I D I A
G A Q A E U L R N M M K Y L E Z D J
L L H S Z Z M E Y A Y K B D Q H C V
G C L U A A A I C H M V L C S S H N
Z A A D Z K M T U A A V P Q Y T U Y
Q Y T X X F X T C R A A A G X H M D
S V I C A Z U B X B I C M Q C Y K L
H C B J R J M S L A T N I A V J S H
I X K M Q O F V M J Y Z O Y G E U A
```

BRITANNICA
BRAINBUSTERS

Word Search

The answers are hidden in the grid of letters below. Answers may be read forwards, backwards, up, down, or diagonally. The answer key will provide the answer to a riddle without giving away the answer's location.

SCIENCE, SPACE & TECHNOLOGY

1 I was the first American to orbit Earth,
A second record I set with my early birth.

2 Medicine was transformed with this radiated beam,
Earning the first Nobel Prize and much worldwide esteem.

U.S. PRESIDENCY & FIRST LADIES

3 "Thomas Jefferson still lives!" I said on my death bed,
Not knowing, hours earlier, he also lay dead.

4 The many stars in my life caused the critics to shout,
But my love for my president was never in doubt.

```
B K S G I F A T O J N S Q A E W Y V
M T M G P G U J F X A C J M Y A Q S
V N S Y J O M Z R R N E Q I J A A U
C G E P J W B X Y B C Q S J S A R J
V J I T T R D Y R W Y C O X G B O X
W F L M G X Q V Q Z R M W Z L H U N
D M V L W R J U F V E O N S N E A W
D R E A V O D W I S A Q B G X S G V
H P P G W W A C Z B G W L T K M T X
F B E B N A C N X N A E N J K G Y Z
D G D V J M Z O L E N I Y B M E O G
I K T V P W W L B N J D J G U I W Q
H N M D A D N C V S M A D A N H O J
R O Z N X V Q P G Z X B J H Z E M A
Q H S Z S J M F V N H F I R I X E F
```

157

Word Search

The answers are hidden in the grid of letters below. Answers may be read forwards, backwards, up, down, or diagonally. The answer key will provide the answer to a riddle without giving away the answer's location.

SCIENCE, SPACE & TECHNOLOGY

1 I am severely disabled in all but mind,
More famous are few scientists of any kind.

2 The space race I launched, leaving Russians to cheer,
But others watched in horror and shook in fear.

FOOD & DRINK

3 V.S., V.S.O.P, even Napoleon I can be,
A noble offshoot of wine, now that would be me.

4 I am a branch of cooking, part of culinary arts,
I deal with the preparing and presenting of meat parts.

```
X Q J N R P Z I M L X N M W Y Y S G
J Q W S O Z P X I E K R N F O B N K
A C C B E A S H E S Z I X Y G I W N
Y L O E F I G P B K S U A V K T N A
T N K X I R P P U G G Y S W U F Z H
B W E K M J T L V T W G A U S M E A
U Z B C Z C G E N H N H P C B J A G
I F J O F W I A Z Y N I N S T F S K
Q B I G K E M D S E S J K V U W K Z
N T U N I W F C H A R C U T E R I E
E A R A O S S P D J U Q V F R O V T
G K M C J S E Y G X Q Z Q Q M D I V
Z Y G V F T Q P C C C U H U P F E R
O U I V S T P G P N B B M O W G J C
G W A G D B T J U T V P C K S O J V
```

BRITANNICA
BRAINBUSTERS

Mind Lines

Try to get from the top line of categories to the bottom in the fewest moves. Check off each box (or mark initials in the box if playing opponents) after each correct answer to a riddle. Once a player "owns" a box, an opponent must find another path.

Fam - FAMOUS & INFAMOUS
Sci - SCIENCE, SPACE & TECHNOLOGY
Lit - LITERATURE & THE ARTS
Pres - U.S. PRESIDENCY & FIRST LADIES
Pop - POP CULTURE & ENTERTAINMENT
Sprt - THE SPORTING LIFE
F&D - FOOD & DRINK

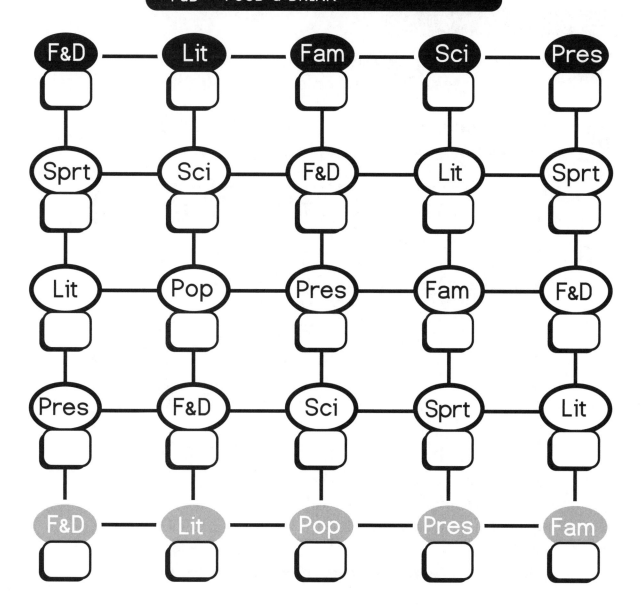

Word Search

The answers are hidden in the grid of letters below. Answers may be read forwards, backwards, up, down, or diagonally. The answer key will provide the answer to a riddle without giving away the answer's location.

U.S. PRESIDENCY & FIRST LADIES

1 110 minus 1 played a role in my life,
As did the beauty and fashions of my wife.

2 A food savior was I, quite famous worldwide,
'Till I turned on war veterans and was crucified.

FAMOUS & INFAMOUS

3 My folks ruled Transylvania, young ladies I killed,
I'm the "Countess Dracula," or so I've been billed.

4 I was learned and famous, a man for any season,
For refusing an oath I was beheaded for treason.

```
E R O M S A M O H T V I J V N S P R
U E R K E S P N P H C O H X Z X X W
R S P H X D K M S O E S I M M D J Y
E O L Q E J C S Y S D H X F G M U A
R N J Z L R Y T S M N F K W B Y E Q
W G O Y T J B Y I B U L D Y I D N F
A S H K O Y X E K K B V B P S V P J
O E N N F F Y R C W T E V U J Z U
K D K V M G S F G T M M P Q S V C M
X M E L I Z A B E T H B A T H O R Y
E F N B H T G X P X V O Q C R A O J
L K N G M S Y P H F O V O Q B U J Z
Z P E R S C O X W S U K N V V Z J X
V U D K J H J Y F Z R C X L E M I K
R E Y M M V J F F G H N G W W R V C
```

Word Search

The answers are hidden in the grid of letters below. Answers may be read forwards, backwards, up, down, or diagonally. The answer key will provide the answer to a riddle without giving away the answer's location.

U.S. PRESIDENCY & FIRST LADIES

1 I was the shortest president, even with my wig,
But when writing the Constitution, I turned up big.

2 I fought in a duel, left a man dead,
Still the country as president I led.

THE SPORTING LIFE

3 The Olympics in this city were full of despair,
With 17 left dead, it was a bloody affair.

4 I'm played on the campo, nearing the target is the aim,
Those closest to the pallino will surely win the game.

```
Z O V D D V J A M E S M A D I S O N
P K Q O D M F A B M V O X V R B O E
H G B N G H Q V I H U A N T A S U D
Q Y B Z S G Y M K P K N V C K S C R
N M I T H D S L J B U L I C H N D T
K M U I K K F L G L G U A C Q L O N
Y P Z R L J B K W D B J F T H M M Q
Q E B K G X J M S U W E H C F A Z V
T C O Y M X K P C E L F Y L B U X N
L G C O R K C R R K R E C X H H G Z
U V C T K S N D F Y P B E C G H O K
G F E F H F N C N P Z B J Y P X O F
Q C K B Z A B S L F X Q Y P L Q Y M
S C D E R K M F J D T V O N A I C X
P Y F P I V Q B Q Y J N N B W Q K I
```

ENCYCLOPÆDIA
Britannica®

Word Search

The answers are hidden in the grid of letters below. Answers may be read forwards, backwards, up, down, or diagonally. The answer key will provide the answer to a riddle without giving away the answer's location.

FOOD & DRINK

1 "I cook with wine," I humorously spewed, "Sometimes I even add it to the food!"

2 I'm sugar, fruit, and water that's frozen and churned, A low-fat alternative for those so concerned.

SCIENCE, SPACE & TECHNOLOGY

3 Although the mission killed me, I was first in space, A hero with statues of a non-human face.

4 My tower brought me and a city great fame, The "magician of iron" was my nickname.

```
I Q W E L E G B M G P T J R Z X Q T
W N X N Q Y A S L U R L Y I V C V X
L X P U G R S A R S L Q W W I Y U F
C U K P Y R R Z H T U T C N A X K O
G K A Z K P W M E A A F K D V S L P
Y P B P Q U N Z F V I X G R N I L I
V Q P X S F O R C E D U E W Z Q X F
K X L G E C G U L E C E T E B R O S
L L K K U J A D A I D K A N Z U K K
L K W Q H O S B E F M D Q F H F V U
S W N K O V A Q W F O Q V P D S H T
Z O Z I O M N K K E N J Y R K G S V
D R X A I R I B I L B W G L D E F O
F P B S H H A B L A N C N Y W S R R
Z U E T E A R F A F L F N K T K F O
```

Word Search

The answers are hidden in the grid of letters below. Answers may be read forwards, backwards, up, down, or diagonally. The answer key will provide the answer to a riddle without giving away the answer's location.

FOOD & DRINK

1 Two things will be broken, said one wise guy,
Promises and this component of pie.

2 I'm a chocolate-flavored drink, a city, and a port,
I'm famous for the coffee my shippers would transport.

POP CULTURE & ENTERTAINMENT

3 My famous final episode would bring me lasting fame,
I'm a show with Vietnam, not Korea, as its aim.

4 Fab and Rob mastered me and ruled the music domain,
But then they used me too much in their legerdemain.

```
J L K I M T R V B Q N W R W O C I A
K I I H E C V D C J W U T Y O R R F
V L V P J E Y I E Y P U Q B V U F H
N J A N S T O P E C S M G U H S A M
L D P T R Y R U L L V J M A T I M
X O K T B D N Z Z S I E A Z G Q O X
G R O J F C R C W Z A V H L H C C O
R E X S H T F Y H H N D F H H Q Y I
C N X E D J T P F I C V A A M S Z O
U F T M M I R R Y J N Q W J N U M I
E L V F Y Q H A U S M G S N O G O A
E A D Z K D U C R W N J J N C Q E K
P R G X A Q C M H A K B I E V O O M
J X T V B N N A N D L U K I K V Y P
P J B R L S F C T S K X M X H K V H
```

Word Search

The answers are hidden in the grid of letters below. Answers may be read forwards, backwards, up, down, or diagonally. The answer key will provide the answer to a riddle without giving away the answer's location.

POP CULTURE & ENTERTAINMENT

1 I was a cat-woman and Bond girl and a star among monsters,
The first African American "Best Actress" at the Oscars.

2 There were Steve, Jack, and Johnny, they came from both coasts,
Jay, Conan and Jimmy would also be my hosts.

U.S. PRESIDENCY & FIRST LADIES

3 "Is it July Fourth?" I asked from my death-bed,
On the holiday of the land I once led.

4 I was president 22 and 24,
And striking rail workers did I fight and abhor.

```
G N T W U M G A J A C J Z B V D B H
M R P E L U Q F J S O V Y M W H A T
Q M O E H S N K N V I L P W T L V O
Y Q W V L H K Q N U O O W P L F H T
S M R T E G U T S J F M S E C V C Q
O N N O F R L V J Y T N B X N Z A X
W U J N Q K C I P G N E N Z I T A B
Z E K I X I D L J M R O P Q I B S W
M T Q G F Z Q Q E R A W A S V W B W
U H H H C U C Q Y V F T C O X H M Y
V V T T H O M A S J E F F E R S O N
L X T S N K S Q H V A L E M P R Y A
K F K H V R Z O T H C A A A G E N S
E I S O D E O D M I H F P N Z I B F
H T J W N V H A Y E N T I H D U H H
```

BRITANNICA
BRAINBUSTERS

Mind Lines

Try to get from the top line of categories to the bottom in the fewest moves. Check off each box (or mark initials in the box if playing opponents) after each correct answer to a riddle. Once a player "owns" a box, an opponent must find another path.

Fam - FAMOUS & INFAMOUS
Sci - SCIENCE, SPACE & TECHNOLOGY
Lit - LITERATURE & THE ARTS
Pres - U.S. PRESIDENCY & FIRST LADIES
Pop - POP CULTURE & ENTERTAINMENT
Sprt - THE SPORTING LIFE
F&D - FOOD & DRINK

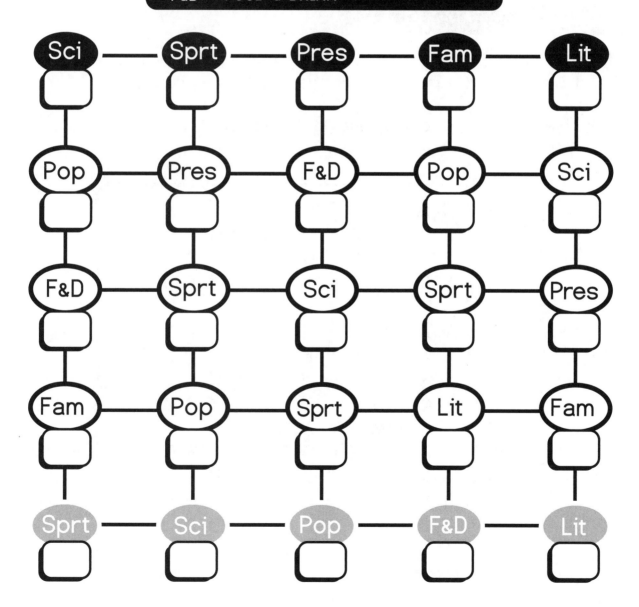

Word Search

The answers are hidden in the grid of letters below. Answers may be read forwards, backwards, up, down, or diagonally. The answer key will provide the answer to a riddle without giving away the answer's location.

POP CULTURE & ENTERTAINMENT

1 When they tried to make me go, I said "No, no, no,"
Then I died after bingeing, singing "I won't go."

2 I hosted dance and game shows and New Year's on the screen,
With young people I mingled as TV's oldest "teen."

FAMOUS & INFAMOUS

3 Feminists defended me, though I never deserved it,
I was indeed a monster, for the charges were legit.

4 In a dark room I'd stay, sitting naked for days,
Watching films, eating bonbons, and peeing in trays.

```
Q H M O J K P P R U A X H V Y L J A
S O Z Z N S L R L Q B E D G O K R F
K W I R K Z L B C G T I S C D T W T
R A O E R T X C A T C D Z R E N C L
K R M U M F L P V K B A I E Y N B I
G D E Y A E V T C I D I B Z L P Q Q
K H B R W A I L E E N W U O R N O S
D U B Y K I A Y H W M Y W U F J J Y
X G W T M R N J X B J D E Z Z K U S
J H E B K B M E A W V N V L U X T Y
U E R Q Z I F G H O F P J U I K L M
F S O O X I N I D O F X V U I B H H
G M S J V P R T U S U E Z G N G V C
A I A C B B Z R J E J S U D P U C R
V F D I X A W M S B L Y E N Y U C Y
```

BRITANNICA
BRAINBUSTERS

Word Search

The answers are hidden in the grid of letters below. Answers may be read forwards, backwards, up, down, or diagonally. The answer key will provide the answer to a riddle without giving away the answer's location.

SCIENCE, SPACE & TECHNOLOGY

1 Squaring and adding my neighbors produces my square,
I'm the famous third side of Pythagoras, I swear!

2 Just seconds into the *Challenger*'s mission,
Disaster struck from my faulty condition.

U.S. PRESIDENCY & FIRST LADIES

3 Thanks to the "Lame Duck Amendment" I was moved,
January 20th was now approved.

4 Into the family of Kennedys I wed,
My legions of workers for peace are widespread.

```
S Y Z R R I O G E Z O S Z F L D N L
M Y F E E E N I B F Y S N O O C R R
F K M Q H I V F R P K B N K M O S F
R T I N R X I I N J A M F K Z A M G
P Y N O P A K E R V J S S B X A B P
L F U M X G G S Q H L T L T D X M V
S U T P R F A U G Q S Z P T X Z Z H
P C Y C D C M N S P J T M S H J P O
X O Q B H Y R E R Y V U N K E B A C
N P M H I B Q T I P Z U N E S R B D
W G J Z F J K O S J K R C C G L F W
C I D X B C T P U S J T N S J R J L
U M I D A T U Y L V V D G Y S Z A X
W N Y S B K M H L M Q A U Q W O O S
Y R O Y A D N O I T A R U G U A N I
```

Word Search

The answers are hidden in the grid of letters below. Answers may be read forwards, backwards, up, down, or diagonally. The answer key will provide the answer to a riddle without giving away the answer's location.

THE SPORTING LIFE

1 The Olympics were considered so sublime,
They even inspired this unit of time.

2 In amateur golf these second chances are rife,
If only these do-overs were common in life.

SCIENCE, SPACE & TECHNOLOGY

3 None of them is bigger, not liver, heart, or brain,
I'm the largest organ in the human domain.

4 The smallest am I among my eight solar mates,
I have the widest swings in temperature states.

```
Y  I  I  F  I  V  I  Z  M  L  S  G  S  Y  F  R  H  D
Z  P  T  B  Y  E  B  O  G  E  E  B  Q  D  R  P  A  I
Y  K  Y  F  W  Q  N  N  N  E  R  X  P  O  C  I  L  V
H  W  W  B  I  J  W  Z  Z  V  R  C  P  M  P  V  S  W
H  P  T  Z  E  S  Y  Y  K  Q  Q  Q  U  M  T  Z  O  R
D  C  U  I  S  H  V  P  R  J  X  D  Y  R  N  F  Z  H
F  F  E  J  Y  H  K  T  H  D  J  L  G  N  Y  Z  Z  I
L  I  B  F  H  T  B  C  R  Z  O  I  C  V  M  T  S  Q
W  A  Q  Z  V  T  C  C  N  G  A  P  C  Q  W  I  A  T
F  Y  W  B  J  R  L  U  C  M  H  M  S  D  E  F  H  B
Q  S  D  O  K  Q  S  O  G  H  M  U  L  L  I  G  A  N
N  K  J  B  A  G  D  A  N  G  A  E  L  D  J  V  E  E
D  I  V  A  R  X  E  V  E  L  Y  M  K  J  Z  Y  B  S
G  N  L  L  D  Q  L  P  S  A  X  L  X  B  P  W  N  U
E  P  I  I  O  S  H  R  U  O  D  I  F  Z  R  P  R  D
```

168

Word Search

The answers are hidden in the grid of letters below. Answers may be read forwards, backwards, up, down, or diagonally. The answer key will provide the answer to a riddle without giving away the answer's location.

U.S. PRESIDENCY & FIRST LADIES

1 Truman's motto was clear for the public to view,
Reflecting a duty few leaders should eschew.

2 My cabinet of advisors was full of crooks,
Women voters I attracted with my good looks.

POP CULTURE & ENTERTAINMENT

3 *Mr. Rogers' Neighborhood* brought me little fame,
But *Night of the Living Dead* established my name.

4 I'm the song that sparked the rock music revolution,
The film that featured me caused riots and confusion.

```
J W P U M Q H A F F Q B P D S Z C U
F A O B J C F K U N A D R F A M L A
O R M O C Y J W H E J I R U U V J Z
Q R T J R H Z K O Y T H Q J X V L U
D E I N X L O R E M O R E G R O E G
A N K C V K S D J L H P U O G T P H
B H C A U R A Y M X R E F F M O E E
X A R N O C Z Y W A X P Q V K S R W
P R T H E B U C K S T O P S H E R E
C D N S Q E F G D W V L A B K B Z H
J I H O P D C O E Q H L R F Z P R K
I N G T T D U F S T K C O G T P E E
M G A J D H C X M M W M A G M G I T
K C O L C E H T D N U O R A K C O R
H L O N P K Q O Y P O C Z P W Y N B
```

Word Search

The answers are hidden in the grid of letters below. Answers may be read forwards, backwards, up, down, or diagonally. The answer key will provide the answer to a riddle without giving away the answer's location.

THE SPORTING LIFE

1 My coveted 18 seems secure for now,
Since my sport's number one imploded, and how!

2 I fired shots from Fort Sumter, the Civil War started forthwith,
I also invented baseball, according to long-standing myth.

FOOD & DRINK

3 Champagne I really did not invent despite what people say,
But I helped to perfect the process by which it's made today.

4 This dessert, said Voltaire, was anything but awful,
What a pity, he noted, it wasn't unlawful.

```
L A I M S U J F K B G A Z A E W J Y
I R C G Y P W D B R W C K Y M M A M
L T E U O I N G O X Q N H T L D B M
L I C Z R C C T J M P H K U E G S I
H I R P R J E Q R E P J A L I L W Q
K R E B B V G L R Z G E B R S Y H S
O L A B N X E F V K I U R Y B U E E
E N M L F T I E S N O P Z I N H C T
C E H T G U N T Z D B R S L G T Q D
N D W J D Y O B R E D I T D T N P W
B F M B D T I E W V I D L V W V O V
O Z U V J Y N X W W K W T A S W R N
N X W U B B J A C K N I C K L A U S
Q X O Y A F P V V Q I F L R J Y L I
T F V Q G Q P U H U E W U D Y G H X
```

Word Search

The answers are hidden in the grid of letters below. Answers may be read forwards, backwards, up, down, or diagonally. The answer key will provide the answer to a riddle without giving away the answer's location.

POP CULTURE & ENTERTAINMENT

1 My "Rat Pack" pals were hip and well-known,
Never they minded my dark skin tone.

2 Schindler and Ryan—their stories I told,
Winning me two famous statues of gold.

LITERATURE & THE ARTS

3 With a minimum of words I could spin a timeless yarn,
About a runaway white bunny and a big red barn.

4 Rags brought me riches, though no one knew me when I died,
But then a sting revived me and spread my work worldwide.

```
S N I L P O J T T O C S Q Z M G T C
N U K N M H C E Y E A T I C G Z C D
P H F P T B H Y G M T E M J Q C F A
T M U R G K A L M Y U V V N P L P W
Y P Q C M Z R Y H E B E T Y R I S Q
J Z F T M O D G Y P Z N S J G W H F
P Y H F N A D U K B T S M L D B R F
F V C U V B L P Y P X P F V W T J O
G O H I S G U N E N P I N P W X E G
N G S Z A B T L O T R E W U D F A Y
A J T S M P T J Y X W L U I H I Q T
R W M V E J J M M G I B G X H L I B
M A R G A R E T W I S E B R O W N O
M N N A C L A C J I G R W P I O F Q
J W F K Z R J D V K F G T L S B J U
```

Word Search

The answers are hidden in the grid of letters below. Answers may be read forwards, backwards, up, down, or diagonally. The answer key will provide the answer to a riddle without giving away the answer's location.

POP CULTURE & ENTERTAINMENT

1 A busty, blonde bombshell, I was a celebrity,
And rear safety bars on trucks are now named after me.

2 "Goodness, what beautiful diamonds," someone said to me,
"Goodness had nothing to do with it," I quipped with glee.

SCIENCE, SPACE & TECHNOLOGY

3 Tornados I measure from zero to five,
And help to keep people aware and alive.

4 Before the seven continents there was only me,
From which the current continents would finally break free.

```
O Z S K I X G S J E J B G H S C V S
K F F W Y D S P J C A F M Y K F V Q
O V H X U I D M O K Y N O N L B F G
Y F U B X C E H G J N X S Q M U C Q
K U X T U I C X J K E V Y U J U F G
N O W M A W O S O J M Y A I R P A E
N Q B I H I W I S E A K T E H J C H
M R O G M V R O X B N A N D G A X P
R G S E B I Y B E W S L G D K N D J
G B G N K L K N W C F X C T Y S A Z
V V P N R C M C A P I Z M C R R J P
T A F E Z K J L T S E Y W Q U C E P
I L D A Z C E U X R L T S E W E A M
A W W A K W L Z D K D Z K P W E T V
U K L B R W I I H X H X M X W I R P
```

BRITANNICA
BRAINBUSTERS

Word Search

The answers are hidden in the grid of letters below. Answers may be read forwards, backwards, up, down, or diagonally. The answer key will provide the answer to a riddle without giving away the answer's location.

LITERATURE & THE ARTS

1 I said when I was 21 I heard a wise man say,
Freely give away your money but not your heart away.

2 I had things to do, promises to keep,
I had miles to go before I'd sleep.

FOOD & DRINK

3 I helped save the Soviet Army as a wartime food,
"Roosevelt sausage" the Russians called me with gratitude.

4 I was first made in China, and my bottom is round,
I make it quite easy to toss food items around.

```
T A N A Z Q X Z F X O U F J A R L N
S H R Q I A B Q F Z N Z V A M Y A W
O U Y S H K U T H R O Z A N B M K J
R V A D J Z D I G T Z D R T S T W R
F T L S K R P G H F S L X U N I P B
T S P S P A M B K B M L O Y X K Q A
R X N N B K B W J P M H M D C W L A
E J N R M A S A C O E H A X O W A R
B S J S W A R E Y A Z G Y P E I N P
O N T U T H K J I D Q W G P S P U Z
R U G A Q R T W R G H D C R Q B N M
W F R D D X S P M C T X O A C I P L
V O W T A K P B B A Q U Q E X M T Y
A Y K U I E S H E H U R R J O C M E
X W L A Z G R U I T S Q P K F B I P
```

Word Search

The answers are hidden in the grid of letters below. Answers may be read forwards, backwards, up, down, or diagonally. The answer key will provide the answer to a riddle without giving away the answer's location.

LITERATURE & THE ARTS

1 B.F. Pinkerton the sailor was the awful cad and meanie,
Who abandoned me with child in this classic by Puccini.

2 I hailed from the brothels, I am very sexy and fast,
Between me and the minuet, our differences are vast.

U.S. PRESIDENCY & FIRST LADIES

3 Not France or Germany, not Mexico or Spain,
None liked my administration's nosey campaign.

4 When I instructed the public to read my lips,
My political life slipped through my fingertips.

```
G N Z K A F S S W U C Z E X B N G C
H E D S Y O I N Y S F Y K V A B F T
M C O V T W C Y Y J G F N G R M L F
E Y Z R S Q T Q K E R T Y S A L Z R
V T K R G O Z D C Q M A Z M C H T J
S U K K H E Q W J Y C R Z K K B S U
R Z U D B O H K S S O S A W O R L Y
F J V H E T X W O G V H E Z B J B K
F Q Q J Q R E Z B I E F Q R A D P P
M X H L C Q E E S U Z O O G M T W V
W N L D Y Z Y V T L S R Z H A T Y T
M O F K V E T M A Q M H M N C D V N
D Y T D Z U R A J D W O G E I N Y Y
Q P K U J N Y M J P V O G C R G M C
V X X M A D A M A B U T T E R F L Y
```

Word Search

The answers are hidden in the grid of letters below. Answers may be read forwards, backwards, up, down, or diagonally. The answer key will provide the answer to a riddle without giving away the answer's location.

THE SPORTING LIFE

1 I wrote *Leaves of Grass* and other poems quite sublime, And claimed baseball as the country's national pastime.

2 "If winners never quit," this famed coach explained, "Then quitters never win," he logically claimed.

POP CULTURE & ENTERTAINMENT

3 I reigned as a king, though some called me a creep, I perished while craving a very deep sleep.

4 Rejected by the army I was considered a zero, Till a serum transformed me into a tri-colored hero.

```
J C A P N W W T K J H Q Q Q N P O I
H D C E P O D G A R I U I B G C D R
L N I K C T S H H A U F E F H R S F
V S R U B T Y K Z F Q F W I A Q S Y
B G E P E E N N C E P O O B K C G K
J V M X P C D D R A R B M M M U D G
X E A M Z H N X T Z J O S X N T L Q
Q W N C H A J I P C L L E O H L F M
J R I P G Y X U A E L T E U I Q V R
M V A M F D A I C B Y V U A I E O E
P K T I U Q X N D I A G D T H O C X
M R P D V W I M W U O M E H M C U O
F Z A T A V J M X H I A J F J D I A
X H C G K C R V D Z Z Q P X N H V M
S H H I H X P W A L T W H I T M A N
```

Word Search

The answers are hidden in the grid of letters below. Answers may be read forwards, backwards, up, down, or diagonally. The answer key will provide the answer to a riddle without giving away the answer's location.

POP CULTURE & ENTERTAINMENT

1 Racial barriers I broke as an Oscar nominee,
The famed gold statue I would win for my role as Mammy.

2 Orson Welles broadcast me—a Martian invasion,
Terrifying listeners across the nation.

LITERATURE & THE ARTS

3 Of forms of music I'm hardly new,
I'm low and guttural, through and through.

4 451 is the key, Ray Bradbury exclaims,
To sending up this product and our freedoms in flames.

```
U Q L B T E S D C G U V S T F N R N
Y B T D N H I C Q N X A D U Y D X W
X L L W Y R R Z D J P M L Z I J C L
P K X N B R C W P D M F R Q M M J W
A M N W I O U P Z K F E O H M C A O
U D N B L V D J I M L M W G X R A J
Y M X I L E I N A D C M E I T T A H
W U Z M M C P Q A P M B H Q J I J G
E E V C T E S S E I B C T A V E X S
J W B M K W X O X B I O F P D I O J
F D H X Z W G B C V L Y O G V I A F
F R H K V I C A O S Z F R K W J T I
U K A R H T X J I Q T X A V S F Z D
Z T O R M N N O E P N J W R R E C S
J D W R T H R O A T S I N G I N G M
```

BRITANNICA
BRAINBUSTERS

Word Search

The answers are hidden in the grid of letters below. Answers may be read forwards, backwards, up, down, or diagonally. The answer key will provide the answer to a riddle without giving away the answer's location.

FAMOUS & INFAMOUS

1 The Norwegians hate me most, and I clearly realize why,
I'm synonymous with treachery—I mastered the lie.

2 With 23 stab wounds did my empire fall,
The thrust from my friend hurting deepest of all.

FOOD & DRINK

3 I'm the master of the beautiful meal,
And even cooked up an insider deal.

4 I'm tart and sweet, from the Sunshine State,
A taste of the islands on your plate.

```
J C C I M U R J Y A A G D V J E Q G
D U P B I B R R G U M O T U D H N V
A K L X E J F C Q V A R J V H I F Z
V E M I E T R J C K I E P C L V W M
Y Y Y C U M W T A K P A E S M E E G
A L Y J J S O G M O O O I O I J H R
W I T M M V C K Q C R U P C U E R A
S M B F R S E A I A Q D D U X B L U
A E H S E B X T E N B R T F Y G T K
U P Y L M Y S F U S T D Z W Z X P N
V I V Y H P Q K R M A O Y T Y H V X
J E V Z Y J D N U R D R I J O O A G
V J L H P I K Z H X W F R C F G D X
Q R H F V M A R T H A S T E W A R T
C H R H S O Y A U M S F T M V P M N
```

Mind Lines

Try to get from the top line of categories to the bottom in the fewest moves. Check off each box (or mark initials in the box if playing opponents) after each correct answer to a riddle. Once a player "owns" a box, an opponent must find another path.

Fam - FAMOUS & INFAMOUS
Sci - SCIENCE, SPACE & TECHNOLOGY
Lit - LITERATURE & THE ARTS
Pres - U.S. PRESIDENCY & FIRST LADIES
Pop - POP CULTURE & ENTERTAINMENT
Sprt - THE SPORTING LIFE
F&D - FOOD & DRINK

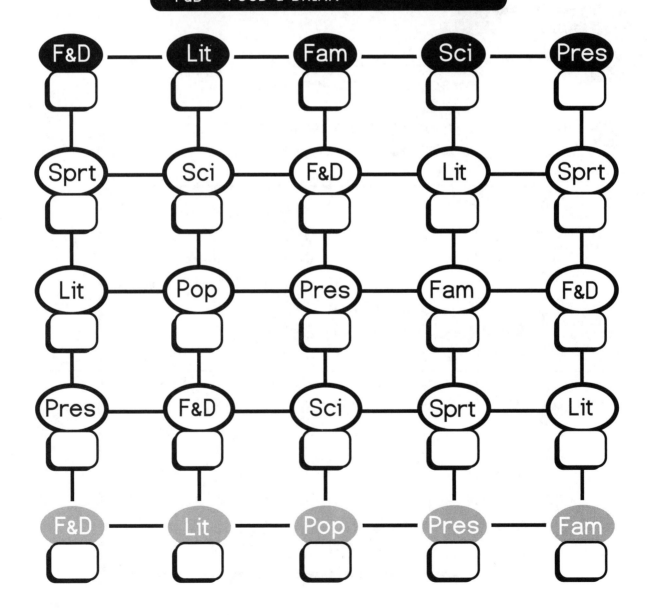

WORD SEARCH
Answer Key

Page 141

1. When **Jimmy Carter** admitted in an interview with *Playboy* that he committed the Biblical sin of adultery (by lusting in his heart), he was admitting to a feeling most people have experienced. But political pundits saw such honesty as foolhardy during a presidential campaign.

2. The Pledge of Allegiance to the U.S. flag was officially recognized by the U.S. government in 1942, and in 1954, at President Eisenhower's urging, Congress legislated that "**under God**" be added to the pledge, upsetting those who favored strict separation of church and state.

3. Prominent chemist, financier, and public administrator Antoine-Laurent Lavoisier coauthored the modern system for naming chemical substances and then was guillotined, in 1794, along with other intellectuals during the **French Revolution**.

4. **Steve Jobs** (1955-2011), cofounder of Apple Computer, was a pioneer of the personal computer revolution. After only six months of full-time college, he dropped out and audited an array of classes, including calligraphy; without the calligraphy class, he said, "the Mac [personal computer] would have never had multiple typefaces."

Page 142

1. Scottish author **J.M. Barrie** (1860-1937) is best known for *Peter Pan,* his tale of the boy who refused to grow up. Barrie possessed a strong childlike quality throughout his life, and he never truly got over the tragedy of the death of his brother when Barrie was just six years old and the devastating effect it had on his mother.

2. Italian painter, sculptor, architect, and engineer **Leonardo da Vinci** epitomized the Italian Renaissance. His *Last Supper* (1495-98) and *Mona Lisa* (*c.* 1503-06) are among the most widely recognized paintings in the world, and his famed notebooks, in which the left-handed artist wrote from right to left, reveal technological ideas that were centuries ahead of their time.

3. In the origin story of **Batman**, which debuted in *Detective Comics* #27 in May 1939, wealthy Bruce Wayne creates Batman as his crime-fighting alter ego after witnessing the murder of his parents on the streets of Gotham City.

4. **Charlie Chaplin** (1889-1977) was a tabloid favorite, making headlines for his pioneering role in the film industry as well as for his attraction to young girls, multiple marriages, and high-profile divorces. He was also, like many in the film industry, a special target of the House Un-American Activities Committee for supposed communist affiliations.

Page 143

1. Polish astronomer **Nicolaus Copernicus** (1473-1543) is the father of the heliocentric (Sun-centered) cosmology of the universe. His proposition that Earth was just one planet among many that revolved around a fixed Sun ran counter to the geocentric (Earth-centered) conception of the heavens long considered sacrosanct by the Church.

2. **Enrico Fermi**, one of the architects of the nuclear age, won the 1938 Nobel Prize for Physics and directed the first controlled chain reaction involving nuclear fission, a breakthrough that led to the production of the atomic bombs dropped on Japan in August 1945, ending World War II.

3. **Frank Sinatra** was one of the most sought-after singers and actors of the 20th century. Throngs of screaming, young female fans in the 1940s, called "bobby-soxers," swooned in his presence. He loved to sing "saloon songs" best, and he was popularly dubbed the "chairman of the board" due to his acclaim.

4. American comedian and writer **Jay Leno**, host of *The Tonight Show* from 1992-2009 and again from 2010-14, is famously recognized by his large chin (anatomically, the "mental" region). In fact, he entitled his 1996 memoir *Leading with My Chin.*

Page 144

1. British ethologist **Jane Goodall**, famous for her extensive research on the chimpanzees of Tanzania, showed that animal behavior was more complex and developed than previously thought. Goodall was made Dame of the British Empire in 2003.

2. A "**blue moon**" is the name for the second full moon in a calendar month. Because one full moon follows another in about 29.5 days, a blue moon is impossible in February. The moon may occasionally appear greenish or blue when there is just the right amount of dust in the air, hence the saying for something rare, "once in a blue moon."

3. **Abigail Adams** was first lady (1797-1801) for John Adams, second U.S. president, and mother of John Quincy Adams, sixth U.S. president. Active in the political debates of her day, she reminded her husband, as he and others worked on the Declaration of Independence, to "remember the ladies and be more generous and favorable to them than your ancestors."

4. **George Washington** fathered no children of his own but did adopt his wife Martha's two children. More famously, he became known as the "Father of His Country" because he commanded the colonial armies in the American Revolution (1775-83) and served as the first president of the United States (1789-97).

Page 145

1. The Steven Spielberg-directed *Jaws* (1975) was the prototypical summer blockbuster, spawning a genre of fast-paced thrillers designed for a summer mass audience. The mechanical shark's enormous jaws, and the film's alternating, two-note "shark theme," which today is synonymous with approaching danger, were two of the most noted features of the film.

2. **Kelsey Grammer**'s acting has encompassed soap operas, Shakespeare, long-running TV series, and voice-acting in cartoons and animated series such as *The Simpsons*. But he is best known for playing Dr. Frasier Crane, a role that began on the TV series *Cheers* in 1984 and continued on *Frasier* until 2004, tying the TV record for the longest-running, prime-time TV character.

3. When President Warren G. Harding grew sick after eating seafood on a tour of the West and then died on Aug. 2, 1923, from a heart attack spurred by his doctor's misdiagnosis and prescription of stimulants, First Lady **Florence Harding** came under suspicion, especially after she destroyed her husband's papers and refused an autopsy.

4. First Lady **Barbara Bush**, wife of President George H.W. Bush and mother of President George W. Bush, wrote two books about her family from the perspective of her dogs: *C. Fred's Story* (1984) and *Millie's Book: As Dictated to Barbara Bush* (1990).

Page 146

1. **Lucille Ball** is best remembered for her classic TV comedy series *I Love Lucy* (1951-57). When questioned in 1953 about the Communist Party voter registration she signed in 1936, Ball said she did so only to placate her socialist grandfather. As her husband Desi Arnaz famously quipped, "The only thing red about Lucy is her hair, and even that's not legitimate."

2. The Academy Award's famed gold-plated, 13.5-inch statuette is officially named the Academy Award of Merit. The origins of its nickname, **Oscar**, have long been debated. Some credit the Academy's librarian, or a columnist, for the moniker, but Bette Davis claimed it derived from her observation that the backside of the statuette looked like that of her husband, Harmon *Oscar* Nelson.

3. **Sue,** the nickname for the most complete and best-preserved skeleton of a Tyrannosaurus rex ever found, was discovered in 1990. For the next ten years, the dinosaur was the subject of an intense custody battle, which ultimately ended in an auction, at which the Field Museum in Chicago bought her for some $8.3 million.

4. Followers of cult-leader **Charles Manson** carried out several vicious murders, including the killing of actress Sharon Tate, wife of film director Roman Polanski, in the late 1960s, inspiring the best-selling book *Helter Skelter* (1974). Manson's cult and followers were called the "Family."

Page 148

1. **Chocolate** contains a chemical compound, theobromine, that can be toxic to dogs. The risk to the animal, like the risk of drug overdose in humans, generally depends on the size of the animal and the level of toxin digested. Milk chocolate, for example, has far less theobromine than unsweetened (baker's) chocolate.

2. One of America's greatest writers and humorists, **Mark Twain** (1835-1910) could muster a witticism on nearly any subject. Having suffered through tragedy so often in his life—bad investments, bankruptcy, and the death of three of his four children along with his wife—he saw "humor [as] the great thing, the saving thing after all."

3. Brazilian football (soccer) star **Pelé** was the most famous and possibly the best-paid athlete in the world during his heyday. He was part of the Brazilian national teams that won World Cup championships in three decades (1958, 1962, and 1970).

4. African American track-and-field star **Jesse Owens** won four gold medals at the 1936 Olympic Games in Berlin, Germany. His victories undercut Adolf Hitler's intention to use the Games to demonstrate Aryan superiority. His world record in the running broad jump (long jump) stood for 25 years.

Page 149

1. **Pasteurization**, the heat treatment that destroys microorganisms in certain foods and beverages, was named after scientist Louis Pasteur, who originated the process. Pasteur's contributions to science, technology, and medicine are unparalleled.

2. **Honey** is a source of the bacteria spores that can lead to botulism. These bacteria are harmless to older kids and adults, whose digestive tracks are more developed, but in infants the bacteria may germinate, multiply, and produce a toxin that could dangerously affect breathing and muscle movement.

3. **Auschwitz**, in southern Poland, was Nazi Germany's largest concentration camp and extermination center. Between 1.1 and 1.5 million people died there, 90 percent of whom were Jews. As the most lethal of the Nazi extermination camps, Auschwitz became synonymous with the Holocaust in general.

4. In the 1860s, Swedish industrialist **Alfred Nobel** invented blasting caps and dynamite, becoming a very wealthy man. It is widely believed that, after a newspaper mistook his brother's death for his and ran an obituary headlined "The Merchant of Death Is Dead," Nobel created his prizes for scholarship and peace to avoid precisely this sort of posthumous reputation.

Page 150

1. In 1985 **Pete Rose** broke Ty Cobb's long-standing record for career hits in baseball. Called "Charlie Hustle" for his fierce competitiveness, Rose soon became better known for the gambling accusations that led to his banishment from the sport in 1989. After years of denying the allegations, Rose finally admitted, in a 2004 autobiography, that he had indeed bet on baseball.

2. **O.J. Simpson** was a Hall of Fame football player and a star of movies and TV (famously running through airports in a car rental commercial), but he will forever be known for the murder charges leveled against him in one of the most celebrated trials in history. Although considered guilty by many in the court of public opinion, he was acquitted of criminal charges in 1995.

3. Theodore Kaczynski (dubbed the **Unabomber** because his first targets worked for *u*niversities and *a*irliners and were victims of *bomb*ings) killed 3 people and wounded 23 others between 1978 and 1995. In a letter to the *New York Times*, he said the attacks would cease if a newspaper published his anti-technology manifesto, and the *Washington Post* did so on September 19, 1995.

4. Gangster **Al Capone** ruled organized crime in Chicago from 1925 to 1931 and is widely considered the mastermind behind the St. Valentine's Day Massacre, at which seven members of the rival Bugs Moran gang were machine-gunned to death in a North-Side garage on Feb. 14, 1929.

Page 151

1. **Michael Jordan** is widely considered the greatest basketball player in the history of the game. He led the Chicago Bulls to six championships (1991-93, 1996-98). In his basketball (professional and Olympic) and brief baseball careers, Jordan wore numbers 9, 12, 35, 45, and, most famously, 23.

2. In 1973, **Secretariat** became the ninth winner of the U.S. horse-racing Triple Crown (the Kentucky Derby, the Preakness Stakes, and Belmont Stakes). He set the record that year for the fastest time at the Derby (1:59.40) and won the Belmont by an unprecedented 31 lengths. In his 16-month career, he won 16 times.

3. Tabloids love to create portmanteaus for celebrity couples: "Tomkat," for Tom Cruise and Katie Holmes; "Billary," for Bill and Hillary Clinton; and **Brangelina**," for Brad Pitt and Angelina Jolie who starred together in the film *Mr. & Mrs. Smith* (2005).

4. **James Bond**—that peerless spy, notorious womanizer, and masculine icon—was the creation of British novelist Ian Fleming, who introduced the character in his 1953 novel *Casino Royale*. Bond is famous, especially in the film franchise spawned by the books, for his high-tech gadgetry and for particular idiosyncrasies, such as repeating his name, "Bond, James Bond."

Page 152

1. George Washington, in his famous **Farewell Address** of 1796, warned the nation to stay clear of political parties and permanent, entangling alliances with other countries. The address laid the foundation for American isolationist foreign policy.

2. **Harry S. Truman** told newspapermen in 1962 that the period in his name should be omitted since the "S" stood for nothing and was merely a compromise between the names of his grandfathers, Anderson Shipp Truman and Solomon Young. The period was often used, nonetheless, in deference to convention.

3. Originating in Punjab, northwest India, **lassi** is a creamy, frothy yogurt-based drink blended with water, fruits, or spices. Most lassi drinks are sweet (blended with curd or fruit or whisked with sugar), salted, or spiced.

4. *Ratatouille*, the 2007 computer-animated film that won the Academy Award for Best Animated Feature, features a rat named Remy who dreams of becoming a world-class chef. The film's name is both a reference to the famed French dish of stewed vegetables, which Remy serves at the end of the film, and a play on words about the rodent.

Page 154

1. Born in Riga, Latvia, in 1948, **Mikhail Baryshnikov** was a ballet star in the Soviet Union when he defected to the West while on tour in Toronto in 1974. He then starred on stage as well as in movies, eventually landing a role in the hit American TV series *Sex in the City*.

2. The illustrated children's books by **Maurice Sendak** are among the most famous ever published. After drawing for comic books and designing window displays for a toy store, Sendak hit his stride illustrating children's books and even writing his own, such as *Where the Wild Things Are* (1963).

3. Mildred "**Babe**" **Didrikson** earned her moniker when someone compared her baseball prowess to that of Babe Ruth's. Called the greatest female American athlete, Didrikson excelled at basketball, baseball, track and field, swimming, figure skating, billiards, and (especially) golf. She won two gold medals and one silver in track and field at the 1932 Olympic Games and was the leading money winner among women golfers from 1948 through 1951, winning three U.S. Opens.

4. The **World Cup** of football (soccer), the most watched and followed sporting event in the world, has been held quadrennially (except during World War II) since 1930. International sectional tournaments lead to a final elimination event, held in one country, for 32 national teams.

Page 155

1. **Shirley Temple** was one of the biggest Hollywood stars of the 1930s, but rumors persisted (especially in Europe) that she really wasn't a child but a little adult. No child, some thought, could speak and dance so well. So they pulled her hair (to see if it was real), checked to see if she had baby teeth, and the Vatican even interviewed her mother.

2. **Joseph Stalin** dictatorially ruled the Soviet Union for a quarter century, until his death in 1953. He, U.S. President Franklin Roosevelt, and British Prime Minister Winston Churchill met at the Yalta Conference in Feb. 1945 to plan for the forthcoming defeat and occupation of Nazi Germany.

3. In six seasons (1935-40), the American racehorse **Seabiscuit** earned $437,730, a record for American Thoroughbreds of the day. His unlikely success (he was undersized, and he won only 5 of his first 35 starts) proved a welcome diversion to millions during the Great Depression. Although certainly not more famous than President Franklin Roosevelt, Seabiscuit nonetheless became a national phenomenon.

4. The **biathlon** is a winter sport combining cross-country skiing with rifle marksmanship. The sport is rooted in Scandinavia's skiing and military traditions. Norwegian and Swedish ski units battled in the Second Northern War (1700–21), and the first recorded biathlon competition took place along the Norway-Sweden border between patrol companies in 1767.

Page 156

1. When U.S. Rep. Leo Ryan of California visited Guyana to investigate the Jonestown commune in Nov. 1978, cult leader **Jim Jones** knew the end was near. Ryan and four others were shot dead as they tried to leave, sparking the Jonestown Massacre of November 18, in which 913 of Jones's followers, including 276 children, died from a lethal drink of cyanide-laced punch.

2. The prophet **Abraham** of the Hebrew Bible, Christian Old Testament, and Islamic Koran is seen as the father of all three major monotheistic religions of the world. Jews and Christians trace their origins to Abraham through his son Isaac, while Muslims connect the Prophet Muhammad to Abraham via his other son Ishmael.

3. Beginning in the 1880s, **Nikola Tesla** famously battled Thomas Edison in the so-called "War of the Currents." The competition pitted Edison's direct current (DC) method of electrical transmission against Tesla's alternating current (AC). Edison's (ultimately futile) campaign against AC was so fervent that his allies even staged public electrocutions of stray animals, ostensibly proving the dangers of AC currents.

4. Zoologist **Dian Fossey** was the world's leading authority on the mountain gorilla when she was murdered, likely by poachers opposed to her work, near her camp in Rwanda on Dec. 26, 1985. Her life was dramatized in the Academy Award-nominated film *Gorillas in the Mist* (1988), which starred Sigourney Weaver as Fossey.

Page 157

1. **John Glenn** was the first U.S. astronaut to orbit Earth, completing three orbits in 1962. When he returned to space as a payload specialist on a nine-day mission aboard the space shuttle *Discovery* in 1998, Glenn, age 77, became the oldest person to enter space.

2. German physicist Wilhelm Röntgen received the first Nobel Prize for Physics in 1901 for his discovery of the **X-ray**, which

revolutionized diagnostic medicine. His first X-ray photographs, in 1895, were of the interiors of metal objects and of the bones in his wife's hand.

3. **John Adams** and Thomas Jefferson both died on July 4, 1826. It was the 50th anniversary of the founding of the country that each man once led as president. As Adams lay dying he uttered, "Thomas Jefferson still lives." Unbeknownst to Adams, Jefferson had died a couple of hours earlier.

4. Critics of First Lady **Nancy Reagan** had long perceived her as snobbish and shallow. They accused her of lavish spending and called attention to her ties to Hollywood stars. After the attempt on her husband's life, she began aligning his schedule in consultation with an astrologer, angering key presidential advisors and attracting even more mockery and vitriol.

Page 158

1. English theoretical physicist **Stephen Hawking** (b. 1942), who is paralyzed due to an incurable degenerative neuromuscular disease, is perhaps the world's most famous scientist. He became famous for his theory about exploding black holes, for making cosmology accessible through popular books, and for his often startling comments and poignant questions on everything from God's existence to Earth's future survival.

2. The Soviet Union shocked the world with its successful launch of the first artificial satellite, **Sputnik** 1, on Oct. 4, 1957. This feat both terrified and outraged the American people and led directly to the founding of the National Aeronautics and Space Administration (NASA) in 1958.

3. **Cognac**, the most famous type of brandy in the world, is named for the town in west-central France that produces it. The age of cognacs is reflected on their labels, such as V.S. (Very Special, two years), V.S.O.P. (Very Special or Superior Old Pale, four years), Napoleon (five years), and older varieties including Extra, XO (Extra Old), and Réserve.

4. The culinary specialty of "**charcuterie**" originated as a way to prepare and preserve meat products before the age of refrigeration (by drying with salt). Today it involves not just classic pork products such as bacon, ham, and sausage ("charcuterie" translates to "pork butcher") but also assorted fat-and-meat mixed creations such as pâtes and terrines.

Page 160

1. On Aug. 2, 1943, **John Kennedy**'s PT-109 ("Patrol Torpedo" boat) was rammed and split apart by a Japanese destroyer. Two of Kennedy's men were killed. Kennedy rallied the survivors and organized their swim to an island three and half miles away. This heroic tale, along with his personal charisma and glamorous wife, all proved useful in his political career.

2. **Herbert Hoover** became famous as the "Great Engineer" who organized food deliveries to impoverished Belgium during World War I and to war-ravaged Europe after the armistice. But his inability to alleviate hunger and joblessness in his own country during the early days of the Great Depression—and his use of military force against needy war veterans camping out near the Capitol—tarnished his administration.

3. Hungarian countess **Elizabeth Báthory** (1560-1614), whose family controlled Transylvania and whose uncle was king of Poland, purportedly tortured and murdered more than 600 young women. Her servants were put on trial for the murders in 1611, and three were executed. Although never tried, Báthory was confined to her

castle chambers and remained there until her death. Some have dubbed her "Countess Dracula."

4. **Thomas More**, King Henry VIII's counselor, was beheaded in 1535 after opposing the English king's decision to break away from the Roman Catholic Church and divorce his wife. For his courage and commitment, More was sainted by the Catholic Church in 1935, and for remaining true to his beliefs amid all circumstances and times he was dubbed "a man for all seasons."

Page 161

1. At 5'4", **James Madison** was the shortest U.S. president. But few Founding Fathers made a bigger contribution to the needs of the new nation. Besides serving two terms as U.S. president (1809-17), he composed most of the U.S. Constitution and all of the Bill of Rights.

2. **Andrew Jackson** was a hero of the War of 1812, the first president to come from the area west of the Appalachians, and the first to gain office by a direct appeal to the masses (called Jacksonian Democracy). The hot-headed Jackson was also fond of dueling. In 1806, he killed a man who had insulted Jackson's wife.

3. Tragedy struck the 1972 Olympics in **Munich**, Germany, when eight Palestinian terrorists invaded the Olympic Village and killed two members of the Israeli team. Nine other Israelis were held hostage as the terrorists bargained for the release of Palestinian prisoners. All of the hostages, five of their captors, and a West German policeman were slain during a failed rescue attempt.

4. **Bocce** is the popular game of Italian bowling. It is played on a long bocce court, or *campo,* enclosed with boarded ends and sides. Four wooden, metal, or composition balls are rolled or tossed, and the closest balls to the target—the smaller *pallino* ball tossed at the start of each match—receive a point.

Page 162

1. Film comedian **W. C. Fields**, star of such shorts as *The Golf Specialist* (1930) and *The Dentist* (1932) and feature films such as *My Little Chickadee* (1940), was noted for his humorously cantankerous persona and fondness, on-screen and off, for alcohol.

2. **Sorbet**, enjoyed as either a dessert or as a palate cleanser in more formal meals, is a churned and frozen mixture of fruit, sugar, and water. The end product is smooth and often brightly colored, with less fat content than many ice cream desserts.

3. The Soviet satellite Sputnik 2, launched on Nov. 3, 1957, carried into space and Earth's orbit the first living creature—a dog named **Laika**. Although the Soviets said the animal died painlessly a week or so into the mission, the truth came out in 2002, when Russian scientists confirmed that Laika had died from overheating and panic mere hours after takeoff.

4. **Gustave Eiffel** was a French civil engineer and bridge builder who will forever be known for the Parisian landmark he built and that bears his name: the Eiffel Tower (1887-89). The structure earned him the nickname "the magician of iron." Less well-known is that he also designed the framework for the Statue of Liberty.

Page 163

1. Anglo-Irish writer Jonathan Swift reportedly uttered this quip about promises and pie **crust**. Swift is best known for *Gulliver's Travels* (1726) and "A Modest Proposal" (1729), the latter a brilliant work of satire, presented as a serious economic treatise, in which Swift

suggested that poverty could be ameliorated by butchering poor children and selling them as food to the wealthy.

2. **Mocha**, a port city on the Red Sea coast of Yemen in southwest Arabia, was the world's foremost outlet of coffee from the 15th-17th centuries. The rich coffee cultivated in Yemen and shipped from Mocha had a distinctive chocolate aftertaste.

3. The American TV series *M*A*S*H*, famous for its biting humor and witty dialogue, ran for 11 seasons (1972-83). The series' last show drew the largest audience in history for a TV series' finale. Although set during the Korean War, *M*A*S*H* began its run during the Vietnam War, and the show's antiwar message was never far from viewers' minds.

4. The popular dance pop duo of "Fab" and "Rob" were better known by their stage name, Milli Vanilli. They won the Grammy Award for Best New Artist of 1989. But when news broke that they were not only **lip-synching** on stage, which many performers do, but also had not sung the vocals on their albums, the group was stripped of their Grammy.

Page 164

1. **Halle Berry** was the first African American to win the Academy Award for Best Actress. She received the honor for her poignant role in *Monster's Ball* (2001). She later played a Bond girl in *Die Another Day* (2002) and the star of the Batman spin-off *Catwoman* (2004), among other roles.

2. The *Tonight Show* has long been a cornerstone of late-night American television. The show has had two main locations—New York City and the Los Angeles metro area—and six principal hosts: Steve Allen (1954–57), Jack Paar (1957–62), Johnny Carson (1962–92), Jay Leno (1992–2009, 2010–14), Conan O'Brien (2009–10), and Jimmy Fallon (2014–).

3. **Thomas Jefferson** died on July 4, 1826, the 50th anniversary of the country he once led. His last conscious words were, "Is it the Fourth?" Remarkably, dying on the same day was his old rival and compatriot, John Adams, whose last words were, "Thomas Jefferson still lives."

4. **Grover Cleveland**, the 22nd and 24th president (1885-89, 1893-97), was the only chief executive to serve two discontinuous terms. Although widely respected as one of the few principled politicians during the Gilded Age, his refusal to use government to help the public during the depression of the 1890s, and his siding with management against workers in the Pullman Strike, eroded support for him.

Page 166

1. British singer-songwriter **Amy Winehouse** won rave reviews with her critically acclaimed debut album, *Frank* (2003). Her smoky, evocative vocals drew comparisons to jazz and rhythm-and-blues legends Sarah Vaughan, Dinah Washington, and Billie Holiday. Tragically, her signature song, the Grammy Award-winning "Rehab," in which she announces her refusal to return to rehab, foreshadowed her end. She died from alcohol poisoning in 2011.

2. **Dick Clark**, often called the "world's oldest teenager," introduced rock-and-roll to millions of Americans as host (1956-89) of the popular TV show *American Bandstand*. He also hosted numerous TV games shows over a 40-year period, and he was the producer and longtime host of the annual *New Year's Rockin' Eve* from New York's Times Square.

3. In 1989-90, **Aileen Wuornos** killed at least seven male motorists while posing as a hitchhiking prostitute. Her case became a cause célèbre after she claimed she killed the men in self-defense, bringing feminist activists to her side. She later admitted to killing for rank profit. Charlize Theron's portrayal of Wuornos in *Monster* (2003) earned her the Academy Award for Best Actress.

4. Famed aviator, tycoon, and film producer **Howard Hughes** took extreme precautions to ensure privacy. A germaphobe with an obsessive-compulsive disorder, he would hole up in a luxury hotel and go for days without sleep, unkempt and often naked, in a black-curtained room. He became emaciated from the effects of a meager diet, his inattention to his health, and from an excess of drugs. He died in 1976.

Page 167

1. The Pythagorean theorem, concerning the three sides of a right triangle, is one of the most famous in all mathematics. It states that the square of the **hypotenuse** (the side opposite the right angle that is usually labeled "c") is equal to the sum of the squares of the other two sides (labeled "a" and "b").

2. Just 73 seconds after liftoff on Jan. 28, 1986, the space shuttle *Challenger* exploded, killing all seven crew members, including schoolteacher Christa McAuliffe. It was later determined that a rubber **O-ring,** which had hardened due to the cold weather before launch, had allowed high-temperature gas to escape from a joint in the right solid rocket booster, causing the explosion.

3. By tradition, a new president's term began on March 4— **Inauguration Day**. This was the date of George Washington's second inaugural and the day that he peacefully transferred power to the next president, John Adams. To shorten the "lame duck" period between a new president's election in November and the beginning of his term, the 20th Amendment (1933) moved Inauguration Day to Jan. 20.

4. In 1953, R. **Sargent Shriver** married Joseph Kennedy's daughter Eunice. In 1961, Shriver was appointed by his brother-in-law, President John Kennedy, to serve as the first director of a new agency of volunteers called the Peace Corps. By 2011, more than 200,000 Peace Corps volunteers had served in some 140 developing nations.

Page 168

1. Of all the athletic contests held throughout ancient Greece, the Olympic Games were the most famous. Held in Olympia every four years between August 6 and September 19, they were so important that in late antiquity historians even measured time by the interval between them—an **Olympiad**.

2. A **mulligan** is an unpenalized "do-over" stroke in golf. Although illegal in competitive and professional golf, it is commonly employed during friendly rounds of golf among friends and at charity events, where mulligans may be sold as an additional way of raising money. The term evolved in the 1920s or '30s.

3. **Skin** is the largest organ in the human body, and it continues to grow all the time. On an average adult, skin encompasses a surface area of more than 20 square feet. The second largest human organ is also the largest *internal* organ: the liver.

4. **Mercury** is the smallest and innermost (closest to the Sun) of the eight planets of the solar system. Because it has nearly no atmosphere to capture heat, it also experiences the widest range of temperatures, from nearly -300° F at night to 800° F during the day.

1. When Harry Truman assumed the presidency upon the sudden death of Franklin Roosevelt on April 12, 1945, he told reporters that he felt as if "the moon, the stars, and all the planets had fallen" on him and asked them to pray for him. A sign on his desk read, "**The Buck Stops Here.**"

2. **Warren Harding** won the presidency with his charm, good looks, and promise to return the country to "normalcy" in the wake of World War I. His brief administration (1921-23; he died during his third year in office) accomplished little, and soon after his death a series of scandals doomed the Harding presidency to be judged among the worst in American history.

3. After graduating in 1961 from the Carnegie Institute of Technology in Pittsburgh, **George Romero** filmed short segments for *Mr. Rogers' Neighborhood*, a TV series produced in Pittsburgh. In 1968, he directed the cult horror classic *Night of the Living Dead.* His production was unique: he disassociated his monsters from Vodou zombies and used contemporary settings (rural Pennsylvania), thereby establishing the pattern for modern zombie movies.

4. The film *Blackboard Jungle* (1955) dramatized violence in urban schools. The film resonated with the restless teens of the day, and fights and riots broke out in theaters showing the film. It was also the first major film to feature rock music on its sound track, and its hit song, "**Rock Around the Clock**" by Bill Haley and His Comets, helped spark the rock-and-roll revolution.

1. Many observers assumed that Tiger Woods was the golfer who would inevitably break **Jack Nicklaus**'s imposing record of 18 victories in the four major tournaments. But then Woods suddenly left competitive golf in 2009 amid a media frenzy sparked by news of his extramarital affairs. His game, hindered also by several injuries, never fully recovered, leaving Nicklaus's record secure for now.

2. Wanting to quell any notion that America's "national pastime" derived from the English game of rounders, a 1907 commission headed by sporting goods magnate A.G. Spalding erroneously concluded that **Abner Doubleday** invented baseball at Cooperstown, New York, in 1839. Doubleday was a commander at Fort Sumter in South Carolina on the day the Civil War began.

3. Champagne is the name of the most famous sparkling wine and of the French region where it is made. French Benedictine monk and cellar master **Dom Perignon** (1638-1715) of the Abbey of Hautvillers, overlooking Epernay in the region of Champagne, is known as the "Father of Champagne" for his contributions to the wine-making process.

4. Voltaire (1694-1778) was one of the most influential of all French writers and intellectuals. His life was rich and varied. Besides discoursing on the virtues of **ice cream**, he once quarreled with a member of a prominent French family who had made fun of his name and was then beaten, imprisoned, and exiled to England.

1. Singer, dancer, musician, comedian, and actor **Sammy Davis, Jr.**, was one of the most versatile of American performers. He began in vaudeville at age three, studied tap dancing under Bill ("Bojangles") Robinson, and performed in such films, with his "Rat Pack" brothers, as *Ocean's Eleven* (1960). He was one of the first African American stars to achieve wide popularity.

2. Few film directors and producers have enjoyed more popularity and critical success than the Oscar-winning **Steven Spielberg**, whose diverse films range from thrillers (*Jaws*, 1975; *Raiders of the Lost Ark*, 1981) and science fiction (*Close Encounters of the Third Kind*, 1977; *E.T.: the Extra-Terrestrial*, 1982) to historical dramas (*Saving Private Ryan*, 1998; *Lincoln*, 2012).

3. **Margaret Wise Brown** was a highly prolific author and one of the most successful writers of children's stories. Her books number more than 100, including such classics as *The Runaway Bunny* (1942), *Goodnight Moon* (1947), and (posthumously) *The Big Red Barn* (1956).

4. **Scott Joplin** was the "King of Ragtime," famous for such works as "The Entertainer" and "The Maple Leaf Rag." Although he died a forgotten man in a mental institution in 1917, his work was revived worldwide when used in the Academy Award-winning score to the film *The Sting* (1973).

1. Actress **Jayne Mansfield** died on June 29, 1967, when the car she was riding in hit and slid under a tractor-trailer, nearly decapitating her; surviving the accident was her daughter Mariska Hargitay, future star of *Law and Order*. The gruesome death spurred widespread use of the low safety guards now routinely seen on the back of trucks, commonly called "Mansfield Bars."

2. **Mae West** was an early film sex symbol whose frank sensuality, suggestive postures, and blasé wisecracking became her trademarks. She costarred with W.C. Fields in the comic western *My Little Chickadee* (1940). During World War II, Allied soldiers called their inflatable life jackets "Mae Wests" in honor of her voluptuousness.

3. The **Fujita Scale**, named after the meteorologist Theodore Fujita who developed it in 1971, classifies tornado intensity based on damage to structures and vegetation. The scale was revised in 2004 into the so-called Enhanced Fujita Scale, which offers more precision in rating tornadoes and their power.

4. About 270 million years ago, a single "supercontinent" called **Pangea** (from a Greek word meaning "all the Earth") was formed. It began to break apart 200 million years ago into the seven continents that we know today. Current plate motions are bringing the continents together once again, and at some point in the future another Pangea will form.

1. "When I Was One-and-Twenty," published in *A Shropshire Lad* by **A.E. Housman** in 1896, is one of the most famous poems in English literature. It deals with the cocksureness of youth and with unrequited love.

2. **Robert Frost**, one of America's most revered poets, won the Pulitzer Prize for poetry four times between 1924 and 1943. He was famous for his depictions of New England life and for such poems as "Stopping by Woods on a Snowy Evening," in which the traveler has "miles to go before I sleep."

3. **Spam**, canned spiced ham produced by the Hormel Company, became internationally famous during World War II. Hormel sent Spam and related canned meats not only to American soldiers overseas but to the armies of Allied countries, including Russia, where the meat was dubbed "Roosevelt sausage."

4. Invented in China, the **wok** is a thin-walled cooking pan that is shaped like a shallow bowl with handles. Because the wok has a round bottom that concentrates heat, food may be moved up the

pan's sloping side to stay warm without cooking further, while other food can continue to cook at the bottom.

Page 174

1. *Madama Butterfly* by Giacomo Puccini is among the most beloved operas of all time. Set in modern-day Nagasaki (the opera premiered in 1904), it's the tale of an American naval officer who marries a Japanese girl in a ceremony that he views as a farce. He returns home and marries a "real wife," leaving Butterfly to wait years, with the son she bore, for his return.

2. Many believe the modern **tango** evolved about 1880 in the brothels of Buenos Aires, Argentina. Others say it was simply in the brothels that the dance or music was first widely encountered before becoming socially acceptable in the early 1900s. In either case, by 1915, the dance style had spread and become all the rage in fashionable European circles.

3. Part of the classified information released by National Security Agency contractor Edward Snowden in 2013 was the revelation that the United States had been spying on friendly allies, such as France, Germany, Mexico, and Spain, and even tapping their leader's personal cell phone conversations. **Barack Obama** acknowledged the spying but denied approving it.

4. The famed pledge by **George H.W. Bush** that helped him win the presidency in 1988—"Read my lips: no new taxes"—later haunted him after he indeed raised taxes in 1990. Thrown back at him by his chief opponent, Bill Clinton, the infamous one-liner helped doom Bush's bid for reelection in 1992.

Page 175

1. "It's our game," exclaimed American poet **Walt Whitman** about baseball. It's "America's game," for it "has the snap, go, fling of the American atmosphere—belongs as much to our institutions, fits into them as significantly, as our constitutions, laws: is just as important in the sum total of our historic life. It is the place where memory gathers."

2. **Vince Lombardi**, as head coach of the previously moribund Green Bay Packers, led the football team to greatness. In nine seasons with Lombardi as their coach (1959-67), the Packers won five national championships and the first two Super Bowls. An inspirational speaker whose aphorisms are often quoted, he became a national symbol of single-minded determination to win.

3. The singer, dancer, and songwriter **Michael Jackson** reigned worldwide as the "King of Pop." He had unparalleled influence on the entertainment industry for four decades despite his eccentric personal life, his drastic cosmetic surgeries, and the charges of pedophilia that long shadowed him. In 2009, he died accidently from a doctor-injected sleep aid.

4. Steve Rogers, **Captain America**'s alter-ego, was a would-be enlistee rejected by the U.S. Army who volunteered to receive a top-secret serum that transformed him into a "super soldier." Dubbed "Captain America" and clad in a red, white, and blue costume, he debuted in *Captain America Comics* No. 1 in March 1941.

Page 176

1. **Hattie McDaniel** was the first African American to be nominated for, and to win, an Academy Award. For her role as Mammie in *Gone with the Wind* (1939), she won the Oscar for Best Supporting Actress. At the film's premiere in Atlanta, Georgia, on Dec. 15, 1939, she was not allowed to sit with the white stars of the film, such as Clark Gable.

2. On Halloween night, 1938, Orson Welles and his radio team of Mercury Players performed H.G. Wells's The *War of the Worlds*—about a Martian invasion—as a simulated news broadcast. Although reports of mass panic were exaggerated, many listeners were fooled into thinking the invasion was real. The national coverage of the incident led to a Hollywood movie contract for Welles.

3. **Throat-singing** may be one of the oldest forms of music. In this guttural vocalization, a singer can produce two or more notes simultaneously and can even create harmonies. It is practiced by the indigenous tribes of Siberia and Mongolia and by the native peoples of Canada and South Africa.

4. In Ray Bradbury's dystopian novel *Fahrenheit 451* (1953), **books** are banned and burned in keeping with the government's intolerance of dissent. The title refers to the temperature at which paper burns.

Page 177

1. Norwegian army officer **Vidkun Quisling** infamously collaborated with Nazi Germany in its occupation of his country during World War II, transforming his name into a synonym for "traitor." Responsible for sending some 1,000 Jews to their deaths in concentration camps, he was arrested, tried, and executed after the war in 1945.

2. On the "Ides of March" (March 15), 44 BC, ruler **Julius Caesar** was stabbed 23 times in the Senate House of Rome. He was killed by nobles who feared his growing power. As dramatized by Shakespeare, the Roman leader's final words were, "*Et tu, Brute?*" ("And you, Brutus?"), a reproach to his trusted friend who had joined the assassins.

3. **Martha Stewart,** a former fashion model, turned her acumen for cooking and decorating into a media empire. When her company, Martha Stewart Living Omnimedia, went public in 1999, her personal wealth topped $1 billion. She was then convicted, in 2004, of obstructing justice during the investigation of an insider-investment deal. She served five months in prison and five months of house arrest.

4. The sweet and tart **Key Lime pie** reportedly originated in Key West, Florida, in the late 19th century. One of its essential ingredients, sweetened condensed milk, was probably used because fresh milk and refrigeration were rare in the isolated Keys until the 1930s. It was named the official pie of Florida in 2006.

Page 141

```
H Y B J T B N J Q Y J O G K Y F X N
Y H S H T G K L L R Q F Q D E X K K
G S F R E N C H R E V O L U T I O N
W P R Z I H Q J A E U D O F U N C S
I P C H D W Q L I T Q R M N Q G U T
Y Y J F R B B W Q M M D D E R G X E
F I P Y W B F Q F H M E R W L T W V
M N X U Y S L S V R R Y R K U B I E
E U E U Y L U J A G B V C U J O K J
N Q E Z P E B A O N N H P A W T I O
I L J C I I C D L B O H B O R H V B
P N E E Y E L Q L P Z H C Q Z T T S
K T Q K P R C T I C M S I U B T E D
E V F H O B P N F D T S F T G R E R
I T K B R H J B C R S V U T M V A K
```

Page 142

```
U Y G T J L J I T R W J Z S C L C E
O P U Z J E P V Q M W V I H K Y O H
E Y Y U J O E I R Q D K A P E U A I
G D U D N N K G O N H R D K B H R N
H H I K H A Y T N V L F M I Q C P J
L I M E W R M G P I E I R R A B M J
L V G Z N D A T E I V X L Q F Q H D
W W X Q H O F C A J E K I A T G B Z
I N V U R D H D K B S M H O N X C C
B T S Q O A X Z B L D F T Y U S Y G
B M R B P V U O I Y X U R E I L S A
B D K L C I O H L V N P U S X T W W
X E I B O N L Z B Q K Q U Z U O Q U
D N G R W C V S K Q I O Z I W K N C
L T W M F I H R J R V Q H C K W L T
```

Page 143

```
K M I T B A W Q S F M O X X B S F M
K E M V C B B L J Z I Y H O J E L J
R R R A Q Z I C L G E B N K D A J B
S J E H R L D G H Y P E E N G W M F
S Z F P R T G B Y V L B K I O T N P
G L O X M X A L A Y U K B O U J I P
L N C R L C V N A Y M A O I H U P X
S Y I A T D G J I I N I J K C Y P J
Y B R Y W L U V I S H X X A M R E G
H A N R K X J G A Y K E T V A N S Y
G V E I G M Z X R F W N C V W R Q J
S U C I N R E P O C S U A L O C I N
W J E I U Y Y U J W A E E R O K E R
D Z R K S H S I H O W N R C F Y M L
Z T A F L W U D V P U P B N W Z U W
```

Page 144

```
W W L J A S M V I H I D H B J C E C
X G X X R B L X X U Y O H O E F G V
E B Z B T D I W C S H R T A E R A F
Y C N E R X O G J Q B I B G N B M B
Y G E O R G E W A S H I N G T O N S
C J D F K P Z B N I C U H V E Z X R
V M J M S R L O E N L V O M B S K R
X R C K M U P W G W X A N S Y U V Z
Q V U K E I N B O M W I D B D V L H
P Q Q M Y L A T O N F A H A R L X E
W H O D G Z R W D O H Q E T M E V Y
F O E B K U K C A A L N J S S S N D
N L K P H M T H L J E R A F A A X C
Q E J D H O A S L Y B Y K F H S M C
K C W F C W F K U C U I K V Q L U H
```

Page 145

```
L X H P E Z F I D U G K A R Q T W G
O O X H Z F D W D B T E E J L O P N
D F P W R C H H T K B M Y W A C B I
O R Y O C W J Y H C M B Q H G W H D
G S U X Q B B L A A T M M B F K S R
Q K A I Y A B A R B A R A B U S H A
N F X V X N X G W E E T R G U U V H
T M L N C J Y A N G W N Y Y P C W E
R C I R N E K T G W R Y Y Y I N E C
M C V O S O Y B V S N G A S R D P N
C X N L U W T Q Y P L J G J O W D E
H I E E B G R X C H T J G T H U O E R
S K R T Y S W X I Y D V I V M N O O
W A S J O I R N J B W T I P M H S L
W Y S M F M I Z C Y F Z H M O Y M F
```

Page 146

```
V T X R L N N N M M H G A M H J C M
G D Y F L L O P K W O N V V P M J N
F T T D A X I S V X J V G X Q E X E
P O B T B Z U J N T J U H U T W P M
U D S U E V T O A A N Q M R A I B P
P O P A L Q B B K L M Q M Q H J S J
V U M I L F U J V W Q S N P A G N C
G A L Q I U H J N J U X E W G F B O
Y Z C X C N Q Y L G G Q I L V Q V J
J T F M U M I A V J W D J L R Y V N
E E N C L H S H M Y W H C R Y A Z P
I B Z B E A Y C Y Z M U A U Z Q H I
L O X V T T Y F F B G C Z Z W H L C
W E U X Z G U C K C S O H G U B S E
B V F W N Q H V K O A Z U W A S M U
```

Page 148

```
U S N X O Q F S Q U R G U F B G Y S
Q V H D J F W X S M E H X X I L N Q
K J F R T M N V Y V A O R K P E M P
O O R W I Z O F Z W C R N G W S Z D
E I Z P M D P G W N L P K O H X S O
R S J N Q V G L T S M Z E T W H P M
F N C H O C O L A T E S L B W J R U
N U W V A P R D P J S P N K U A G L
G S M Y H E I R Y E R B E D T B I X
P S Q Y L L X W J L D T F S O A J N
Y K O W T E C S M E V V Z C G A H R
B R K R D M K A R O W S J F N J S Q
U O Z F A R S A S L Y F Q A K O C A
Z Y B H K J G A D R E I H D N C J K
G U S T O N P W P J M I U O W Z X C
```

Page 149

```
H W F L E B O N D E R F L A Y U A P
S N L Z T V Y E J R D N H E I O A P
D T C A R G E H A P W D Z V I S C X
N K L D I R N A E Z O N Y P T Y E T
O M Z A E A O O O T Z V Z E V K I Q
Y Q J Z J G H D E E Q Z U T J H B K
S U Z T T G S T U I N R I V J X Y B
I L Y Z C I U V K O I A D A L M C T
Q K F S V V W W K Z J M V O F C F L
N E N H Q M Z H A Z P Q M L I I R C
V O C I F Q E T C R Y Z S I H N M B
U I D E V I I O F S P K X B L T L Z
A J J M R O V O B K U Q H C B J N G
A S F U N L Y C S S N A Z C P L A H
N U V L E P E D I S D P O X I W Y Z
```

Page 150

```
P N X E T Z G S S E E U S B V C N O
O G P N D Y V J S X N S L Z M I J S
X G D O R L C C Z G Z U O X Y S O Y
G S A P D B W Q G F S Q S R I Y O W
D O L A P N N V J H X L H M E U Y A
B D A C Y Y S E S D D A P R Z T T T
H U A L M A W Q G U G S H O Q W E B
J V G A D B P H T B O G O H U W T P
C H L D T O L G D N T Y I J I S X E
N X A K O B N R Y R E B M O B A N U
C A X C U K W X F O N M X D E L M J
V Y Y C C Y P I Z J G Y G U A K P F
G X G S J F O Q F M F Q D E P L X R
M J D K F J B D O E I V I O C W J Q
Y T J E I W S Z B W N H B K P M P N
```

Page 151

```
G B A C Z R G K W A E W Q C W M H S
Q P T N T R Z X M U Z H O U I L P G
M L A J I N X K W T R N S C O J A O
Y W X H C L R R C X B G H C R Y H Q
X N Z A D T E R K P U A I M A Z L I
V W U D N Z A G V O E B C Z G P Y X
Q C R B O I N T N L K D Y L M D M Y
N A X A B G C Y J A T Z J G X G F K
N E M O S O D O F J R I X Q M R V N
F V Y W E Y R C Z R X B Y U N H R G
V R Q G M D W N H V H Y F N Q E F U
E D B M A O K T A I R A T E R C E S
Z J Z N J G D E X Q B L M B O Y X V
W W Z H N W W B B B N P A N I G L U
B E H K R H C W J J U B I R X R Y H
```

Page 152

```
Z F O F A I T G W A J J P C P F H O
W N Q R A R Y N Y T S V U E F Z A H
A E O R M R D A C Z U V V L B R E
C T S F O L E F R B X D B D B A R O
O W D H Z G W W D Q P X W O T E Y W
Q Q B G W L V G E C M M U A G K S R
N U D L E C P D V L G J T N A C T K
P Y Z S E Z W O Q V L O Z R C W R A
M G V U I P X K S E U A U G E L U I
Y X V G O W G G M I Q D D O X W M Y
A B G K K T C M L P G J L D Z Z A U
H F I I S S A L W K E Z X W R O N K
Z J X I X L E S M N N K K W J E O V
P U R L F E G P I R X X L C D S S T
M W B D W M J Z J V G X C W A L Y S
```

Page 154

```
E W I L A W S D T W G C Q J B H A O
B A V M W J K U Z M E K N D E P M P
J A G Z R Q A A L Y R V A U M S T L
Z K B N I G Y M K K X C A G A R B M
C D L E G Z P L M G X P T K U O Z L
T C B V D D L T K E W K S J R T Z G
M I K H A I L B A R Y S H N I K O V
Z T K S F G D U Q L S W Y K C S I X
B H O D V Y Y R R J S X W E Q C D
F R S M O R A P I R U D E P S F X R
S E Z U T C Z K L K N P L X E H C H
M Q T K K M T D M L S I G K N P W Y
W J J U K B C H J R S O W D N F A
L J B Z L U Y E E C G J N Z A D M F
I L Z Q P A Q Q C J E C Z F K B J E
```

Page 155

```
Q M S N P Z W K G H H L L C L Z J J
N V H A G Z E C V S O V U F M G O D
F I I K W C Q U B Y N J Z N D S A J
W G R J K R Q H E O D O I J E T C H
V N L Z Q R N O T R X I L P O D Q L
F W E R T A I J V P W S H H A J T H
P Z Y G S R Y E Q P L S E R T N I A
R D T K Z W X D D A T Y F P Q A D O
R K E J V G K J E A V S Z R D B I I
Z A M F Z Z S E L H G R V K I E V B
P O P X C D U I X Y Z V Q B T O L U
C U L Y W R N G U A V I D X T M P G
H U E K I T F N T I U C S I B A E S
P A R K A B Y M U H V P M L L Y M V
Q G J R H G C B Y A C D V C V P K W
```

Page 156

```
J W X E Q W D C C Z S N M G X E V J
K G D W J Q K U D H I E V S G R S N
G N E N L Y J E J K G K N G Z B Q R
A N E M V H W G O O O N E O B P W L
L K O Y M L D L W R N V L T J C A U
Z I C W G R A Z D O U T L W R M A M
G O S T Z T Y E S S O F N A I D I A
G A Q A E U L R N M M K Y L E Z D J
L L H S Z Z M E Y A Y K B D Q H C V
G C L U A A A I C H M V L C S S H S
Z A A D Z K M T U A A V P Q Y T U Y
Q Y T X X F X T C R A A A G X H M D
S V I C A Z U B X B I C M Q C Y K L
H C B J R J M S L A T N I A V J S H
I X K M Q O F V M J Y Z O Y G E U A
```

Page 157

```
B K S G I F A T O J N S Q A E W Y V
M T M G P G U J F X A C J M Y A Q S
V N S Y J O M Z R R N E Q I J A A U
C G E P J W B X Y B C Q S J S A R J
V J I T T R D Y R W Y C O X G B O X
W F L M G X Q V Q Z R M W Z L H U N
D M V L W R J U F V E O N S N E A W
D R E A V O D W I S A Q B G X S G V
H P P G W W A C Z B G W L T K M T X
F B E B N A C N X N A E N J K G Y Z
D G D V J M Z O L E N I Y B M E O G
I K T V P W W L B N J D J G U I W Q
H N M D A D N C V S M A D A N H O J
R O Z N X V Q P Z X B J H Z E M A
Q H S Z S J M F V N H F I R I X E F
```

Page 158

```
X Q J N R P Z I M L X N M W Y Y S G
J Q W S O Z P X I E K R N F O B N K
A C C B E A S H E S Z I X Y G I W N
Y L O E F I G P B K S U A V K T N A
T N K X I R P U G G Y S W U F Z H
B W E K M J T L V T W G A U S M E A
U Z B C Z C G E N H N H P C B J A G
I F J O F W I A Z Y N I N S T F S K
Q B I G K E M D S E S J K V U W K Z
N T U N I W F C H A R C U T E R I E
E A R A O S S P D J U Q V F R O V T
G K M C J S E Y G X Q Z Q Q M D I V
Z Y G V F T Q P C C C U H U P F E R
O U I V S T P G P N B B M O W G J C
G W A G D B T J U T V P C K S O J V
```

Page 160

```
E R O M S A M O H T V I J V N S P R
U E R K E S P N P H C O H X Z X X W
R S P H X D K M S O E S I M M D J Y
E O L Q E J C S Y S D H X F G M U A
R N J Z L R Y T S M N F K W B Y E Q
W G O Y T J B Y I B U L D Y I D N F
A S H K O Y X E K K B V B P S V P J
O E N N N F F Y R C W T E V U J Z U
K D K V M G S F G T M M P Q S V C M
X M E L I Z A B E T H B A T H O R Y
E F N B H T G X P X V O Q C R A O J
L K N G M S Y P H F O V O Q B U J J
Z P E R S C O X W S U K N V V Z J X
V U D K J H J Y F Z R C X L E M I K
R E Y M M V J F F G H N G W W R V C
```

Page 161

```
Z O V D D V J A M E S M A D I S O N
P K Q O D M F A B M V O X V R B O E
H G B N G H Q V I H U A N T A S U D
Q Y B Z S G Y M K P K N V C K S C R
N M I T H D S L J B U L I C H N D T
K M U I K K F L G L G U A C Q L O N
Y P Z R L J B K W D B J F T H M M Q
Q E B K G X J M S U W E H C F A Z V
T C O Y M X K P C E L F Y L B U X N
L G C O R K C R R K R E C X H H G Z
U V C T K S N D F Y P B E C G H O K
G F E F H F N C N P Z B J Y P X O F
Q C K B Z A B S L F X Q Y L O D M
S C D E R K M F J D T V O N A I C X
P Y F P I V Q B Q Y J N N B W Q K I
```

Page 162

```
I Q W E L E G B M G P T J R Z X Q T
W N X N Q Y A S L U R L Y I V C V X
L X P U G R S A R S L Q W W I Y U F
C U K P Y R R Z H T U T C N A X K O
G K A Z K P W M E A A F K D V S L P
Y P B P Q U N Z F V I X G R N I L I
V Q P X S F O R C E D U E W Z Q X F
K X L G E C G U L E C E T E B R O S
L L K K U J A D A I D K A N Z A H D
L K W Q H O S B E F M D Q F H F V U
S W N K O V A Q W F O Q V P D S H T
Z O Z I O M N K K E N J Y R K G S V
D R X A I R I B I L B W G L D E F O
F P B S H H A B L A N C N Y W S R R
Z U E T E A R F A F L F N K T K F O
```

Page 163

```
J L K I M T R V B Q N W R W O C I A
K I I H E C V D C J W U T Y O R R F
V L V P J E Y I E Y P U Q B V U F H
N J A N S T O P E C S M G U H S A M
L D P T R Y R U L L L V J M A T I M
X O K T B D N Z Z S I E A Z G Q O X
G R O J F C R C W Z A V H L H C C O
R E X S H T F Y H H N D F H H Q Y I
C N X E D J T P F I C V A A M S Z O
U F T M M I R R Y J N Q W J N U M I
E L V F Y Q H A U S M G S N O G O A
E A D Z K D U C R W N J J N C Q E K
P R G X A Q C M H A K B I E V O O M
J X T V B N N A N D L U K I K V Y P
P J B R L S F C T S K X M X H K V H
```

Page 164

```
G N T W U M G A J A C J Z B V D B H
M R P E L U Q F J S O V Y M W H A T
Q M O E H S N K N V I L P W T L V O
Y Q W V L H K Q N U O O W P L F H T
S M R T E G U T S J F M S E C V C Q
O N N O F R L V J Y T N B X N Z A X
W U J N Q K C I P G N E N Z I T A B
Z E K I X I D L J M R O P Q I B S W
M T Q G F Z Q Q E R A W A S V W B W
U H H H C U C Q Y V F T C O X H M Y
V V T T H O M A S J E F F E R S O N
L X T S N K S Q H V A L E M P R Y A
K F K H V R Z O T H C A A A G E N S
E I S O D E O D M I H F P N Z I B F
H T J W N V H A Y E N T I H D U H H
```

Page 166

```
Q H M O J K P P R U A X H V Y L J A
S O Z Z N S L R L Q B E D G O K R F
K W I R K Z L B C G T I S C D T W T
R A O E R T X C A T C D Z R E N C L
K R M U M F L P V K B A I E Y N B I
G D E Y A E V T C I D I B Z L P Q Q
K H B R W A I L E E N W U O R N O S
D U B Y K I A Y H W M Y W U F J J Y
X G W T M R N J X B J D E Z Z K U S
J H E B K B M E A W N V L U X T Y
U E R Q Z I F G H O F P J U I K L M
F S O O X I N I D O F X V U I B H H
G M S J V P R T U S U E Z G N G V C
A I A C B B Z R J E J S U D P U C R
V F D I X A W M S B L Y E N Y U C Y
```

Page 167

```
S Y Z R R I O G E Z O S Z F L D N L
M Y F E E N I B F Y S N O O C R R
F K M Q H I V F R P K B N K M O S F
R T I N R X I I N J A M F K Z A M G
P Y N O P A K E R V J S S B X A B P
L F U M X G G S Q H L T L T D X M V
S U T P R F A U G Q S Z P T X Z Z H
P C Y C D C M S P J T M S H J P O
X O Q B H Y R E R Y V U N K E B A C
N P M H I B Q T I P Z U N E S R B D
W G J Z F J K O S J K R C C G L F W
C I D X B C T P U S J T N S J R J L
U M I D A T U Y L V V D G Y S Z A X
W N Y S B K M H L M Q A U Q W O O S
Y R O Y A D N O I T A R U G U A N I
```

Page 168

```
Y I I F I V I Z M L S G S Y F R H D
Z P T B Y E B O G E E B Q D R P A I
Y K Y F W Q N N N E R X P O C I L V
H W W B I J W Z Z V R C P M P V S W
H P T Z E S Y Y K Q Q Q U M T Z O R
D C U I S H V P R J X D Y R N F Z H
F F E J Y H K T H D J L G N Y Z Z I
L I B F H T B C R Z O I C V M T S Q
W A Q Z V T C C N G A P C Q W I A T
F Y W B J R L U C M H M S D E F H B
Q S D O K Q S O G H M U L L I G A N
N K J B A G D A N G A E L D J V E E
D I V A R X E V E L Y M K J Z Y B S
G N L L D Q L P S A X L X B P W N U
E P I I O S H R U O D I F Z R P R D
```

Page 169

```
J W P U M Q H A F F Q B P D S Z C U
F A O B J C F K U N A D R F A M L A
O R M O C Y J W H E J I R U U V J Z
Q R T J R H Z K O Y T H Q J X V L U
D E I N X L O R E M O R E G R O E G
A N K C V K S D J L H P U O G T P H
B H C A U R A Y M X R E F F M O E E
X A R N O C Z Y W A X P Q V K S R W
P R T H E B U C K S T O P S H E R E
C D N S Q E F G D W V L A B K B Z H
J I H O P D C O E Q H L R F Z P R K
I N G T T D U F S T K C O G T P E E
M G A J D H C X M M W M A G M G I T
K C O L C E H T D N U O R A K C O R
H L O N P K Q O Y P O C Z P W Y N B
```

Page 170

```
L A I M S U J F K B G A Z A E W J Y
I R C G Y P W D B R W C K Y M M A M
L T E U O I N G O X N H T L D B M
L I C Z R C C T J M P H K U E G S I
H I R P R J E Q R E P J A L I L W Q
K R E B B V G L R Z G E B R S Y H S
O L A B N X E F V K I U R Y B U E E
E N M L F T I E S N O P Z I N H C T
C E H T G U N T Z D B R S L G T Q D
N D W J D Y O B R E D I T D T N P W
B F M B D T I E W V I D L V W V O V
O Z U V J N X W W K W T A S W R N
N X W U B B J A C K N I C K L A U S
Q X O Y A F P V V Q I F L R J Y L I
T F V Q G Q P U H U E W U D Y G H X
```

Page 171

```
S N I L P O J T T O C S Q Z M G T C
N U K N M H C E Y E A T I C G Z C D
P H F P T B H Y G M T E M J Q C F A
T M U R G K A L M Y U V V N P L P W
Y P Q C M Z R Y H E B E T Y R I S Q
J Z F T M O D G Y P Z N S J G W H F
P Y H F N A D U K B T S M L D B R F
F V C U V B L P Y P X P F V W T J O
G O H I S G U N E N P I N P W X E G
N G S Z A B T L O T R E W U D F A Y
A J T S M P T J Y X W L U I H I Q T
R W M V E J J M M G I B G X H L I B
M A R G A R E T W I S E B R O W N O
M N N A C L A C J I G R W P I O F Q
J W F K Z R J D V K F G T L S B J U
```

Page 172

```
O Z S K I X G S J E J B G H S C V S
K F F W Y D S P J C A F M Y K F V Q
O V H X U I D M O K Y N O N L B F G
Y F U B X C E H G J N X S Q M U C Q
N O W M A W O S O J M Y A I R P A E
N Q B I H I W I S E A K T E H J C H
M R O G M V R O X B N A N D G A X P
R G S E B I Y B E W S L G D K N D J
G B G N K L K N W C F X C T Y S A Z
V V P N R C M C A P I Z M C R R J P
T A F E Z K J L T S E Y W Q U C E P
I L D A Z C E U X R L T S E W E A M
A W W A K W L Z D K Z K P W E T V
U K L B R W I I H X H X M X W I R P
```

Page 173

```
T A N A Z Q X Z F X O U F J A R L N
S H R Q I A B Q F Z N Z V A M Y A W
O U Y S H K U T H R O Z A N B M K J
R V A D J Z D I G T Z D R T S T W R
F T L S K R P G H F S L X U N I P B
T S P S P A M B K B M L O Y X K Q A
R X N N B K B W J P M H M D C W L A
E J N R M A S A C O E H A X O W A R
B S J S W A R E Y A Z G Y P E I N P
O N T U T H K J I D Q W G P S P U Z
R U G A Q R T W R G H D C R Q B N M
W F R D D X S P M C T X O A C I P L
V O W T A K P B B A Q U Q E X M T Y
A Y K U I E S H E H U R R J O C M E
X W L A Z G R U I T S Q P K F B I P
```

Page 174

```
G N Z K A F S S W U C Z E X B N G C
H E D S Y O I N Y S F Y K V A B F T
M C O V T W C Y Y J G F N G R M L F
E Y Z R S Q T Q K E R T Y S A L Z R
V T K R G O Z D C Q M A Z M C H T J
S U K K H E Q W J Y C R Z K K B S U
R Z U D B O H K S S O S A W O R L Y
F J V H E T X W O G V H E Z B J B K
F Q Q J Q R E Z B I E F Q R A D P P
M X H L C Q E E S U Z O O G M T W V
W N L D Y Z Y V T L S R Z H A T Y T
M O F K V E T M A Q M H M H C N B A
D Y T D Z U R A J D W O G E I N Y
Q P K U J N Y M J P V O G C R G M C
V X X M A D A M A B U T T E R F L Y
```

```
J C A P N W W T K J H Q Q Q N P O I
H D C E P O D G A R I U I B G C D R
L N I K C T S H H A U F E F H R S F
V S R U B T Y K Z F Q F W I A Q S Y
B G E P E E N C E P O O B K C G K
J V M X P C D D R A R B M M M U D G
X E A M Z H N X T Z J O S X N T L Q
Q W N C H A J I P C L L E O H L F M
J R I P G Y X U A E L T E U I Q V R
M V A M F D A I C B Y V U A I E O E
P K T I U Q X N D I A G D T H O C X
M R P D V W I M W U O M E H M C U O
F Z A T A V J M X H I A J F J D I A
X H C G K C R V D Z Z Q P X N H V M
S H H I H X P W A L T W H I T M A N
```

```
U Q L B T E S D C G U V S T F N R N
Y B T D N H I C Q N X A D U Y D X W
X L L W Y R R Z D J P M L Z I J C L
P K X N B R C W P D M F R Q M M J W
A M N W I O U P Z K F E O H M C A O
U D N B L V D J I M L M W G X R A J
Y M X I L E I N A D C M E I T T A H
W U Z M M C P Q A P M B H Q J I J G
E E V C T E S S E I B C T A V E X S
J W B M K W X O X B I O F P D I O J
F D H X Z W G B C V L Y O G V I A F
F R H K V I C A O S Z F R K W J T I
U K A R H T X J I Q T X A V S F Z D
Z T O R M N N O E P N J W R R E C S
J D W R T H R O A T S I N G I N G M
```

```
J C C I M U R J Y A A G D V J E Q G
D U P B I B R R G U M O T U D H N V
A K L X E J F C Q V A R J V H I F Z
V E M I E T R J C K I E P C L V W M
Y Y Y C U M W T A K P A E S M E E G
A L Y J J S O G M O O O I O I J H R
W I T M M V C K Q C R U P C U E R A
S M B F R S E A I A Q D D U X B L U
A E H S E B X T E N B R T F Y G T K
U P Y L M Y S F U S T D Z W Z X P N
V I V Y H P Q K R M A O Y T Y H V X
J E V Z Y J D N U R D R I J O O A G
V J L H P I K Z H X W F R C F G D X
Q R H F V M A R T H A S T E W A R T
C H R H S O Y A U M S F T M V P M N
```